INFORMATION SYSTEMS AND BUSINESS DYNAMICS

INFORMATION SYSTEMS AND BUSINESS DYNAMICS

Robert B. Walford

ADDISON-WESLEY PUBLISHING COMPANY, INC.
Reading, Massachusetts Menlo Park, California New York
Don Mills, Ontario Wokingham, England Amsterdam Bonn
Sydney Singapore Tokyo Madrid San Juan

Many of the designations used by manufacturers and sellers to distinguish their products are claimed as trademarks. Where those designations appear in this book and Addison-Wesley was aware of a trademark claim, the designations have been printed in initial capital letters (for example, Knowledge Craft) or all capital letters (for example, KEE).

Library of Congress Cataloging-in-Publication Data
Walford, Robert B.
Information systems and business dynamics / Robert B. Walford.
p. cm.
Includes bibliographical references.
ISBN 0-201-52408-2
1. Business — Communication systems. 2. Systems design.
3. Information networks. I. Title.
HF5548.2.W2922 1990
650'.028'546 — dc20 90-31909
CIP

Jacket design by Mike Fender
Text design by Patricia Dunbar
Sponsoring editor: Ted Buswick
Set in 11 point Trump Mediaeval by DEKR Corporation

ABCDEFGHIJ–MA–9543210
First printing, April 1990

This book and its companion volumes are dedicated to my wife

Carolyn Mary

and our children

Ann, Roberta, Jim, Dennis, Christopher, Randall, and Mary

who endured this project with humor, patience, and understanding. They helped me balance the discipline of writing, university duties, office responsibilities, and most of all, the family. Without their help, this book never would have been written.

CONTENTS

TWO INFORMATION NETWORKS AND SYSTEMS

THREE THE DEVELOPMENT PROCESS

TABLES

CHAPTER ONE

CHAPTER TWO

CHAPTER THREE

CHAPTER FOUR

CHAPTER FIVE

CHAPTER SIX

CHAPTER SEVEN

FIGURES

CHAPTER ONE

CHAPTER TWO

CHAPTER THREE

CHAPTER FOUR

CHAPTER FIVE

CHAPTER SIX

CHAPTER SEVEN

PREFACE

This book, along with its companion volumes, *Network System Architecture* and *Information Networks: A Design and Implementation Methodology*, is a presentation of technical, business, and related considerations that impact the development of information networks and systems. The focus in these books is, of necessity, somewhat different than that expected in classical engineering presentations that are devoted entirely to a discussion of a specific technology area. Information network and system technology is described and discussed in considerable detail, because it is the foundation on which all information networks are built, but nontechnical aspects that have considerable influence over design decisions are also considered. A discussion of only the engineering aspects, without an appreciation of the business environment (including the regulatory and competitive conditions) in which the technology must exist, is not especially useful.

Most of the current intense interest in information networks has occurred because of the recognition that such networks are — or could be — an important component of the enterprise structure and strategy. The recent emphasis on the use of information as a strategic asset (or weapon if you prefer) in the conduct of business is a case in point. Utilizing information networks in this way requires that the effort be approached from many different directions in an integrated fashion. Thus, the discussion in this book balances the purely engineering aspects of information network technology with the associated business aspects in order to present a complete treatment of the subject.

The discussion in this series of books is oriented toward the point of view of the user. This is important because the whole purpose of the network in providing information services is to support the end user. Users must have access to all information and services that are needed to perform their required activities. Thus, the design engineer must serve the needs of the users, rather than the users having to adapt their procedures to the engineering design — a condition that is more prevalent than anyone would care to admit.

A third aspect of information networks that makes it best to take a non-traditional approach to discussing such networks is the fact that information technology subsumes a large number of other technologies. These technologies, which include telecommunications, human factors, and software engineering, serve as components to information network technology. They must be closely integrated and coordinated and yet remain separated enough to allow each component to evolve independently without increasing the system's overall complexity beyond that which can be effectively assimilated.

The last and probably most important reason for a different treatment of information networks and systems is that the design and development process is affected significantly by three areas of intense change: the technology itself, the business environment in which the network must operate, and the products and services that are available to implement the network. Because of the large costs involved, any design and implementation effort must guard against premature obsolescence. At the same time, the design approach must allow for rapid change in all of the network's technologies, and it must be able to accommodate any reasonable directions taken by these technologies. Changes in the business or regulatory environment may also force changes in the technological directions that are utilized. Such changes must also be accommodated in a cost-effective way.

This need to accommodate constant and sometimes radical change when discussing information networks and systems is in contrast to the demands imposed by discussions of more mature technologies, which can focus on well-known and well-understood theory that does not change radically over time.

In order to accomplish these purposes, the major focus of the discussion presented in these three volumes is on the topics of environment, architecture, and methodology. The environment, discussed in this volume, encompasses technical and nontechnical constraints and requirements that are central to the proper development and use of the information network technologies. Discussion of the environment concentrates on the integration of technologies, both among themselves and with the requirements of the business they serve.

The architecture is discussed in the second volume of the series; this volume contains the knowledge necessary to develop suitable products, and its approach is designed to provide a framework that is flexible and yet provides enough structure so that design and implementation decisions can be made effectively. These decisions are determined and evaluated by means of principles which are derived from the architecture definition and structure.

Methodology, discussed in the third volume, provides the means of developing products and services that are consistent with the architecture, cost-effective for the organization, and able to meet the needs of the marketplace effectively. As the last phase of the development process, the methodology must also bridge the gap between the consistent and orderly architecture and the rough and tumble conditions of the real world.

Dividing the discussion into three volumes as mentioned above helps organize the discussion and keeps it from becoming unmanageably complex. In addition, it makes it easier to identify quickly the location of the information of immediate interest. Because each book is designed to be a "stand-alone" discussion of the major topic addressed, it is not necessary to read the books in serial fashion; the appropriate book can be consulted directly. Of course, information presented in one of the other volumes may be necessary for a full understanding of the topic in its complete context.

In this book, the first of the series, the technical and business environment in which system development must take place is presented. Emphasis is placed on the necessity of integrating many technologies along with the underlying business requirements. The discussion is divided into two halves, each with a different emphasis. The first half (chapters 1 through 4) presents a general overview of the technical and business aspects of the development process, including its historical background. The impact of terminology on the integration process is addressed, with some advice as to the resolution of this problem. The historical perspective of the third-, fourth-, and fifth-generation concepts of network evolution are considered. This is important to the design and development of an information network system, because that system must coexist with past, current, and future products and services.

Next, various key philosophies of development are examined and characterized in order to determine the optimum approach to network system design and implementation. This discussion also leads to a definition of architecture and methodology, explaining these concepts in the context of the overall development environment. A brief discussion of the structure and philosophy of both architecture and methodology is presented. (A more complete discussion of these topics is found in the companion volumes.)

The emphasis in the remainder of the first half of this book is on the technical issues involved. This includes a discussion of several technologies that are an integral part of any information network, including human factors, telecommunications, and artificial intelligence, among others. These discussions are not intended to be exhaustive presentations. However, the material provides a minimum amount of knowledge as a prerequisite to the general discussion of architecture and methodology. This discussion emphasizes the integration of the technologies, rather than treating each one as an isolated entity. This is in keeping with one of the major themes of the presentations — that the integration of the component technologies is a necessary ingredient for significant progress in the network area.

The second half of this book is oriented toward the business environment and its impact on the design and implementation process. First, a comprehensive treatment of technology management is presented. *Technology management* is a critical and often neglected part of development that requires a careful integration of business and technical aspects. Proper attention to technology management will ensure that investment in technology will be leveraged to the maximum extent possible, allowing cost-effective use of technology in the products and services produced by the enterprise.

This presentation is followed by detailed consideration of a number of issues that significantly affect the cost of development. Without close control over these areas, technically perfect products can be developed that will cause the enterprise to fail. This book concludes with an overview of the dynamics of a technically oriented business; this discussion ties together the topics discussed previously. Among the business factors considered are mission and strategy, organization dynamics, marketing, and the overall management process employed by the enterprise. It is hoped that this discussion will motivate the business personnel of an enterprise to communicate their concepts and thinking to the technical personnel, and conversely, that it will help the technical personnel to realize that much more than technology is involved in the successful enterprise. Above all, engineers and business managers should talk to one another so that each understands the other's needs and wants. The global environment and competition demand no less.

The first companion volume, *Network System Architecture,* contains an in-depth discussion of the architecture structure and its implications. The basic requirements for the design of any architecture are discussed and used to design a specific example architecture. As a part of the example architecture, a large number of principles that can be used to direct the design and structure of information network systems are developed.

The second companion volume, *Information Networks: A Design and Implementation Methodology,* presents a comprehensive methodology that contains design and implementation techniques specifically defined to utilize the output principles of the network system architecture. Each step of the methodology is carefully defined, and the reasons for including each step are explained in detail. These definitions and explanations will help ensure that the resultant procedures will provide the results necessary, advancing the development in an optimum fashion.

The information presented in this book and its companion volumes has been designed to assist professionals involved in the research, design, and development of information networks and systems. It will also effectively serve the needs of students in a classroom or self-study environment. The method of use will be somewhat different in each case. In a business setting, the main uses of this book will be (1) to provide an organized approach to the design of an information network and services that will serve the specific needs and strategies of the organization; (2) to serve as a reference manual for those individuals responsible for providing network-based products and services; (3) to form a basis on which to direct the research and development of the concepts and structures needed for new information networks and systems; and (4) to provide a mechanism by which technical and business people can communicate more effectively.

Although there are no study questions given at the end of each chapter, these volumes are also appropriate for classroom use in advanced courses in software engineering. A three-semester sequence, one for each volume, would be necessary to delve into the subject matter in some depth. If desired, the books could be augmented by a discussion of the more popular classical methodologies to complete the historical positioning of the current environment. If only the major concepts and results were covered, the material could be reduced to a two-semester sequence, if desired. I have taught a course based on this latter sequence at the University of South Florida with excellent results.

In either type of sequence, assignments would consist of example designs and possible alternatives to the procedures and methodologies presented. As in actual practice, there are few single or simple answers to most questions, and the instructor must look for the validity of the approach and conclusions reached in determining the absorption of the material. In this regard, I must give special thanks to Dr. Murali Varanassi, chair of the computer science and engineering department at the University of South Florida, for giving me the freedom to experiment with new ways of providing students with an understanding of the needs of modern software engineering and practice.

I would like to express my deep appreciation to Don Peeples, former president of GTE Data Services, Dan Lawson, former vice president of information sciences, and Jim Hamrick, my current vice-president. They provided the opportunity and environment that enabled me to research and develop the concepts presented in these volumes. Their encouragement and aid are gratefully acknowledged.

Thanks and recognition are also richly deserved by several of my current or former associates on the technical staff of GTE Data Services, who contributed in diverse ways to the formation of this book. They participated in many discussions, arguments, and brainstorming sessions that greatly helped to solidify the concepts and ideas presented. The many late nights they spent reading and proofing are also appreciated. These individuals included Bill Livesey, who kept me honest in the data engineering area and who insisted that proper attention be given to modeling; Bill Berry, an expert in software engineering, who contributed much to the discussion of applications development; Scott Shipper, the human intelligence on fifth-generation artificial intelligence; and Pat Jordan, who thinks technology planning should take over the world.

I would also like to thank Ed Daly, former director of technology management, our chief "devil's advocate," who wouldn't take "it's obvious" for an answer. Bob Staretz, my director at GTE Data Services during the start of this effort, deserves considerable credit for steering me in the right directions. Recognition is also due Paul Yamashita, who helped with the important gateway discussion, and Rick Ahlgren, who served as the large computer system expert. Scott Shipper also contributed significantly to early versions of the architecture definition and structure, as did John Janis, a former colleague. Other staff members who should be mentioned are Paul Heller, who kept me focused on the end user, and John Ruble, the organization administrative specialist who kept things flowing smoothly. All of the above individuals, as well as the many I am unable to mention by name, are dedicated hard-working professionals, and I am proud to have been associated with them in the writing of this volume.

I would also like to give a special thank you to Evelyn Banks, who was my secretary and administrative assistant as the writing progressed. Without her skill and dedicated effort, there would be no book.

Robert B. Walford
September, 1989

INTRODUCTION

In the beginning, there was the mainframe, which was attended by a priesthood of programmers and operators. So that the mainframe and its attendants received the proper homage and respect, the mainframe was located within a room of windows (affectionately called the glass house) so that all could come and observe the workings of this wondrous machine. Of course, the ordinary people outside the glass walls could not converse directly with the mainframe. If they had a need and dared ask it a question, they were required to inscribe their request on paper cards or tape for presentation to the mainframe. This request would be devoured by the mainframe at its leisure, and, if it was so inclined, the mainframe would eventually produce an answer on still more paper cards or tape.

If the answer was not forthcoming or was in error, well, this was "State-of-the-Art-Technology," and the attendants could not bother to explain. Anyway, ordinary people should be glad that the mainframe talked to them sometimes. Did not the ordinary people realize that only a member of the priesthood could understand the workings of the mainframe?

Inhabitants of the modern world, of course, are much too smart and sophisticated to believe in this old concept. And yet, if we examine most of our sophisticated computers, the networks we have built to obtain access to them, and our attitudes toward them, we will find that, in reality, very little has changed. We haven't distanced ourselves very far from the past, even though a great deal of technology has been utilized and the glass house has turned into a concrete bunker. There are, of course, many reasons for this failure: some technically complex and some more emotional than real.

With all of the publicity given in recent years to "user friendly" interfaces, computers, for the most part, are still difficult to use. A mystique still surrounds the mainframe, even though the all-pervasive personal computer sits on the desktop. Legions of systems programmers are required if an organization is to utilize mainframes effectively. "Information Centers," staffed with experts, have been developed to ease the pain of using computers, personal and otherwise. The "priesthood" still exists. Users still have great difficulty in talking to the mainframe, even using the other computers sitting on their desks. Just witness the many products that are constantly being developed to allow "easy communication."

Even if modern computers rarely give wrong answers as a result of hardware problems, programming errors abound. They provide interesting error conditions in software, so that the use of a computer system is still an adventure in "high technology."

In addition to these long-lived problems related to computer use, a few new ones are now common:

- Requirements and specifications for large systems take years to develop. In some cases, the technology or business has changed so much after this initial period that the proposed system is no longer useful.
- New systems define equipment, network, software, and data needs independent of what already exists. Information already available in machine-readable form is rekeyed by manual means, because the two processors are incompatible and no transfer mechanism has been defined or implemented. In addition, although available equipment is not

used to capacity, new hardware is purchased. This drives up costs and prevents many systems from being cost-effective.

- A significant number of network and system users have multiple terminals on their desks because the systems they use on a day-to-day basis are incompatible (to say nothing about being incomprehensible!).
- Software development is based primarily on manual techniques, with the result that most systems have huge cost overruns and are delivered and deployed late. Bugs and inconsistencies abound in released operational software. Computer-based techniques, which would allow increases in productivity and improve the quality of software development and implementation, are not utilized effectively. Many computer-based development aids are nothing more than a manual process implemented on a computer. Little value is added through the use of this tool, which is still as difficult to use as the manual method. This lack of reliance on computer-based development techniques occurs even though most businesses of a significant size have integrated computers into their operations totally and would literally fail if they did not utilize computer-based operations. The network and system development businesses are not nearly as advanced as the businesses they serve!

This book is much needed to show that a way can indeed be found to eventually advance beyond the current primitive beginnings. These improvements will make it possible to do the following:

- Develop systems efficiently and effectively
- Take full advantage of the network environment in the delivery of services
- Make systems "user friendly" in practice as well as theory
- Reduce the need for legions of professionals to develop, maintain, and run the corporate networks and systems
- Within the constraints of the business need, use what already exists to the maximum extent before buying more.

One positive sign of success in this quest will be if general disagreement occurs as to whether this book is a engineering text, a business study, a design road map, or a consultant's report — for it is necessary that it be collectively all of these and individually none of them. If we are indeed to escape from the restrictions and problems of the past, the development of new systems must be considered from an integrated approach using all of the information and experience available to us, regardless of source and fundamental discipline.

The path to the future requires more than a linear extension of prior experience and knowledge. This is the approach used most often, and it only results in a casting of the same difficulties in a different format. Merely throwing technology at the problems does not help. The approach needs to be one that allows large changes in previous concept, scope, and philosophy. Integrating a number of disciplines, including accounting, business administration, engineering, psychology, and law, will enable us to make a start in this direction.

This integration will be successful only if the network system development process is itself considered and treated as a system. Pieces of the design and implementation process cannot be considered in isolation but must be taken as an interconnected part of the entire procedure.

The specific approach taken in this book and its companion volumes (the integration of the technical and business development environments, the utilization of a comprehensive architecture rooted in modern technology and business practices, and a sophisticated methodology tightly coupled with the architecture) is designed to take maximum advantage of the latest advances in the foundation disciplines while eventually allowing significant automatic generation of networks and systems through the use of artificial intelligence. Although much of the technology needed to automate the development procedure is still being developed, the necessary constructs must be put in place now if new advances are to be utilized effectively.

INFORMATION SYSTEMS AND BUSINESS DYNAMICS

ONE

IN PREPARATION

INTRODUCTION

Because of the complexity of the subject matter that is discussed, and because this material requires a knowledge of some topics that are not always presented as a part of an engineering or business education, the major concepts of a number of topics that are fundamental to this book will be presented in this chapter. This discussion is not intended to be a comprehensive treatment of the selected areas. However, enough detail is presented to enable the reader to follow the philosophy and reasoning behind the presentations contained in the book. Readers who are already familiar with the information in these discussions may skip them without losing continuity with the presentations contained in the other chapters of the book.

Of course, additional areas of knowledge that are not presented explicitly here are also required to assimilate the information contained herein. Knowledge of these areas will generally be known as a result of a comprehensive engineering and/or business curriculum. However, if it is obvious from a particular presentation that additional background knowledge is required, an appropriate source should be consulted before continuing. If readers lack the appropriate level of background information, the presentations will lose a great deal of their impact, and some amount of the information could be misunderstood.

The discussions contained in this chapter cover terminology, product definition, standards, and government regulation. Each topic will be presented separately, although there is close coupling between them, as will be indicated as necessary during the course of the discussions. In my experience, although most people believe that they understand these topics, misinformation abounds. The result is confusion and considerable inefficiency in the development process.

TERMINOLOGY

Networks and network systems, along with many other fields of endeavor, utilize a specialized language that describes certain activities, procedures, and events that are unique to this particular technology. This language has developed over a considerable period of time and practitioners in the field utilize it with the same familiarity as they do their natural language. Any specialized vocabulary is sometimes lamented by the laity because they feel that it is employed to keep them from understanding information that could be useful to them. Although it generally takes a great deal of time, effort, and study to become familiar with specialized terminology, it takes even more time to learn the field itself. However, this latter fact is sometimes forgotten.

In addition to this "public relations" problem, there is another, even greater, difficulty attached to the use of specialized terminology, or *jargon*. This occurs when the same words or phrases mean different things to different people within the sphere of the technology under study. This can occur for a variety of reasons, some of which are accidental because of independent development, others because of the desire to differentiate the work of one author from that of another. As in the case of natural language dialects, there can also be geographical differences. In many cases there have been "West

Coast" versus "East Coast" differentiations both in approach and terminology.

To some extent, this rivalry is good competition. It keeps everyone alert and allows for a full discussion of the relative merits of the approaches to the technology. When the use of alternate terminology tends to confuse rather than enlighten, however, a problem is born. Add this to the peculiarities and deficiencies of the English language (or any other natural language) in making precise definitions, and an even greater difficulty exists.

A third difficulty with specialized language occurs when the same word has divergent meanings in different technologies. When the concepts and structures of these technologies are integrated, a great deal of confusion can result.

This discussion is not intended to discourage the use of specialized language and terminology where appropriate. There are many good reasons why these languages will continue to flourish and be utilized: They represent a shorthand for the experts in the field; they enable complex subjects and concepts to be referred to in a concise way; and given the needs of human nature, they allow one expert in a field to identify another expert without much difficulty.

In a book such as this, where a great deal of terminology from several different fields, is introduced and utilized, it is important to ensure that the terminology is properly identified and defined. As indicated above, the same words may have completely different meanings in different fields. When the technologies of these fields must be integrated to produce new products and services, a clash of terminology can have disastrous effects on the process and may actually defeat the integration attempt.

This clash of terminology is particularly evident in the data processing and telecommunications technologies. Two areas are central to the discussions in this book. To show the confusion that can result, some examples of the conflict are presented in table 1.1.

I have tried to be careful in this book to ensure that all the

TABLE 1.1 TERMINOLOGY CLASHES

	Meaning	
Term	*Telecommunications*	*Data Processing*
Tandem	Telephone switch used to switch trunks from class 5 offices	Particular brand of computer system
Channel	Talking path or transmission circuit	Connection between main processor and closely coupled external device
Transaction	Call attempt	Message processing
Mainframe	Structure for running jumper wires	Large-scale computer

terminology that can possibly be confused or misinterpreted is well defined. In some cases this definition may not agree with current popular usage(s) in one or more fields. This occurs because a current definition can be confused or can conflict with a definition in another field. Also, its underlying concept or common usage may not be entirely clear and must be rigorously defined.

Because of the importance of the subject, the difficulties inherent in terminology are further explored in the following discussion. This will illustrate effectively the problems and peculiarities of terminology when the exact definitions are not known and the interpretation is somewhat imprecise and not universally accepted. Consider the confusion that can result from the use of a single word — *simulation* — that is widely used in system design but whose definition is little understood. Understanding the problems caused by this word is important because of the reliance on simulation techniques as part of the development methodology. In addition, it will help demonstrate what can occur when different technologies and their associated jargon must be integrated.

When Terminology Fails

Consider the following scenario, which repeats itself daily in research and engineering organizations across the world.

> An engineer enters his manager's office and says, "I have completed the assignment you gave me. I have simulated the XYZ system so that prospective users can get a good idea of the XYZ system capabilities." The manager thanks the engineer, goes to see the simulation, and is suitably impressed as to its depth and its realistic presentation. Prospective users are then invited to see the simulation, and they too are impressed, not only with the proposed capabilities of the system, but also with the simulation that represents it.

At this point, however, an interesting phenomenon tends to occur. The users, because they are looking at the first physical embodiment of their system, tend to equate the simulation with the system. The scenario continues:

> The users then say to the manager, "That's good, you've done a wonderful job. When will you deliver it?" The manager replies, "This is just a simulation, the real system will take two years to develop and deploy."

The reaction among the users can then cover a wide range:

- A feeling of astonishment
- A feeling they are getting "ripped off"
- A feeling that the development organization is incompetent
- A feeling that all that's going to be added to the program are "bells and whistles."
- A feeling that they would be perfectly happy to get along with what they have just seen — so why can't they have it?

This problem results from a misunderstanding of the use of the word *simulation*, in addition to a misunderstanding as to what it takes to design and implement a product. Because both of these concepts are important considerations to the presentations in this book as well as its companion volumes, each of them will be examined in some detail.

The scenario can have several endings — not all of them happy, from either the user's or the developer's perspective. If the users prevail, they will be stuck with an unmaintainable system of poor quality and limited functionality. If the developers prevail, at best, there will be some amount of animosity between the users and developers, and, at worst, the system will be cancelled. The best result is a negotiated ending that satisfies both groups. To achieve this, each must understand a great deal of the other's point of view. This discussion hopefully will increase the awareness of these considerations among personnel and organizations that are the users, designers, and implementors of network systems.

Now You Understand It — Now You Don't

The use of the word *simulation* can engender several different interpretations of what is really being said. Some of the words that are sometimes thought to be synonyms of the word *simulation* are listed below:

- Emulation
- Synthetic
- Artificial
- Illusion
- Substitute
- Prototype
- Demonstration
- Model
- Mock-up
- Temporary
- Low quality
- Inadequate

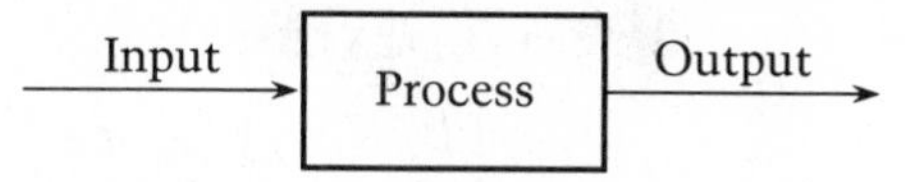

FIGURE 1.1 PROCESS MODEL

As an example, in the scenario of the previous section, the engineer considered the simulation as a concept *demonstration* for the system. The manager presented it to the users as a *prototype,* and the users in a sense considered the simulation to be a *substitute.* In addition, both the engineer and the manager considered it to be *temporary* and an inadequate embodiment of the system, and the users thought that it could be adequate for their needs and could serve as a permanent replacement.

The fact that these problems occur has been lamented on many occasions, not only in scientific papers, but in the popular press. Much more than just recognition of this difficulty is needed, however. This terminology problem needs to be structured so that it can be attacked from an engineering perspective. Although this probably would be extremely difficult in general, in this particular case a way does exist to structure the problem and make some progress in identifying and defining words that are causing the difficulty. The process of identifying and defining such words should also "raise the consciousness" of the reader as to the difficulties inherent in even familiar terms.

An Approach to the Terminology Problem

The familiar system process model will be utilized in this approach to structuring the terminology problem; this model is shown in figure 1.1. The model, which consists of three components — input, process, and output — will be used to define the "real" or "true" system as well as those systems that are "not real" in some sense. The word *model* in this context is defined as an *explanation* of the input, output, and

TABLE 1.2 CONNOTATION MATRIX

System Type	*Input*	*Process*	*Output*
Real	Real	Real	Real
Artificial	Simulated	Real	Real
Prototype Emulation	*	Restricted	Real
Synthetic Simulator	*	Simulated	Real
Illusion Illustration	*	*	Simulated

*Either a real or a simulated condition

process of a system. Because the real system contains the real input, the real process, and the real output, a system that is not real must contain alterations to at least one of these entities. A system component that has been altered is said to be *simulated,* and a system that contains at least one simulated component is itself said to be simulated. By defining words that indicate simulations of each of these components, an organized approach to the problem of terminology in this specific domain can be generated.

Consider the chart shown in table 1.2. In this chart, specific words are used to describe the process model in terms of the real system and associated simulated systems when each of the components of the system are simulated. Notice that if none of the system's components — the input, process, and output — are simulated, the system is considered to be real. The special case of a restricted real system will also be defined.

This table also illustrates the major difference between a prototype and a simulator. A prototype is considered to be a restricted version of the real system. This means that not all of the features and functions that are a part of the final system requirements and specifications have been implemented. However, whatever functionality is available has been implemented in such a way that real or simulated input can be used to produce real output. The prototype, in essence, consists of a real system with reduced functionality.

A simulator need not resemble any structural aspect of the real system. Its sole use is to provide information about the behavior of the real system, and it is not a physical embodiment of the system. Simulators can therefore be based on mathematical or statistical models and can produce output in the form of data that describes the operation of the system, rather than the normal system output.

Unfortunately, the line between a simulator and a prototype is not always clearly defined. A simulator of the proper design can be used to process real or simulated input to produce real output, and a prototype can be used to gather information about the behavior of the system. Usually, it is not necessary to determine rigorously whether a process is a simulator or a prototype unless it is being advertised as having a set of capabilities that meet the criteria of one or the other as specified above.

If the output is not real, the resultant system is called an *illusion* or an *illustration.* This usually occurs in the beginning stages of a project, when the design is not yet started but the output requirements are known. An illustration is sometimes referred to as a *simulator* or *prototype,* but technically neither is correct. Such usage should not be confusing, however.

If the process is not real (complete or restricted), the resultant system is *synthetic* or an *emulation.* It should be noted here that in some cases it is not possible to tell among two competing systems which of the process components is real and which is not. In this case, the system that is actually being utilized to perform the function for which it is intended is defined to be real and the other system becomes a *substitute.* If the two systems should switch roles, their definitions would, of course, also switch.

If the input is not real, the word *artificial* is used to describe the system. If more than one component is not real, the

TABLE 1.3 SIMULATED SYSTEM ATTRIBUTES

Simulated Component	*Real System Output*	*Simulated System Output*
Input	Natural pearls	Cultured pearls
Process	Human speech	Machine speech
Output	Leather	Naugahyde

descriptions of each individual component can be concatenated. Thus, if both the input and the process are simulated, but real output is available, the model is artificial and synthetic. However, the system is not illusionary or an illustration, because the real output is shown. The output could have been recorded or obtained as a result of previous systems operation or by another means.

If all of the components are simulated, the resultant system is usually called a *demonstration* or a *mock-up*. Mock-ups are used whenever the aesthetic properties of the system are of significant importance. The embodiment of a mock-up is usually such that it is not mistaken for the real system. Mock-ups of network systems are generally produced as sales vehicles to illustrate to potential customers the anticipated capabilities.

Some examples that illustrate the concepts presented above can be taken from familiar, nontechnical situations. These are shown in table 1.3. In the first case, the difference between a cultured pearl and a natural pearl is not in either the process or the output. The oyster works the same way and the pearl consists of the same material in either case. Instead, the difference is in the input, or the method by which the original impurity was placed into the oyster. In a natural pearl, the process occurs as a result of the natural environment of the oyster in the sea. In the case of cultured pearls, that input is performed manually. Although the process and the output are identical, a differentiation is still made between the two — especially in price.

In the second type of case described earlier, the input and output are real but the process is simulated. An example of this is human speech as compared to computer-generated speech. Speech that is uttered by a human is real, whereas speech generated by use of a computer is simulated. The input (such as text) can be the same in either case, as is the output — recognizable speech.

In the case of simulated output or illusion, it may not really matter whether the input and process are real or simulated, because they bear no real connection to the output. An example of this is shown in the third example in table 1.3. Leather is the output from the real system, and naugahyde is the output from the non-real system. It is a simulated output, or, in other words, simulated leather. It is designed to look like leather and function somewhat like leather but, of course, it is not leather.

That brings us to the interesting examination of ads sometimes found on late-night TV. These ads contain words to the effect that the product being sold consists of genuine naugahyde. That implies that naugahyde now becomes the real system and that there are other products, presumably cheaper, that can be used in place of naugahyde (that is, another simulation of the output that is not as good as naugahyde). This puts us at least three levels down from where we started with leather. Thus, the definition of what the real system is (that is, the requirements and/or specifications) becomes extremely important when the problem deals with entities that are simulated but that could be misrepresented as the real system.

The following list is presented to give you some practice in using the concepts that were just discussed to sort out the various implications of the process model on terminology. This list presents some relatively well-known products resulting from systems that are simulations of the "real" system, as well as some examples from network systems. Which of these products are simulated? What are the names of the real products for the simulations?

- Soyburgers
- Plastic flowers
- Generic cola
- Sparkling wine
- Ice milk
- Flight simulator
- Javarik-7 heart
- Hot standby processor
- FORTRAN interpreter
- Replicated database
- Null Modem
- Stored digitized voice
- System field trial
- Expert system

Depending on assumptions, there are multiple answers to each item in this table. If you find this exercise hard, remember that it is simple compared to the identification of similar conditions in actual use in the network and its systems.

Implications

What does the previous discussion mean to implementers of network systems? Because of the profound effect that terminology and its individual definition has on the system design and development process, this book devotes considerable effort to insuring that each term is defined adequately and unambiguously so that the discussions can be followed and interpreted as intended. Unfortunately, in some cases, this requires definitions that do not quite agree with "common" usage. In my experience, however, common usage can vary from person to person, from place to place, and from organization to organization.

I also recognize, however, that in a work of this size and complexity, inconsistencies and contradictions may occur occasionally. These are unfortunate, of course, but they do not invalidate the general premise of the work — that the entire design and implementation process can be placed on a sound business and engineering footing; and that without adequate definition and input from both of these fundamental disciplines, the enterprise cannot be efficient and effective enough to remain competitive in the marketplace.

PRODUCT REQUIREMENTS

The interpretation of the definition of a product (or service) is not always the same to different groups of people. It is true that if a market exists for a specific item, that item can be considered a product in some sense of the word. However, an item usually should not be considered a product unless it has certain attributes. These attributes generally relate to these facts: the product has a life cycle; the product must be maintained; and the responsibility for the product must be able to be transferred between various groups of people and/or organizations. Some of the attributes a product should have are listed here:

- Requirements
- Specifications
- Design documentation
- Operations documentation
- Maintainable structure

If one or more of these attributes is missing, the offering cannot be considered a product in the strict sense of the word. That does not mean, however, that it cannot be sold or transferred to a customer. It does mean that the organization will have a more difficult time servicing the customer with that particular product. For example, if the documentation concerning a potential product is lacking or nonexistent, the enterprise cannot respond adequately to the customer's needs and questions concerning the product that arise during normal operation.

Another aspect to the definition of product is not a function of any single product but occurs across the product line. This aspect is the interaction between products. If a suitable set of common technical and business guidelines is not utilized for the development of each product in an organization's product line, the product line tends to become confused and disorganized. This can prevent an organization from competing successfully in the marketplace, and it considerably raises the cost of maintaining and adding to the product line.

Again, if an organization defines a product to be anything that can be sold to a customer, these considerations do not necessarily apply. If, however, a definition of product is included to contain the need for efficient production, maintenance, and additions to the product line, then all of the attributes and considerations mentioned in this discussion must be addressed.

Returning to the scenario presented earlier, in which the users and engineers are upset with each other because of differences in their concepts of a simulation, it is obvious that each of the groups interested in the development of the new system also has different ideas of the definition of product. The engineer and manager are utilizing the expanded definition of product as presented in this section. The users have the definition of product as any available entity. To avoid this confusion, the organization must adopt for itself the particular definition of product that best suits its market and customer characteristics.

However, because of the increasingly rapid changes in technology, as well as the increased competition and government regulation, the expanded definition of product seems to fit most current markets. This extended definition of product must be used if an organization is to maintain its credibility in the market place and its viability as a competitor.

The assumption in this book is that the expanded definition of product is to be used by all parties concerned with the system definition, development, and implementation.

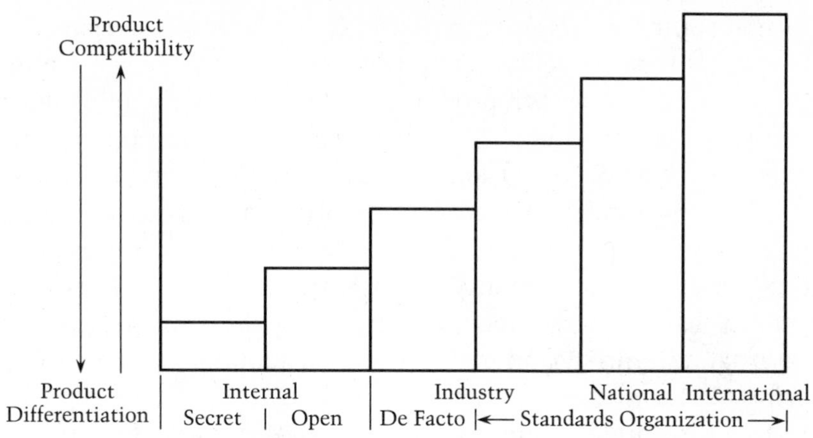

FIGURE 1.2 STANDARDS TYPES

STANDARDS

Because of the complexity of modern technology, the number of competitors providing products and services, and the user's desire to be able to pick and choose products from any or all of these competitors, there is a growing emphasis on formal standards within the engineering and business community. Although engineering design standards have always been important for a variety of reasons, historically closely related to safety concerns, there is a renewed emphasis on standards, especially in the area of information networks. This emphasis covers both the telephone and data communications aspects of networks. This has resulted from the divestiture of AT&T and the increased competition it engendered. Because many enterprises can now provide network products and services, standards are deemed necessary to allow interworking among them.

Standards Development

Standards develop in many ways. Figure 1.2 illustrates a number of these ways along with their major characteristics. The formal standards organizations are, of course, only one source. Standards may be defined by a particular enterprise for use in interworking their own products. Depending on the perceived competitive advantage in doing so, these internal enterprise standards may be either kept as a trade secret or published as an "open" standard to encourage other manufacturers and product vendors to utilize the standard and make compatible products. This is generally a marketing decision and is not usually based on the technical merit of the standard. More internal enterprise standards should be adopted, because they bring to the enterprise discipline and structure.

As an example of open versus closed enterprise standards, consider the approaches of Apple and IBM in providing personal computers. For many years, the Apple line of personal computers has had a "closed" software system to restrict third-party development of compatible software products and to allow Apple to perform most required development. For marketing and competitive reasons, this position was altered toward more open interfaces. On the other side, IBM from the beginning adopted an "open" software system for their Personal Computer, and consequently many products from third-party developers are available.

Other standards come into widespread use because they were promulgated by the dominant company in a particular field or industry. These standards are usually called *de facto standards*, because they have been adopted on an informal basis by most of the relevant industry. As an example, IBM has developed many standards that have been adopted by other organizations in the data processing field. Among these are the SNA network architecture and the DIA/DCA architectures for document distribution. In the telecommunications industry, AT&T set the standards for almost the entire industry until it was divested of its operating companies in 1983. General Motors has established the Manufacturing Access Protocol (MAP) for factory automation, and it has been adopted as a standard by most of the manufacturing industry.

With increased competition in the future, no one organization is likely to dominate an entire industry as IBM, AT&T, and GM have dominated theirs. This increases the importance of industry standards that are developed on a formal basis, utilizing input from all the organizations in that industry and perhaps allied industries, both national and international. Other standards organizations probably will come into being, especially in the areas of application software that is used in a network environment. Some standards are currently available in this area, including those for the distribution of electronic mail and other forms of commercial information, such as invoices and purchase orders. These standards will become even more necessary as networks are used increasingly to communicate between different firms in the same and/or different industries.

Standards Organizations

Many organizations, national and international, provide formal standards for use in the network environment. Some of these organizations are shown in the following list:

- *International*
  CCITT: International Telegraph and Telephone, Consultative Committee
  ISO: International Standards Organization
- *National*
  ANSI: American National Standards Institute
  NIST: National Institute of Technology and Standards (Formally National Bureau of Standards)
  IEEE: Institute of Electrical and Electronic Engineers
  UL: Underwriters Laboratories
  ECSA: Exchange Carrier Standards Association (Through the T1 Organization charted by ECSA)
  EIA: Electronic Industries Association

The two major organizations concerned with network standards are the CCITT, which is responsible for international standards, and ANSI, which, through the ECSA-sponsored T1 committee, is responsible for the United States national network standards. These standards organizations have been in existence for some time, and their current role in defining network standards is merely an extension of their historical role.

Other organizations concerned with standards have recently come into existence to meet a particular need. One of these is the Corporation for Open Systems (COS), which is a consortium of a number of computer manufacturers in the United States. The purpose of this consortium is to provide standardized interfaces for both hardware and software so that the users can use computers and peripherals from various manufacturers in the same systems, especially in network systems.

Utilization

Individual manufacturers have long attempted to differentiate themselves from the competition by utilizing specifications and design techniques for their products that are different from those of their competitors. This approach historically has had two results: (1) Aggressive firms try to be the first to market to gain market share and possibly force competitors to follow their initial lead. (2) After a product has gained initial acceptance, customers are required to purchase additional equipment from the original supplier if all equipment is to interconnect properly.

When products and services from different vendors need not interact with one another, these practices are not a problem and may even serve to enhance competition to the benefit of all customers. In the modern networking environment, however, where there is generally no such entity as a standalone product or service, the need for interworking becomes critical. Thus, many manufacturers, in order to increase the market for their products and services, have de-emphasized the need for product differentiation through unique designs and specifications and have allowed themselves to become a part of a formal standardization process. Differentiation then comes in the form of cost, quality, and customer service.

Standardization not only allows for interworking of components but also helps define terms and concepts that were previously ambiguous. Although this definition process is a by-product of the standards process, it is nevertheless of great value to the industry and will help alleviate some of the problems with terminology expressed previously in this chapter.

Standards Difficulties

There are two problems with utilizing standards in networks and their associated systems. First, because of the number of standards organizations and the varying interest of the organizations involved, there are usually several competing standards that can be utilized. For example, in local area networks two standards have been promulgated by the Institute of Electrical and Electronics Engineers (IEEE): the token ring standard and Ethernet. Either of them could be used in a local area network, and each has advantages and disadvantages that must be taken into account in a particular situation. Unfortunately, systems built using the two different standards cannot interwork directly.

The other major disadvantage of certain standards is that, even if a single standard is selected in a particular area, that standard may allow for a number of options. Two systems that use the same standard could be incapable of interworking because they have adopted different values for the options allowed.

Thus, standards that are broader than those developed within and for a particular enterprise must be used with some caution. Within an enterprise, such broad standards are certainly no substitute for a comprehensive architecture and implementation methodology. They form only one component in the design and implementation procedure and must be considered in that light. Throughout this book, some standards will be identified as being useful or even of strategic importance. However, they will never be considered as a substitute for an architecture and implementation methodology.

Standards that apply to an entire industry or group of industries must also be differentiated from standards that apply to the practices of a particular organization. As indicated previously, these standards are utilized only to apply to the products or methodologies of the defining organization and have no validity beyond the enterprise. In fact, the standards may themselves constitute a trade secret that a particular enterprise would not want to be known to other organizations. The architecture defined in this book contains a number of standards that are presented as part of its output principles. Unless otherwise indicated, these standards should be assumed to apply only to the enterprise using the architecture, not to the industry as a whole.

GOVERNMENT REGULATIONS

Whereas standards imply a type of voluntary constraint on vendors of networks and network products, government regulations impose required or statutory constraints on permissible offerings and operations. The constraints imposed by government are generally in a state of change because of the political atmosphere in which these regulations are proposed and imposed. For this reason, as well as because of the sheer volume of regulations, it is impossible within the limits imposed by this book to do more than mention some of the more universal concepts inherent in the regulation of networks and their associated products. However, it is wise for any vendor or potential vendor to seek appropriate legal counsel before venturing too far into the networking arena.

Although the current trend is away from government regulation and toward increasing competition, some form of regulation is likely to be with us for some time. The form and scope of this regulation may change. However, some fundamental regulatory concepts are in widespread use, and their existence and possible effect should be understood by everyone concerned with information networks and systems.

Different types and scopes of regulation are exercised by various concerned governmental jurisdictions. In the United States this would be at the federal, state, and local levels. In other countries, of course, these jurisdictions will change. However, most of the regulation of information networks outside of the U.S. is accomplished by government entities known as PTTs — Postal Telegraph & Telephone regulatory bodies.

In the United States, the federal-level organization charged with the regulation of networks is the Federal Communications Commission (FCC). At the state level, regulation is accomplished by state Public Utility Commissions (PUCs). At the local level, the county board, city council, or equivalent organization is responsible for appropriate regulation.

The following sections present some of the regulatory concepts that influence the design and operation of information networks and their associated products and services. Because these concepts are subject to a great deal of change in their details, only the overall concepts will be discussed. For more information, consult one or more of the publications available on government regulation in the networking area (see the bibliography).

Common Carrier

One of the most important concepts in the government regulation of network vendors is that of a common carrier. In nonlegalistic terms, a common carrier is a network operator that offers the use of its network to the public — either the general public or a specific subset, such as members of a particular industry. Common carrier status is conferred as a result of government operation, and not all requests may be honored. In many cases, only a specific number of common carriers serving a particular industry or segment will be allowed.

License

Common carrier status is granted by a license that gives specific authority to the licensee. The authority granted determines the scope and type of services that may be offered, and disregard of these restrictions may result in the revocation of the license and may cause the business enterprise to fail.

Tariff

A tariff is the list of services and prices that the common carrier will offer to the public being served. A common carrier can offer only those services that are tariffed. If additional services or changes to existing ones are to be offered, they must be tariffed. This process may be quite lengthy, because proposed tariffs are subject to the scrutiny of the regulatory body and any interested parties, who may then file objections or other comments. These must be considered before any decision is rendered.

When technology is changing rapidly, and new innovative services must be offered and altered to suit the technology and marketplace in order for the enterprise to remain competitive, this tariff process can have a negative effect on the business. This is one of the reasons that government is currently looking to replace the regulatory process with competition where possible.

Franchise

A franchise gives an enterprise the authority to serve a specified geographic area, usually as a monopoly and almost always at the local governmental level. This is done when it is deemed uneconomical for more than one business to serve the area involved. Historically, this has usually been reserved for utilities such as telephone and electric companies. Recently, however, other entities, such as cable TV providers, have also been granted franchises. Although it is not expected that the franchise system will be utilized for information networks, it is necessary to understand this concept because the local telephone companies that may provide some of the facilities utilized in such networks are still bound by this concept, although it is being loosened considerably at this time.

Uniform Access

This is a new concept that is being promulgated under a variety of different names and specific definitions. However, the basic requirement imposed by this regulatory concept is that all organizations wishing to offer a service have the same access to any service components that are provided by a common carrier. For example, assume that a common carrier wishes to offer a service that utilizes its network, billing process, switch control, and proprietary database. It would then have to offer its network, billing process, and switch control on the same basis and cost as it utilized internally for the service. However, the common carrier would not have to offer its proprietary database. The proposed competitor would have to create its own. Thus, regulated enterprises could not obtain an advantage by use of the common carrier facilities it controls. The advantage could be obtained only through proprietary, or "non-common-carrier" entities, such as a database or specialized processing.

Future Regulatory Concepts

The concept of uniform access will probably undergo considerable evolution as experience is gained, requirements mature, and the regulatory process changes. In addition, other novel concepts will be defined to meet the changing environment. To remain competitive, all providers and users of information networks and products must be cognizant of government regulations at all levels and in all countries in which they are active.

Regulations in the Design Process

Although regulations must be considered in the overall business environment, it would be a mistake to base a complex and expensive system design entirely on a government regulation or a common carrier tariff. Because changes to these entities are not necessarily under the control of the using enterprise, a system design that depends on specific attributes of a regulation or tariff can be made ineffective or uneconomical overnight.

An example of this type of design would be a network service that depended on the structure of "OUT WATS," a tariffed offering of interexchange telephone carriers such as AT&T. If the cost structure of this offering should change or the offering be eliminated by FCC order, a profitable service could be eliminated instantly. The design of a network or service must be able to provide profitable operation under a variety of regulatory and tariff conditions or be flexible enough to accommodate itself to anticipated changes in the regulated environment with a minimum of redesign.

TWO

INFORMATION NETWORKS AND SYSTEMS

GENERAL NETWORK PRINCIPLES

A network can be defined as an interconnected set of entities, usually called *nodes*. Depending on the network type and purpose, both the interconnections and the nodes may have a diverse set of attributes and associated characteristics. Because of their applicability in a wide variety of situations and the relative simplicity of definition, networks have been studied extensively and a great deal of theory exists as to their general properties.

As one type of network realization, information networks inherit the principles of general network theory, and these principles provide a substantial foundation for development. For this reason, a general knowledge of networks is helpful as background to the material in this book. It is beyond the scope of this book to discuss network theory in detail; this information may be obtained from a number of texts (see the bibliography).

Two properties of general network theory are especially applicable to the discussion of information networks, and these will be touched on briefly. The first principle assumes that the network of interest is *directed.* As shown in figure 2.1, a directed network has links in only one direction. A node X is said to be not reachable from another node Y if no

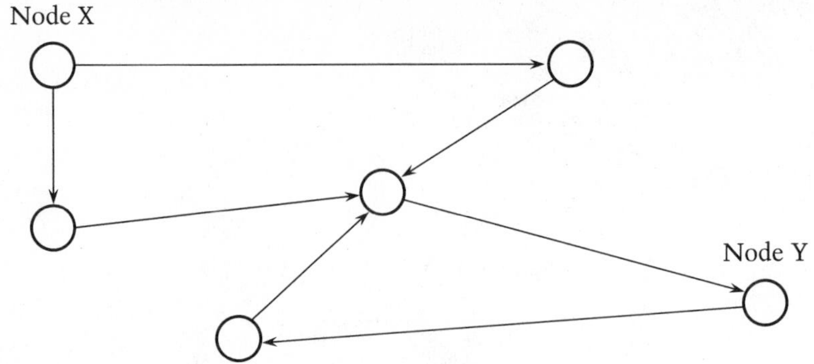

Notes: Node Y is reachable from Node X
Node X is not reachable from Node Y

FIGURE 2.1 DIRECTED NETWORK

path exists, even through intermediate nodes, from Y to X. This does not, in general, preclude node Y from being reachable from X. It is not necessary in a general network for a given node to be reachable from another node. In an information network, for example, it may be possible for one node to be able to send data to another node but not be able to receive data from that node. This will be discussed in more detail shortly.

The second principle is that of *subnetworks.* A subnetwork is a portion of a network that, for some reason, is considered independently of the whole network. Although a subnetwork could be defined to be the entire network, it usually consists of a proper subset of the network (such as a local area network that is part of a larger network). Information networks make considerable use of subnetworks, both on a physical and a logical level.

LEVELS OF ABSTRACTION

Information networks and their components can be characterized with different levels of abstraction. Physical nodes are processors and associated peripherals (printers, voice units, CRT screens, keyboards, etc.), and the physical interconnection paths are electric (including radio and light) circuits through which digital data (or analog data in the short term) can pass. Although the physical level of abstraction must eventually be specified in order for the network to be realized and deployed, the design of an information network usually utilizes a higher level of abstraction known as the *logical level.* Logical nodes and transmission paths depend on the specific design and functions of the network. Logical nodes are usually known as *servers* and are defined on a function basis. Examples of such nodes (servers) are database servers, department servers, LAN servers, and so forth. Logical transmission paths are usually characterized in terms of networks, such as backbone networks, local area networks, dial networks, and broadband networks. Other abstraction levels do exist and are discussed in some detail in the companion volume on network system architecture.

The presentation of pyramid structures in chapter 3 discusses the general theory of abstraction levels and their major interfaces and interaction methods.

INFORMATION NETWORK DESIGN

In general, information networks are comprised of many different types of nodes and subnetworks as described above. Each provides a set of functions and services that can be accessed by the users of the network. The design of the information network is accomplished essentially by integrating the functions and services specified on a logical abstraction level and assigning them to a physical realization of the network. This design process is quite complex and requires the integration of many technologies and business requirements, as well as the establishment of an overall design philosophy. The major thrust of the remainder of this book is the specification of the design philosophy and the associated structures and procedures necessary to produce an effective information network.

INFORMATION NETWORK OBJECTIVES

The main objective of an information network is to serve as a means of providing systems and services that will help an enterprise improve productivity and maintain a competitive edge in a highly competitive business environment. These systems and services may be (1) utilized internally to decrease costs and/or improve efficiency or (2) sold to customers as a commercial offering in order to increase revenue. A single product could, of course, be used in both ways. In this sense, the network and associated applications are crucial to the continued success of the organization.

To meet this objective, the information network must provide: (1) a foundation upon which present systems/services can be enhanced and (2) a standard framework on which new systems/services can be quickly developed and deployed in order to meet the rapidly changing business requirements of the organization and its customers.

The information network must also be effective in allowing the organization to identify and quickly deploy systems that use information to provide a competitive advantage. The success of American Airlines in using the information gathered by its reservations system to define the first frequent flier program is an oft-cited case. It took a great deal of time and effort for the other airlines to match this program. During the time American was the only airline offering this program, the airline had a tremendous advantage.

INFORMATION NETWORK USERS

The ultimate purpose of any system (including an information network) is to support the needs of the end (human) user. The major classes of users, along with the principal classification attributes and values for each class, must be identified to determine the required characteristics and functionality of a network.

An analysis of the end users and the types of problems they

TABLE 2.1 NETWORK USER CLASSES AND CHARACTERISTICS

Class	*Characteristics*
Executive	Problem identification — parameter-oriented, individualized, low volume, menu-driven, graphics-oriented, exception-driven, specialized workstation functions
Management/Professional	Problem solving — ad hoc query, medium volume, end user programming, office services, decision support systems, and intelligent workstations
Clerical/Administrative	Operations-oriented — repetitive, optimized for efficiency, high volume, and text-oriented

deal with suggests an initial partitioning into three major classes: executive, managerial/professional, and clerical/ administrative. The characteristics of these classes are defined in table 2.1.

Although the requirements of the groups are quite different, each needs to access the same data and use many of the same or similar functions while performing their work. The network must provide the mechanisms that will serve these diverse needs. In addition, it must provide standard and consistent user views of the network and services, regardless of physical location, type of workstation, and network interconnection method utilized. A further discussion of how the network accommodates these diverse user needs is contained in chapter 2 of the companion volume on network system architecture, which deals with the architecture of end user services and interfaces.

SCOPE

An information network is defined to encompass all data, data processing, internal telecommunications, and office ser-

TABLE 2.2 APPLICATION FUNCTION CLASSIFICATION EXAMPLES

Classification	*Meaning*
Management Information System (MIS)	A system providing automation of a basic business function, such as order entry, billing, inventory, etc.
Management Support System (MSS)	A system providing business data and analysis tools to enable a manager to make informed and effective decisions
Strategic Information System (SIS)	A system enabling customers and/or suppliers of a business to interact directly with its data processing facilities to make business transactions and inquiries easier and more efficient for both organizations
Network Support System (NSS)	A system in support of network operation and/or management. This type of system does not interact with the user directly but is vital in maintaining a viable network.

vices required by the enterprise. It may support the transmission and processing of voice, text, graphic, and image information in addition to numeric data. The information network also includes access to the network by customers and suppliers to facilitate the orderly transfer of data between the cooperating enterprises.

The network definition does not cover stand-alone devices, such as specialized minicomputers or microprocessors. If it becomes necessary to connect these devices to the network, however, such connection can only be accomplished by using the standard interfaces and protocols defined for the network. In these cases, it is the user's responsibility to ensure conformance with the network standards.

Network data processing applications are sometimes divided into classifications to facilitate definition and development. One such set of classes is shown in table 2.2. Although a classification of this nature may be useful to the enterprise, from a network viewpoint there is no difference between classes. Each application uses the same resources and provides the same type of output regardless of its defined business purpose. In fact, a given application may have functions that belong in different classes, making the assignment of the application into a single category impossible. In any event, the definition of an information network covers all of the listed areas.

ROLE OF TECHNOLOGY

The design of the information network is based on the information technologies available today, as well as those projected for the future. Chapter 4 discusses some of the major technologies and their use in information networks. Because technology is continuously changing, new as well as existing networks must change in an orderly and controlled manner. As an example of the effects of this change, consider the user interface. Instead of the "dumb" terminals utilized previously, intelligent workstations (personal computers) are becoming the equipment of choice for economic and technical reasons.

This evolution has caused the design of information networks and their resident systems to change considerably. Total local processing capability has surpassed that of central computers, allowing more sophisticated and complex user interfaces to be designed. In addition, a substantial number of locally based functions can be utilized.

Integrated voice, graphic, and image information transmission is now possible (although in the early stages of development), as is cooperative processing and database technology. For networks to continue to provide cost-effective and efficient services, these and other new and emerging technologies must be utilized fully and must be considered in the design of new systems.

As these new technologies become commonplace, others

will emerge. The information network must be able to respond to this continuous change efficiently and effectively in order to remain a viable service for the users.

To enable you to understand fully the role of changing technology in satisfying corporate needs through an information network, a discussion of the various stages of the evolution of the information (data) processing industry is presented. A new stage, or *generation* as it is usually called, is defined when a significant change occurs in the development process and receives support from the technical and business community. For the purpose of the discussion the areas considered are network environment, development tools, and methodology.

It will be seen in the next chapter that the characterization of the development process is far more complex than these three areas would suggest. However, they will be more than adequate for presenting the evolution of data networks in a structured manner while at the same time keeping the discussion to a reasonable length. After reading the presentation on the development process in chapter 3, you may want to try describing the other elements of the process in terms of their generation as defined in this chapter.

The following section discusses the latest three generations: the third (current), fourth (emerging), and fifth (work in progress). A sixth generation (early concepts) has also been defined and is discussed in general terms. This sixth generation is considered to be based on systems that can improve their performance by automatically learning how to provide the "correct" response. This technology is still in its infancy, and it is expected that this generation will undergo considerable change in definition and structure before its principles are accepted and deployment begins in practical networks. The first two generations were batch-oriented, and the notion of a network was not relevant. Thus, their definition and study would contribute nothing to our understanding of information networks.

EVOLUTION OF INFORMATION NETWORKS

Although the word *generation* can be overused when describing various states of evolution (consider advertisements for third-generation mattresses — imagine what the first two generations were like!), the word has been applied to data processing and, by extension, information networks. To some extent, there is widespread agreement as to what constitutes these various generations (or *stages*). However, the definitions provided in this discussion contain extensions in order to more fully characterize the generation.

The presentation will examine the three major components of the third, fourth, and fifth generations:

- The environments utilized for deployment and implementation
- The tools that can be utilized in the development process
- The methodology that is followed in the use of these tools

Third Generation

The third generation, which forms most of the current generation of information processing systems, has as its focus the data processing professional. All data processing requests for programming services, features, and functions are directed to the data processing department, where persons specifically trained in data processing are utilized. In addition, the focus is on operational systems utilized by clerical/administrative personnel. These systems are designed for a small number of highly repetitive tasks, usually performed by a substantial number of operators.

Most third-generation systems use on-line real-time processing as opposed to batch processing, which was considered to be the major focus of previous generations. The deployment environment consists of "dumb," or relatively dumb, terminals connected to a processor by a simple network, as

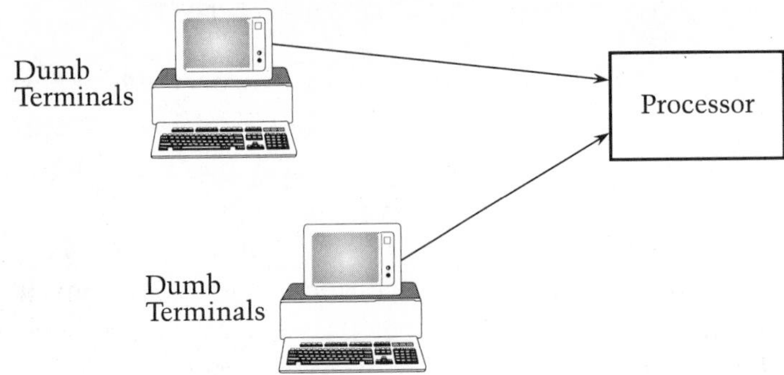

FIGURE 2.2 THIRD-GENERATION DEPLOYMENT ENVIRONMENT

shown in figure 2.2. Although these terminals may have resident microprocessors, they do not provide any independent intelligence as far as the application system is concerned. These processors may be utilized to perform protocol handling or to interpret screen layout instructions, but the terminals themselves are not considered intelligent. The connection of these terminals to the main processor formed the first computer networks and differentiated this generation from those of the past.

In the third generation, the mainframe processors to which the terminals are connected are generally not networked in the classical sense of the word. One or more processors may be physically interconnected and procedures may exist for the transfer of data between these processors. Usually, however, this is done under separate application control and the processors are not considered to be part of an overall network from the users' point of view.

As shown in figure 2.3, the implementation environment is such that application systems are each connected to their own database. When a new application system is defined, the data necessary to give it life is also defined as an integral part of the system development process, and a separate database is developed in which to locate that data. In many cases, this results in the same data being entered into various machines

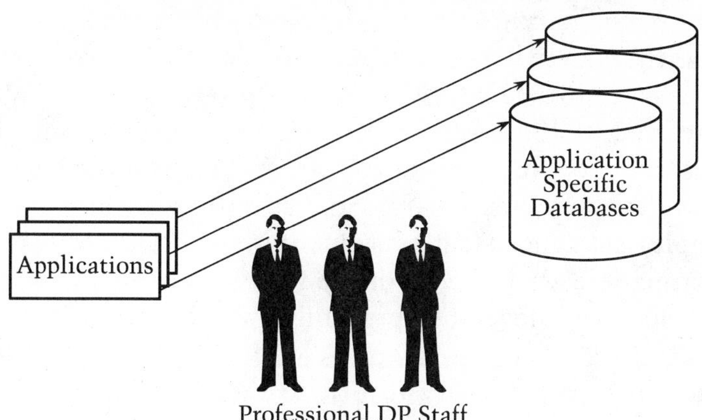

FIGURE 2.3 THIRD-GENERATION IMPLEMENTATION ENVIRONMENT

several times. Because of this, the data easily becomes inconsistent and difficult, if not impossible, to bring into agreement with other instances of the same data. This results in high on-going data maintenance costs and error rates.

The tools available in the third generation are fairly varied in terms of their function and availability, as shown in figure 2.4. These tools have not been used to anywhere near the

- COBOL, FORTRAN, Etc.
- DBMS
- Dictionary
- Report Generator
- Screen Generator
- Utilities
  Debug
  Testing

Characteristics:
—Not Integrated
—Poor User Interface
—Single Skill Level
—Reinvention of the Wheel

FIGURE 2.4 THIRD-GENERATION TOOLS

degree possible, however, and their early promise of providing a breakthrough in data processing has not been realized. There are basically three reasons for this lack of use:

The first is that these tools are not integrated. In other words, each tool has been developed separately, in many cases by different vendors, to provide a specific functionality. For example, the data base management system (DBMS) may not be compatible with the report generator or screen generator, which has been developed by another vendor. Because of this lack of integration, programmers are reluctant to go through the extra steps necessary to utilize the functionality of the tools.

Secondly, in many cases, these tools have a poor user interface. Typically, the issue of providing good user interfaces has not been addressed. User interfaces are important for these tools, especially when an unexpected event occurs. Instead of the user being left with a message such as "Unrecoverable System Error," the system should give the user some indication as to what went wrong and how it can be corrected. Although some tools do have this capability, it is unfortunately true that the vast majority do not.

The third problem with the use of third-generation tools is that, in general, these tools have a single skill level — expert. For a user to interact with the tools and utilize them effectively, they must become very conversant with the tools. This usually involves reading a lengthy, and often incomplete, manual, as well as spending a great deal of time interacting with the tool to find out what the quirks, problems, and difficulties are. The user of these tools must also spend time consulting with experts, either from within the organization or from the vendor, when problems are reached that cannot be solved through conventional means.

Because of the high skill level required to use these tools, many programmers either do not want to take the time, or do not have the time, to learn how to use them properly. They simply do not use the tools. In order to perform their

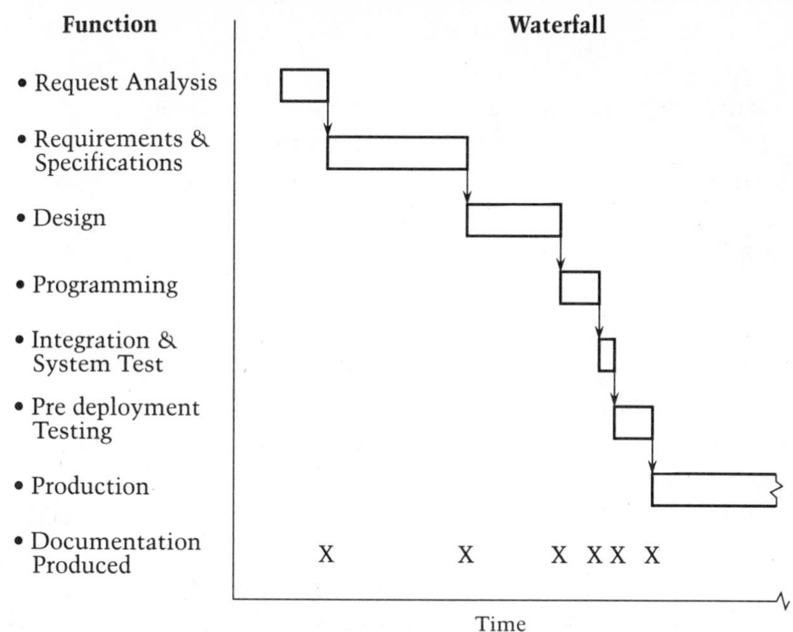

FIGURE 2.5 THIRD-GENERATION METHODOLOGY

jobs, they fall back on the use of more familiar but less efficient tools. In some cases no tools at all are used.

Given the limitations of the tools of the third generation and the operational problems associated with them, a complex methodology has emerged to enable the tools to be useful in developing applications. The methodology, sometimes called the "Waterfall" methodology, is illustrated in figure 2.5. It will not be discussed in detail in this book. Suffice it to say that the methodology must make up for the limitations of the tools and the restrictions of the environment. This is a lot to ask of any methodology and, as might be expected, the difficulties with the products of this generation remain.

Because of the complexity of the development process and the large amount of up-front work that must be accomplished, application developers usually try to characterize the application system completely before any programming work is started. This forces the end user and/or developer to attempt to define *a priori* all of the features and functions that the system must initially contain, as well as predict how the system will evolve in the future. This must be accomplished without the user and/or developer ever having seen the application in actual use.

What typically happens in this type of environment is that the user and the developer do their best to define the system, but after it is developed and becomes operational, substantial problems will arise. Users will find that (1) although the system may be close to what was asked for, it does not fully meet their needs or (2) the business has changed enough to make the system obsolete. This process could be dramatically improved if the user was able to see the system in action *before* and *during* its development instead of *after*. For the most part, this is not possible for third-generation systems, and that is why most large systems being built today have large cost overruns and inherent user dissatisfaction with the product and development organization.

Fourth Generation

The fourth generation of information systems is currently beginning to emerge in larger development organizations. These fourth-generation systems have several characteristics different than those of the third generation. For one, a major focus is on the end user — the person sitting at a terminal desiring to obtain services. This end user may fall into the clerical/secretarial, managerial/professional, or executive areas of usage as defined previously. Usually, however, the end user falls in the managerial/professional category. The executives are too busy and the clerks and secretaries have no need to program the system.

The fourth generation is *network-based* and allows the end user to obtain many of the required services without going through the systems development organization. This, of

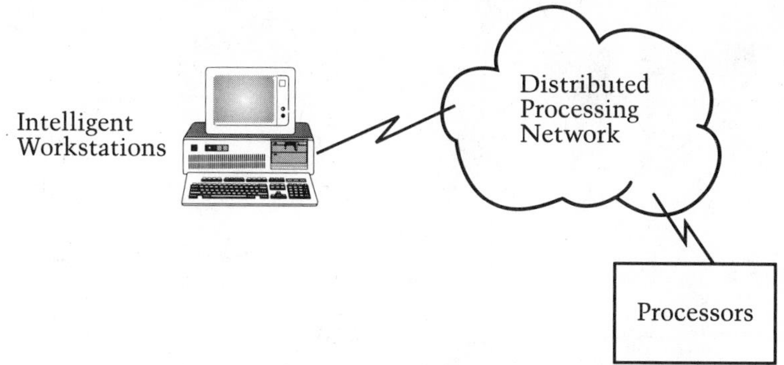

FIGURE 2.6 FOURTH-GENERATION DEPLOYMENT ENVIRONMENT

course, requires a different development philosophy and associated set of tools than were previously available.

The fourth generation also focuses on increasing system development *productivity* for those large integrated systems which do require the services of a professional systems development organization. Currently, it has been estimated that the backlog for information systems is on the order of ten years. To reduce this backlog, it is necessary to increase the productivity of the individual development professional. The fourth generation has the tools and procedures necessary to address this problem.

The fourth-generation deployment environment is completely different from that of the third, as indicated in figure 2.6. Instead of dumb terminals, end user workstations are now intelligent, having a data processing capability of their own that provides the end user with a substantial amount of processing power. Also, instead of being connected to a single processor, these workstations are now connected to an information network that consists of many main processors. The term *main processor* as used in this context is meant only to distinguish them from workstation processors. These main processors can be of varying types, capabilities, and powers, and all are reachable from the end users' workstations by means of the network that contains shared transport facili-

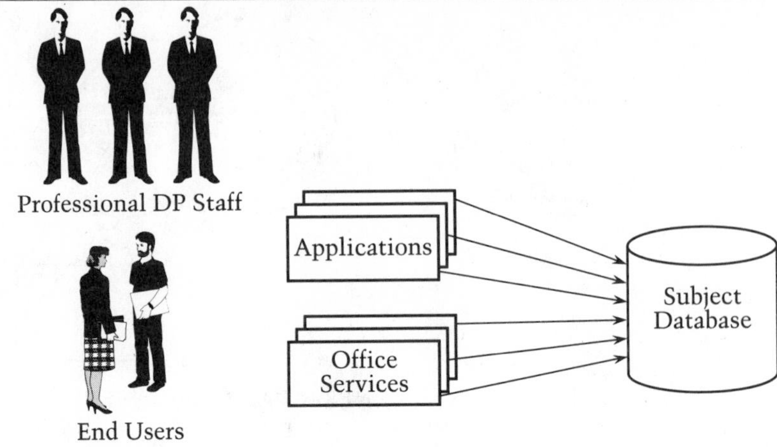

FIGURE 2.7 FOURTH-GENERATION IMPLEMENTATION ENVIRONMENT

ties. This does not imply that security measures may prevent certain users from utilizing specific processors, features, or functions on the network. In this context, a new logical network is defined that has a different reachability structure than the physical network.

The implementation environment is shown in figure 2.7. Systems that run on this network do not have individual databases. They utilize a single logical database that contains, at most, one official occurrence of each data entity. The physical implementation may, of course, contain replicated data, be distributed across multiple processors, etc. If this official data entity is correct, it will be seen as correct by all the systems that require the use of that data entity. This does not mean that data cannot be copied. However, when it is copied, it is considered to be owned by a specific system and is no longer considered to be part of the shared database that is accessed by all systems. This shared database is designed, implemented, and managed separately from the development and deployment of network system functionality.

The shared availability of all of the data necessary for the operation of the business allows many services that are defined on this data to be offered to the end user. These services are generally classified as management support systems (MSS). A large set of services offered under this heading consists of those handling the extraction, manipulation, and display of corporate data.

The language utilized by the end user to request these services is generally known by the term *fourth-generation language,* or 4GL. Because these languages are generally nonprocedural, the term 4GL has been extended in common usage to cover any nonprocedural language, no matter how it is defined or used. To a great extent, the term has lost any meaning it ever had as part of the characterization of the fourth generation of system development.

Another set of MSS services is known as "office services" because of the environment in which they are used. These services consist of word processing, document distribution, voice mail, and video conferencing, among others. The network environment and data processing capability of the workstation are, of course, an integral part of providing any of the MSS services.

As in previous generations, in the fourth generation, professional systems development personnel develop applications that are beyond the skill of the end users in scope, size, or complexity. However, when appropriate and desired, end users are allowed access to some of the same tools utilized by the professionals.

Many of the fourth-generation tools are the same as those of the third generation. A key difference, however, is that the three major problems associated with these tools in the third generation have been removed. The tools are now integrated and have user interfaces that are easy to use for users at multiple skill levels, as illustrated in figure 2.8. This means that all of the tools work easily with one another and even a novice can become productive quickly. As the end users gain experience with the tools, they can become more efficient in the utilization of the tools through the use of higher skill level interfaces. Thus, these tools can be utilized by several classes of system developers, including professional develop-

	Information Center		Development Center
	Suitable for End Users	Suitable for Systems Analysts	Suitable for Professional Programmers
• Simple Query Languages	X	X	
• Complex Query and Update Languages		X	X
• Report Generators	X	X	X
• Graphics Languages	X	X	X
• Decision Support Languages	X		
• Application Generators		X	X
• Specification Languages	X	X	X
• Very High Level Programming Languages		X	X
• Parameterized Application Packages	X	X	
• Application Languages	X	X	

FIGURE 2.8 FOURTH-GENERATION TOOLS

ment personnel, end users, and those with skill levels somewhere between them.

The third component of the fourth generation is its methodology. As was mentioned earlier, the third generation has a complex methodology as a result of the inherent limitations of its tools and environment. The fourth generation, with its much richer environment and tool set, allows an addition to the methodology — the rapid prototyping approach to system development.

Fourth-generation tool sets, as well as a networking environment, provide a foundation for the rapid prototyping of systems, as shown in figure 2.9. A prototype can be developed quickly with enough functionality to indicate to the end user what the system will look like when it is fully developed. If the system is not adequate, the user can discover any differ-

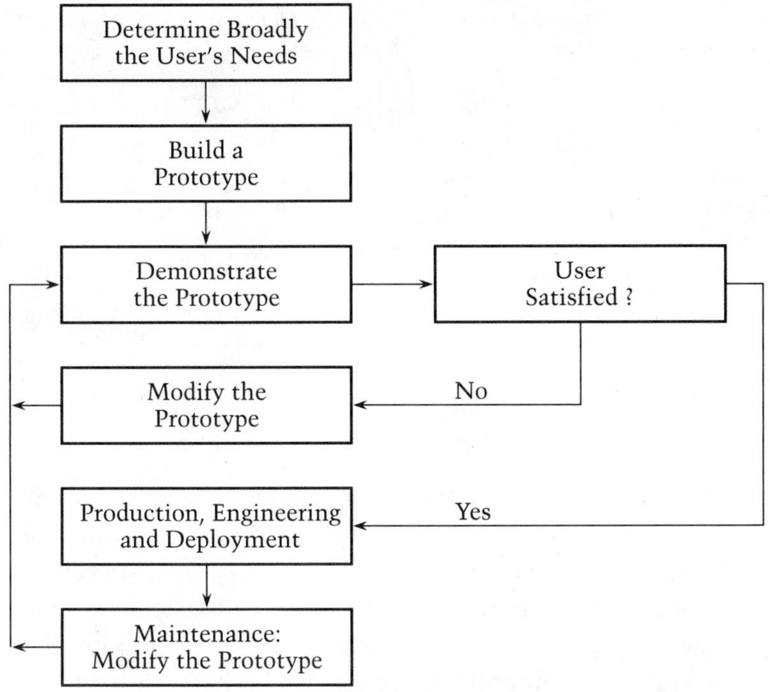

FIGURE 2.9 FOURTH-GENERATION METHODOLOGY (RAPID PROTOTYPING)

ences immediately and indicate them to the system developer, whether it be the user or another organization or person. The changes can then be made quickly and the altered system shown to the user. This process can continue until the user is happy with the system. At this point, the prototype system becomes the system definition from the user's point of view, and it becomes a large part of the requirements documentation. If desirable, the prototype can form the basis for the commercial system, including hardening, testing, documentation, and error detection and recovery. For large systems, the standard waterfall or other appropriate methodology can be adopted at this point. In either case, there is a great advantage in having the users see and approve the functionality before the remainder of the development is accomplished.

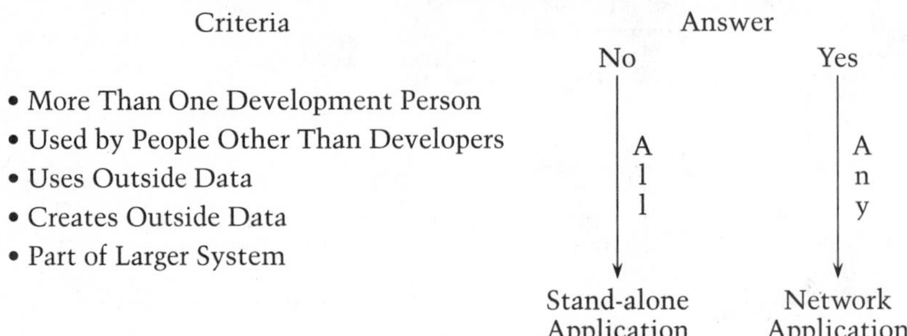

FIGURE 2.10 FOURTH GENERATION COMPUTING SCOPE

Although rapid prototyping does add a great deal to the use of any development methodology, defining a methodology that considers the concept of prototyping as an integral part of its operation is the best overall solution to the development problem. This will be discussed in more detail in chapter 3.

The major consideration that must be kept in mind when using rapid prototyping is that this technique is a tool — it is not the answer to every problem. Its use must be part of a systematic efficient approach to the overall development process.

Another important principle of the fourth-generation philosophy is concerned with stand-alone computing versus participation in the network environment. The network environment imposes constraints and obligations on any network hardware or software element that seeks to make use of the environment or provide services through it. Because of this, some end users and/or developers who wish to avoid these constraints declare that their particular systems and computing requirements are such that they do not need the network environment and will operate solely on a stand-alone basis.

As shown in the chart in figure 2.10, few applications are truly stand-alone in nature and will not at one point or another be utilized by another person or share in network resources. For this reason, all enterprise systems should be treated as shared applications, and the network requirements should be respected. Although there may be isolated incidents of true stand-alone applications, these are probably rare and are not worth the time and trouble needed to separate them. In addition, the constraints and obligations imposed by the network are good ones to observe even for stand-alone applications. Again, for this reason, all systems should be considered to be network systems, and the requirements of the network should be enforced as the evolution to the fourth generation progresses.

This discussion of the fourth generation characterized it in ideal terms. In reality, many of the desired characteristics will never materialize because of technology, cost, or time constraints. This in no way compromises the desirability of or need for fourth-generation concepts or philosophy. The transition from single-processor-oriented systems to network-oriented systems must be made, even if it is done with a less than perfect migration.

Fifth Generation

The fifth generation of computer technology is directed at the commercial exploitation of artificial intelligence (AI) capabilities in a network environment. Development of the deployment and implementation environments, tools, and methodologies required by the fifth generation is being pursued by government-sponsored consortiums as well as by computer vendors on a worldwide basis.

Although the strategic goals established for the fifth generation will not be realized for quite some time, a pragmatic set of AI capabilities is currently available for commercial use (although sometimes in very primitive form). These include natural language processing, speech recognition, other advanced human interfaces, and knowledge-based network systems and services.

Natural language (NL) technology provides the capability to establish end user interfaces that understand English language sentence structures. Through applied human factors engineering with NL technology, users can converse with the information network with greater ease and with less training. A whole new technology of "dialoguing" is emerging from this capability. Dialoguing allows the users to engage in a conversation with the network or system to define and satisfy their needs.

Speech recognition is necessary for the effective use of natural language processing as well as for the elimination of confusing equipment interfaces. These include large numbers of buttons and switches, confusing sequences of numbers and letters, and deep menu selection stacks.

Bit-mapped displays and advanced image processing are also providing more efficient user interaction with network services. Large amounts of data can be displayed statically or dynamically to convey insight as to the underlying physical phenomena or process taking place.

Knowledge-based systems capture the expertise and knowledge that highly skilled professionals use to solve complex problems. Once the knowledge is encoded in the form of an expert system, it can be used as a problem-solving aid by personnel of lesser degrees of skill and competence. Expert systems insure that problems are solved efficiently, consistently, and with reliable quality.

The fifth-generation deployment environment is shown in figure 2.11 and consists of a distributed information network with a wide variety of servers attached to it. These servers not only perform the traditional data processing functions but also provide voice and image processing as well as knowledge-based services. Interfaces to the network are through workstations that provide integrated voice, data, and image access and control.

The fifth-generation implementation environment, as shown in figure 2.12, significantly extends the base of services and ease-of-use features offered by the fourth-generation environment. Several capabilities have been added to accom-

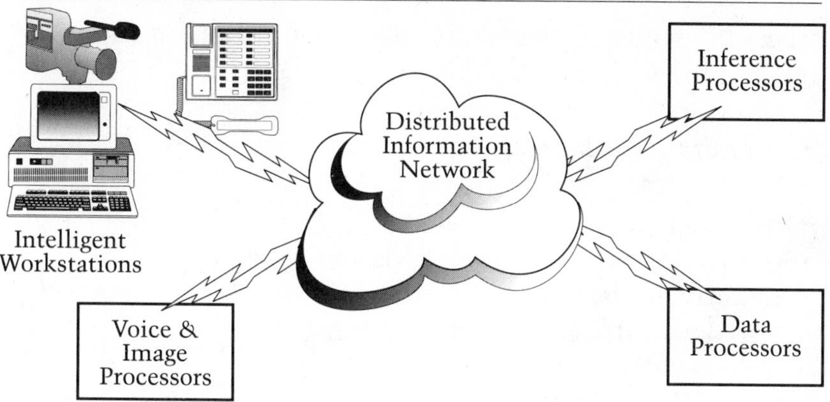

FIGURE 2.11 FIFTH-GENERATION DEPLOYMENT ENVIRONMENT

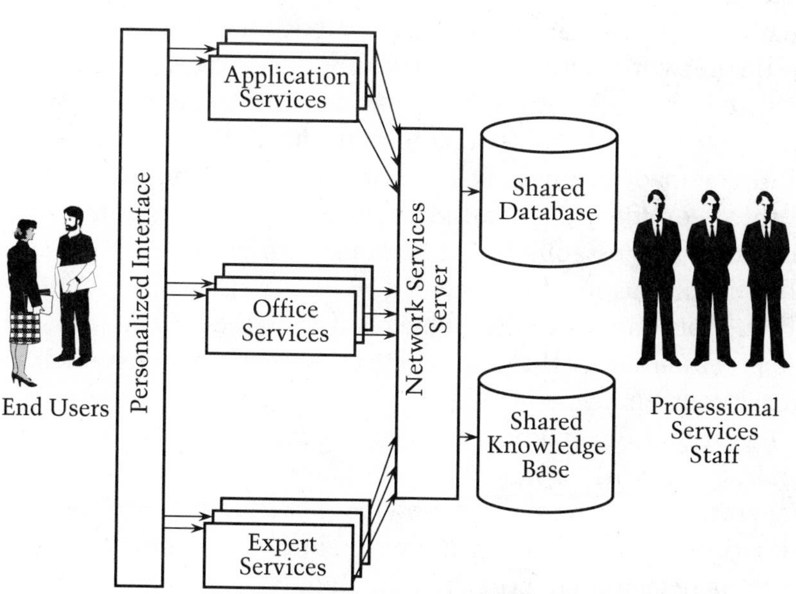

FIGURE 2.12 FIFTH-GENERATION IMPLEMENTATION ENVIRONMENT

plish the evolution from the fourth-generation to the fifth-generation environment:

- A natural language (NL) user interface
- Speech-recognition facilities
- Image generation and presentation
- Knowledge-based services of various types
- An active information directory
- Distributed databases and processing

The user interface provides a common point of interaction with the network services and can be personalized using workstation or network features such as natural language, speech recognition and synthesis, graphics, voice, or a combination of these. Systems implemented in this environment will be designed to use the available services and to connect directly to them as necessary. Interaction between the user interface and the information directory will determine automatically where the requested information or service resides in the network. The information directory expert system will then be charged with scheduling and retrieving the desired information or establishing communication with another component of the network (for example, an office service or a third- or fourth-generation application). The information directory also establishes a common point of control to insure that information is updated and maintained consistently throughout the network. The results of the interaction are then presented in the most effective manner — natural language text, image, or voice.

Incorporation of knowledge-based services into the information network is another important feature of the fifth-generation environment. Knowledge-based services and applications will address complex business problems in areas such as decision support, financial analysis, equipment diagnostics, marketing/sales analysis, and regulatory affairs.

The functional role and flexibility of the intelligent workstation are enhanced in the fifth generation. Features include

	Development Environment	Deployment Environment
	Suitable for Knowledge Engineers/ Implementors	Suitable for End Users
• AI Machines (LISP Processors)	X	
• AI Languages (LISP, PROLOG...)	X	
• Inference Engine Shells (KEE, LOOPS, OPS5)	X	
• Natural Language Retrieval Packages (INTELLECT)		X
• Automated Knowledge Acquisition Packages		X

FIGURE 2.13 FIFTH-GENERATION TOOLS

video conferencing and integrated voice/data/image capabilities that will allow business professionals to tailor the workstation to their personal specifications.

Currently a sharp dichotomy exists between the fifth-generation development environment and the delivery environment. The development environment is characterized by powerful specialized AI hardware and software tools that require extensive training to operate. This is illustrated in figure 2.13. The environment is used by knowledge engineers and experts to develop and test knowledge-based systems.

Significant progress is also being made with respect to general-purpose but customized intelligent workstations for the development of expert system applications. Such workstations are a major step toward the integration of the development and delivery environments.

Deployment of knowledge-based system services should be accomplished with conventional, general-purpose computer technology. This can be achieved by utilizing one of the following strategies:

- The expert system and knowledge base can be compiled in a manner that would allow the system to run on conventional computers.

- The knowledge-based application can be re-engineered and implemented with a conventional high-level language. It can then be made resident on a processor within the network.
- The specialized AI machine can be connected directly to the network to allow transparent access to the expert system application. This solution is suitable only for low-volume applications with noncritical response times.

The fifth-generation methodology capitalizes upon the software engineering experience gained in the third and fourth generations. It also extends and enhances the methodologies and engineering principles of these previous generations and makes full use of the network environment. This is accomplished through the increased power and flexibility offered by fifth-generation environment, technology, techniques, and tools. Because of the sophistication of the fifth-generation development requirements, however, additional preparation must be accomplished before systems of this generation can be designed.

This preparation is generally discussed under the topic of *knowledge transfer.* Knowledge transfer is the methodology by which information or knowledge held by one or more persons is transferred to a form usable by computer software. The general requirements for knowledge transfer are described in greater detail in chapter 6.

The main components of the fifth-generation knowledge transfer methodology, as shown in figure 2.14, are described briefly below.

- *Establish technology base:* Establish an AI technology and experience base that can be used effectively to develop and deploy knowledge-based application capabilities.
- *Knowledge acquisition:* Debriefing an expert to determine the thought process that is used to resolve conflicts, accomplish goals, and obtain objectives in a complex problem domain. The domain expert is debriefed by a knowledge engineer, who is responsible for directing the investigation,

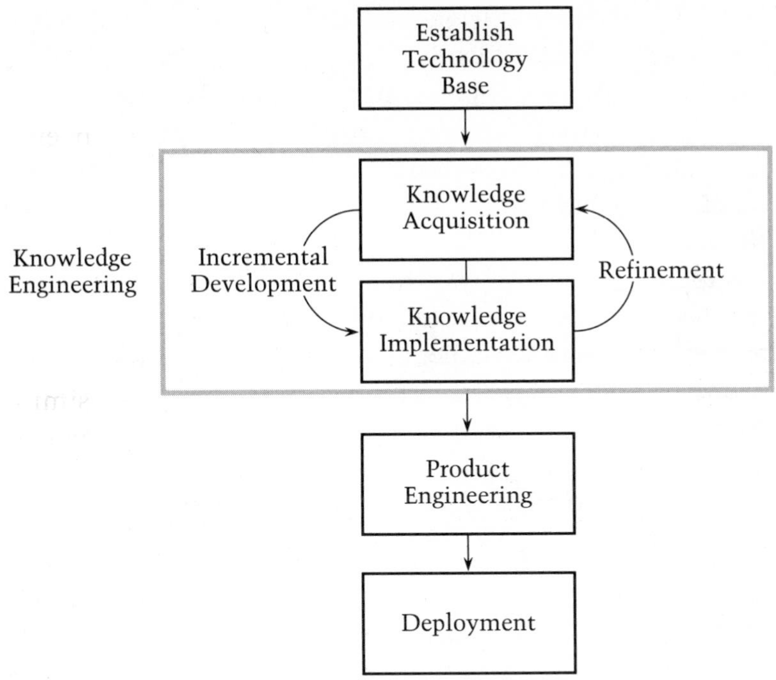

FIGURE 2.14 FIFTH-GENERATION METHODOLOGY (KNOWLEDGE TRANSFER)

documenting the results, and directing the knowledge-implementation phase of the development cycle.

- *Knowledge implementation:* An incremental process that is performed concurrently with knowledge acquisition. It is similar to the rapid prototyping technique of the fourth generation.

However, there are fewer restrictions associated with developing fifth-generation prototypes. The fifth-generation tool set allows operational prototypes to be developed more quickly and with less information about the problem domain (application requirements).

The power inherent in AI languages and tools provides substantial productivity gains over the languages and tools available in the previous generations. Fifth-generation technology is exclusively nonprocedural and does not require extensive data definition and data typing. This provides increased flexibility in developing application prototypes that do not have complete specifications. No penalties are associated with adding (or subtracting) classes of data objects or altering the functional characteristics of the processes to be performed. Fifth-generation technology is extremely flexible.

- *Production engineering:* After a fifth-generation prototype has been field-tested extensively, it is ready to be engineered for production deployment. The production engineering activity is concerned primarily with integrating the application within the network environment, providing appropriate human interface features, and installing control mechanisms to insure the integrity and robustness of the application.

For the sake of brevity, issues related to application and tool selection, documentation standards, and other similar matters have been omitted from this discussion. References concerning these topics have been included in the bibliography at the end of the book.

The system development methodology defined in chapter 3 and specified in detail in the companion book, *Information Networks: A Design and Implementation Methodology*, utilizes many of the principles and technology of the fifth generation.

MIGRATION BETWEEN GENERATIONS

Networks and resident systems typically will consist of software written for more than one generation. This is the price to be paid for utilizing new technology in a rapidly changing environment. When changes must be made to an application or function that was initially produced under a prior generation, several decisions must be made concerning the generation environment of the changes. Although each case must be evaluated independently, the following discussion sets some guidelines for the decision. This discussion will be presented in terms of the third, fourth, and fifth generations, where the transition is currently taking place. However, the principles will hold for any set of future generations.

In general, the changes should be programmed in at least the fourth-generation environment, because it represents the desired state, and the limitations of the methodology, tools, and environments are too great to allow the third generation to be integrated effectively with generations beyond the fourth. The following sections present several possible development scenarios and discuss the environment that should be used for the new software.

New Systems

Software for new systems developed in-house should be developed using the fourth-generation environment (fifth, if the system under development uses knowledge-based components), as it is currently defined. *Software* for new systems *being developed by third-party software vendors,* even though enterprise personnel are not involved in its development, should be developed under the fourth-generation environment. In most cases, this will necessitate the contracting enterprise to provide the development environment to the software developer. The development of software for new systems under the existing third-generation environment is not a good way to proceed toward the goal of having at least a fourth-generation network environment for all software.

Major Changes in Existing Software

This is probably the hardest area in which to specify a migration path. The decision must be based on the merits of the proposed modification(s). If the modifications are such that the modified software cannot be separated from the unmodified software, it probably means that the modification must be accomplished under the current third-generation environment. Insofar as possible, however, the information concerning the modifications, data utilized, etc. should be entered into the data dictionary. If the modified portions of the software can be partitioned into separate modules, the modifications should be done using fourth-generation techniques (as specified earlier), with appropriate links between the current software and the new software. Again, depending on the specifics of the modifications, either one or both of the above techniques may be employed.

Minor Modifications to Existing Software

In most cases, these modifications should continue to be made in a third-generation environment during the life cycle of the product. At the end of the life cycle, the replacement software (which will generally be part of an entirely new project) will, of course, be written under the fourth- or fifth-generation environment.

Existing Data

Because existing programs need the data in current formats, the existing files and databases cannot be eliminated until the programs that use them are retired. However, fourth- and fifth-generation databases can be built that contain the same data and that serve the programs of those generations. The duplication of data can be controlled by specific utilities that populate and update one data occurrence from the other. Deciding which occurrence will be the master and which will be the slave must be handled on a case-by-case basis and will depend on a number of factors, such as the number of fourth- and fifth-generation programs needing access to the data, the programs that require the most recent information, and the physical locations of each of the data occurrences.

The above discussion serves to define and clarify some of the complex issues involved in migrating from the third to the fourth generation (and beyond by extension of the proceeding discussion). Obviously, experience in this area will either reinforce or change any directions in this area as needed by a specific enterprise and/or networks and resident systems.

BEYOND THE FIFTH GENERATION

The design of information networks will continue to evolve at a rapid pace, as will the composition and focus of the generations that are used to describe and categorize them. Each succeeding generation will have a shorter life than the one before it and the evolution process will begin to span three, four, and possibly more generations. Change will have to be designed into networks and systems instead of being addressed only when absolutely necessary.

THREE

THE DEVELOPMENT PROCESS

INTRODUCTION

Networks and network systems can be produced and deployed in a variety of ways. The procedures utilized range from simple and informal "seat-of-the-pants" methods to methods that are formal, highly structured, and complex. The size of a development project can vary from "one person does it all" to organizations that number in the hundreds. The development process will vary considerably with these and other attributes. Examining the development process in a structured format and determining the characteristics of several development types will help us specify suitable processes for the design and implementation of network systems. In some cases, reference will be made to products and services instead of network systems. This will be done when it is desirable to identify systems specifically as the output of the enterprise and the reason for its existence.

This chapter will consider only the technically oriented aspects of the development process. The business aspects will be introduced and considered in chapter 5 through 7. The development processes discussed in this chapter represent only a subset of the overall needs of the business.

The development of hardware-based (electronics-based) systems has a long and well-studied history. The characteristics are well defined and well known to most practitioners. The question is often raised as to why software development does not follow the hardware methodologies. There is probably no single satisfactory answer to that question. Instead, the characteristics of software development as compared to those of hardware development have to be examined to discover why software has never been able to adopt the methodologies that have worked so well for hardware.

The design of electronics hardware is in essence the specification of interconnections of standard components. Through the years, the type and scope of the components may change, but the design philosophy remains the same. The electronics designer is generally not free to design his/her components because of the cost and time involved — even if efficiency could be improved. The hardware designer thus worked under a set of constraints that were well defined by the appropriate engineering principles.

Software design historically has not utilized the concept of components. It instead has tolerated, if not encouraged, the product under development to consist of entirely new software. The use of a development philosophy that emphasized total restart allowed the software to be designed for maximum efficiency. Efficiency was valued greatly because of the high cost of computers and was possible because of the relative ease (compared with hardware) with which software could be created and changed. One of the prices paid for this optimization was a total lack of standards in the development process. This in turn made an engineering approach to the process difficult, although certainly not impossible. The desire to create an engineering approach to software is the force that created and sustains the field of software engineering.

DEVELOPMENT DEFINITION

Before proceeding, it is necessary to define exactly what is meant by the term *development*, because there exists some confusion concerning the definition. Development is defined to be the "deliberate construction of new functionality," where functionality can be considered to be new if it differs in any significant way from existing functionality.

This may seem to be an obvious definition of little use, but a few examples will illustrate the constraining effect that is produced.

Example 1

Researchers discover a new algorithm that will make page swapping more efficient. The discovery was made while searching for better ways of routing printed wiring boards. The algorithm was not produced as a result of a development, because there was no deliberate attempt to produce such an algorithm. Even if the goal had been to produce such an algorithm, the result still would not be the product of a development, because no process could be followed to provide the desired output. In other words, there was no construction process.

The results of research do not come from a *development* process, they come from a *discovery* process.

Example 2

A programmer uses a new compiler to produce code for a computer with an architecture that does not follow von Neumann architecture. The original source code does not change. The resultant code for the new computer is not the result of a development. There is no new functionality inherent in the code. Although the result certainly may be more efficient, it is the result of the compiler and the new computer architecture (which *are* the result of a development), not the original code.

The results of a port from one computer to another do not come from a *development* process; they come from a *manufacturing* process. (*Manufacturing* in this sense refers to a duplication process and not a design process.)

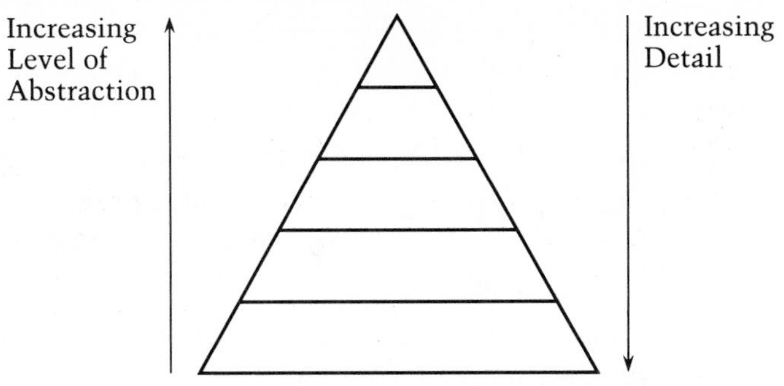

FIGURE 3.1 PYRAMID STRUCTURE

The processes defined for information system implementation should include a minimum of discovery, although the total elimination of discovery is impossible, as will be discussed in the section on methodology. Use of manufacturing processes may be necessary during the deployment phase of the development methodology, but they represent little value added from a development viewpoint.

PYRAMID STRUCTURES

The process of defining a highly abstract concept or need and adding detail in successive steps occurs in many areas of business and technology, including business planning, development methodologies, and architecture. This process can be modeled by a pyramid structure, as illustrated in figure 3.1.

Pyramid structures consist of levels with different amounts of abstraction and detail. The greatest level of abstraction and conversely the least detail are contained in the top level.

Lower levels become successively less abstract and contain larger amounts of detail. Because of the importance of such structures, this section examines their general principles and properties.

Although the pyramid structure is well known and is utilized frequently for a number of purposes, the methods for defining the contents of a lower level based on the information contained in the level above, are not generally discussed explicitly — with one exception noted later. The definition and utilization of these methods, along with the specification of the interfaces between adjacent levels, is of interest in this section. Without such knowledge, it is impossible to understand the characteristics of any process or definition that is based on a pyramid structure.

Four fundamental ways exist for adding detail to an existing level in order to obtain a lower level:

- Decomposition
- Assignment
- Augmentation
- Discovery

In a decomposition process, the contents of the existing level are partitioned and detail is added to each part, forming the lower adjacent level. This is the classical method of adding detail and is the stated basis for most of the current system development methodologies (assignment also plays a significant role but it is usually not identified explicitly). Because the content of the lower level springs directly from that of the higher level, the process that interfaces them is generally called a *mapping process*. Specific content in one level can be mapped directly to that in the adjacent level. This process is illustrated in figure 3.2.

In an assignment process, the contents of the lower level are derived independently of the higher level. Contents of the higher level are assigned to the contents of the lower level according to some predefined procedure, and the suitability of the lower level for supporting the higher level is determined through a verification process. This process is shown schematically in figure 3.3.

An example of this type of process is the development of a business organization structure that will support the mission of the enterprise. The organization structure is generally developed according to historical principles and the general industry of the enterprise. It does not spring directly from the

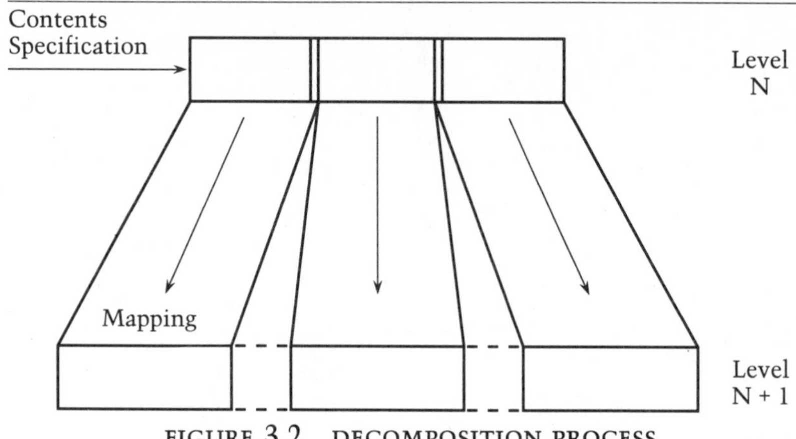

FIGURE 3.2 DECOMPOSITION PROCESS

mission statement. The usefulness of the organization is determined by assigning the needs of the enterprise as contained in the mission statement to one or more of the organization components and verifying that these components can produce the results desired. If either the assignment or the verification fail, the organization must be changed and the process repeated. The key to determining if the relationship between the levels is that of assignment is in determining the independent design of each level. A more complete discussion of this part of the business planning function is provided in chapter 7.

The augmentation process requires an independent source of detail information called a *control set*. The lower level is

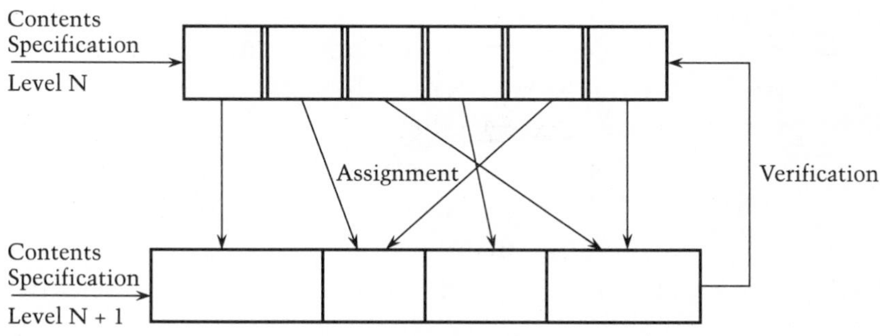

FIGURE 3.3 ASSIGNMENT PROCESS

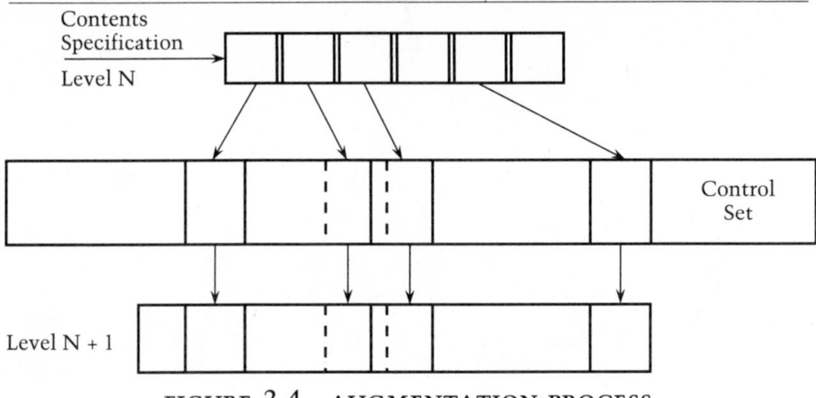

FIGURE 3.4 AUGMENTATION PROCESS

a subset of the information contained in the control set and is selected by using the contents of the higher level as the selection criteria. This process is illustrated in figure 3.4. An example of this process is the use of architectural principles (the control set) to supply technical specifications for a system under development. The business requirements are the contents of the higher level and serve as the guide by which the principles of the architecture are selected. The relevant principles become the nucleus of the specifications. This process is developed in detail in the companion book, *Information Networks: A Design and Implementation Methodology.*

The discovery process is similar to the assignment process. The major difference is that the proposed contents of the lower level do not result from a development process but come from a trial-and-error process. Instead of the relationship between the levels being one of assignment, then verification, the process is reversed and becomes verification, then assignment. This reversal is desirable because the presumption of the discovery process is that the result is not appropriate. This process is illustrated in figure 3.5.

An example of the use of discovery is in the selection of software assets for use in a system under development. A selected asset is placed in a verification process to determine if it meets the requirements of a component specification. Most of the assets tested will not be appropriate and will be

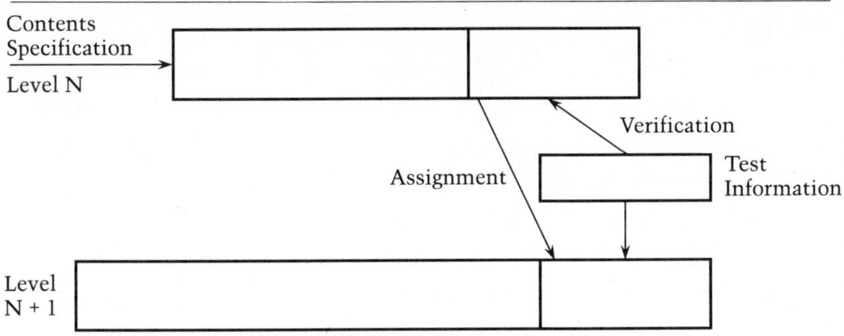

FIGURE 3.5 DISCOVERY PROCESS

eliminated from consideration. Those that survive verification have a component assigned to them.

If this assignment cannot be justified (economically or technically), the asset is also eliminated. Although a comprehensive selection methodology can be defined, as discussed in the companion book, *Information Networks: A Design and Implementation Methodology*, the selection process still retains some of the characteristics of discovery.

Explicit identification and/or selection of a suitable process for the addition of detail is important to the understanding of any development process. If this is not done, or if an inappropriate process is selected, the effectiveness of the results will be compromised.

DEVELOPMENT PROCESS COMPONENTS

One partitioning of the development process is shown in figure 3.6. There are three distinct components in the process:

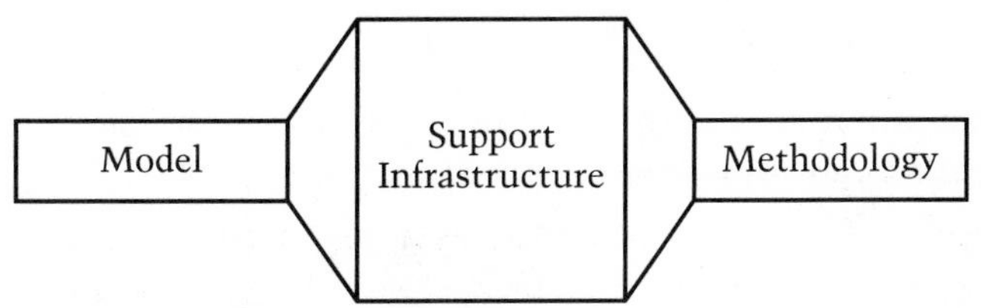

FIGURE 3.6 DEVELOPMENT PROCESS CHARACTERIZATION

model, infrastructure, and methodology. The model represents the philosophy that is adopted by the development organization to define how development will be accomplished. An organization may use one model or several models depending on the particular project being considered. The infrastructure represents the support required in order to utilize the model. Different models will have different infrastructure needs. Finally, a methodology must be defined through which the product will be implemented and which is compatible with the model and associated infrastructure.

Development Models

The product development model is the starting point from which all other development activities are derived. Support functions must provide the proper information and environment for the development to be accomplished in accordance with the model, and the development methodology must utilize the support structure during the implementation process.

The model(s) utilized by a given organization may be the result of history and culture, industry practice, type of product produced, the skill set of the key employees, or an explicit choice to optimize the development efficiency of the product set. Even though an organization does not explicitly pick the model(s) which it will use, one or more implicit models almost always govern the development process.

Hundreds of different models could be specified. However, most of these are variants of one of three major types:

- Job shop model
- Standard product model
- Custom shop model

These particular names come from the traditional hardware manufacturing environment. Although applying them to the development of software requires a slight twist in their usual definition, the names will be retained because they are relatively descriptive of the model philosophy.

The characteristics of these major model types will be discussed in detail so that they can be (1) recognized as part of an organized process and (2) used as appropriate for internal and external development characterization. The importance of this characterization will be demonstrated later in the chapter. It will be shown that one of these models is usually most appropriate for the development of networks and network systems.

Development Model Attributes The attributes that define a development model are listed below:

- Number of product classes
- Intraclass variability
- Change frequency
- Product utilization consistency
- Client/customer expectations
- Production efficiency
- Expertise applied
- Standards defined
- Financial arrangements

The first three attributes in this list indicate the amount of variability in the products produced by the enterprise. The next two indicate the flexibility required by the users. The next three depict the methods that are used to build the products. The last attribute indicates the method of financing the development. These attributes will be used in the following sections to define the characteristics of the major models.

Job Shop Model The first model is that of the job shop. Organizations using this model build all products in their entirety. Each individual product is an entity unto itself, with little or no relationship to previous or future products. With this philosophy, almost all of the components utilized in a product are also designed, developed, and built without using any designs or components from previous jobs. Of course, the experience gained in producing previous products will be of use within the job shop environment in the production of new products. Tools that are used in producing new products are also reused from development to development. For software, these would be compilers, debuggers, automated methodologies, etc. This is the traditional model of the craftsman or artisan who develops each new product as a one-of-a-kind work of art. Because each aspect of the development is directed toward the production of the single product, there is a perception that products produced in this way are superior to those produced using other manufacturing techniques. Although this may or may not be true, because of this perception and for other reasons (such as the desire to retain complete control of the entire development process), the job shop model is probably the most widely used development model in the world.

It is also the model utilized by most software development organizations. As discussed previously, because of the relative ease of software production or the perceived need for efficiency and/or total development control, there is a significant tendency to redesign and reimplement all of the software needed for a particular development. The use of this model may also be connected with the fact that most software development is still a "cottage industry," with many of the characteristics of the business of an individual tradesman or artisan.

The characteristics of this type of development are shown in the following list:

- Any number of product classes
- High intraclass variability
- High change frequency
- Variable product utilization
- Differing client/customer expectations
- Low production efficiency
- High expertise applied
- Few standards defined
- Customer financed

What these characteristics depict is a small number of highly individualized products produced for clients who want them optimized in a variety of different ways. The products are generally customer-financed because of the uniqueness of each development and the close involvement of the customer in the process. Because each product is started anew and the wants of the clients are highly diverse, the amount of general expertise that must be applied to each product is quite high.

These characteristics indicate that the improvement of software productivity in general requires the use of a model other than that of the job shop class. With the job shop model, the amount of possible improvement in productivity is limited.

Standard Product Model At the other end of the spectrum is a product development philosophy that relies on a single product. This standard product is altered to meet specific market and/or customer demands. Although it may be argued that this model is less a development model than it is a manufacturing model, it is nevertheless possible to utilize a standard product and make significant changes to it in order to satisfy a variety of needs. In this respect it is an extremely efficient model, because all of the expertise and experience is concentrated on a single entity. The characteristics of this model are shown in the following list:

- One product class
- One product in class
- High change frequency
- Variable product utilization
- Differing client/customer expectations
- High production efficiency
- Medium expertise applied
- Many standards defined
- Developer financed

This type of model would be suitable for a complex product that requires extensive modifications and tailoring to meet the needs of a specific customer. A network management and control system would fit this situation. Although the basic approach and core software would not change, the package would have to be altered to accommodate the characteristics of the network with which it is used.

This model is viable in a number of different circumstances. Examples would be (1) a new start-up company that initially relies on a single product and (2) the maintenance phase of a mature product. In this latter case, the development organization would probably need multiple development models, because the standard product model is not suitable as the only model for most mature organizations. Organizations of this type usually develop and market a number of different products and would require a different approach to the development process.

Custom Shop Model The final product development model considered here is that of a custom shop. A custom shop utilizes standard components and assembles them in such a way that the resulting product meets the needs of the customer or market. It is a combination of the job shop and the standard product models. The characteristics of the custom shop model are shown in the following list:

- Any number of product classes
- High intraclass variability
- High change frequency
- Variable product utilization
- Differing client/customer expectations
- High production efficiency
- Medium expertise applied
- Many standards defined
- Developer financed

The major function of an organization utilizing the custom shop model is integrating standard components, which are already available, to form a wide variety of products. The number of new components that must be developed to produce a specific product is kept to a minimum. The custom shop model requires that an organization decide which standard components are necessary for the product line(s) of the company. The design and implementation of these standard components must be completed before they can be used in new products.

This development model (1) retains the flexibility required to produce a wide variety of products, (2) imposes a design discipline that can effectively utilize engineering principles in the development of software, and (3) leverages the use of previously developed products. These characteristics make this model the most appropriate for building network systems; it will be used for the remainder of the book. The custom shop model contains elements of the other two models. This allows much of the information that will be developed through the use of the custom shop model to be applied to the other models. However, the full impact of the presentation in this book can be obtained only through the use of the custom shop model.

Development Infrastructure

An infrastructure is usually considered to be a shared set of resources that provides a foundation for performing a set of desirable activities. For example, the infrastructure of a city would be its system of roads, bridges, government, etc., which is used by the citizens to pursue their life and/or deliver products and services. An infrastructure is not an end in itself but a means to make the desired results more efficient and effective.

Because system development is the process of creating products and services (a desired result), an associated development infrastructure can be postulated and utilized successfully. The development infrastructure is different from the deployment infrastructure. The deployment infrastructure is usually the one meant by references to a "network (system)

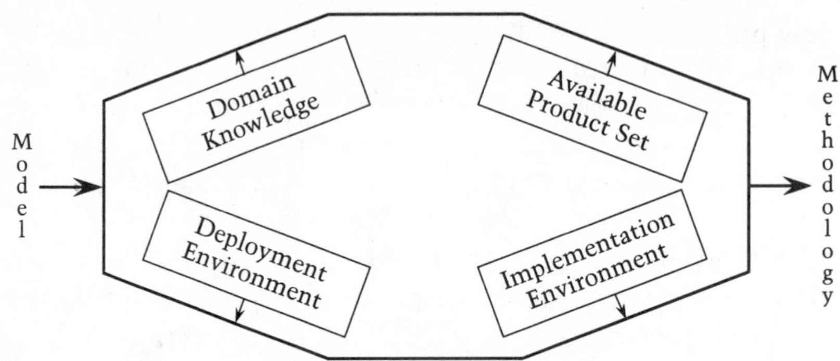

FIGURE 3.7 DEVELOPMENT PROCESS SUPPORT INFRASTRUCTURE ELEMENTS

infrastructure." It consists of elements utilized by the deployed system and will be discussed later in the chapter.

The system development infrastructure contains all of the information and activities that allow the model to be utilized effectively for system development. Each of the models require different infrastructure implementations, although a generic form, which is common to all of the models, does exist. A system development infrastructure has four distinct elements: domain knowledge, available products, deployment environment, and implementation environment, as shown in figure 3.7. The characteristics of these entities, along with their interrelationships, are shown in figures 3.8 through 3.10

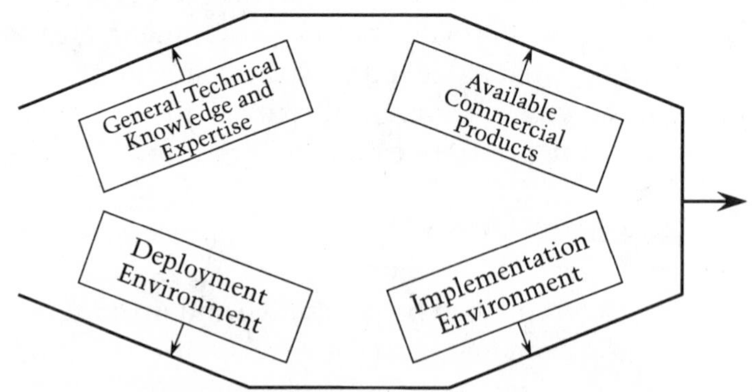

FIGURE 3.8 JOB SHOP MODEL SUPPORT INFRASTRUCTURE

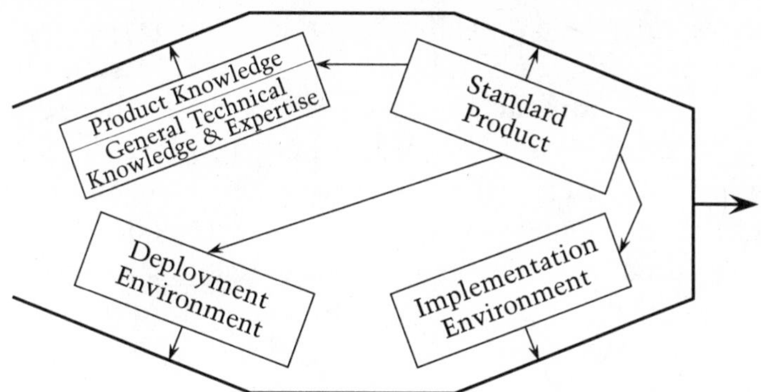

FIGURE 3.9 STANDARD PRODUCT MODEL SUPPORT INFRASTRUCTURE

for each of the three model types. The characteristics of each of these infrastructure components are presented in the following discussion.

Domain Knowledge *Domain knowledge* is that knowledge which is required to produce products in accordance with the model. The type of domain knowledge that is necessary varies considerably from model to model. In the job shop model, it consists of the accumulated technical experience and expertise that can be applied to the current product. Because each

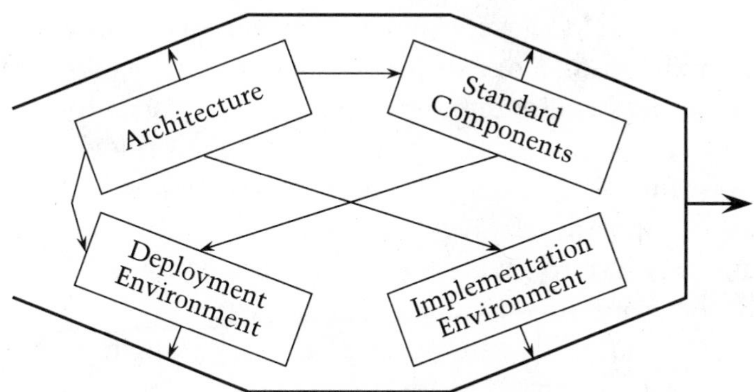

FIGURE 3.10 CUSTOM SHOP MODEL SUPPORT INFRASTRUCTURE

project is independent of all other projects, this type of general knowledge is the only domain knowledge possible. In the standard product model, the general technical experience and expertise are also important, but knowledge of the product itself is of at least equal importance and may in fact be more important. In the custom shop approach, the domain knowledge required in addition to general technical expertise is embodied in an architecture. This architecture provides the principles (strategies, standards, guidelines, and rules) needed to assemble complex systems from standard components. In a very real sense it is an extension of human expertise. Because domain knowledge is shared among products and is required before the development methodology can be initiated, it is considered to be part of the development infrastructure.

Available Products The "available products" part of the development infrastructure is a set of products that can be utilized as part of a new system (or implementation infrastructure) development to produce a usable result. The products may be hardware, software, or a combination of both. Product resources are usually acquired as a separate unit that was not developed specifically for the application system being implemented. For this reason, the addition of detail that occurs when these products are specified is a process of assignment. Knowledge of product availability is required to complete the development process and can certainly be considered part of the infrastructure necessary to develop practical systems. Even systems whose application software is all developed specifically for the project need a processor and system software to give them life. These components would be chosen from an available products list.

In many cases, the number of available products is so large that it must be restricted for efficient and effective use. The restricted list results from an associated management process and is usually called a standard product list. The development and use of such a list is discussed in chapter 6.

Because available (standard) products are defined to be a pool of potentially deployed system (or deployed infrastructure) components, tools used in the implementation or management process are not considered to be part of this group. They belong to the implementation environment, which will be discussed shortly. In addition, products that are in actual use in current systems are considered to be a part of the deployment environment. As such, they are not considered to be available products, because they have already been selected and used.

In the development infrastructure that supports the job shop, the available product pool consists of the hardware and software that is supplied by the processor vendor (or third party) to enable the application system to function. This could include run-time subroutine libraries such as those that perform mathematical functions (sine, square root, linear regression, etc.) as well as user interface functions, such as graphics packages.

In the standard product model, the only available product is the standard product itself. It is assumed that any required hardware or software that comes from outside vendors becomes an integral part of the standard product. As the standard product is changed to fit specific circumstances, these "outside" products are also subject to modification as the conditions warrant.

In the custom shop infrastructure, available products are of two types. The first type is similar to that discussed in the job shop presentation, although most of the available products will be used as part of the deployment infrastructure and will not specifically be made part of an application system. The second type consists of the standard components (assets) from which the system is constructed. Because of their importance in the development process, standard components will be discussed in considerable detail. The technology point of view will be considered later in this chapter. The companion book, *Information Networks: A Design and Implementation Methodology*, will consider standard component use in the development methodology.

Deployment Environment The deployment environment is the current or anticipated environment in which the products must function. Two aspects of this environment must be considered. The first (and most important) is the deployment infrastructure. It consists of any existing deployed set of entities through which the system under development will operate. Existing networks, computers, specific software functions, and other products that have additional capacity and that could be used by the new system are examples of this type of entity. In general, the deployment infrastructure entities are shared physical or operational resources put in place for the purpose of serving current and future products/services. This particular part of the infrastructure is especially critical from an economic viewpoint.

The second aspect consists of the operational characteristics that are imposed on systems by the enterprise and that form a set of constraints that must be followed for the product to meet the requirements of the enterprise. These constraints arise from a need to use specific existing or anticipated facilities or to follow a corporate deployment strategy. Without a knowledge of this aspect of the environment, a product cannot be implemented.

As an example of a corporate deployment strategy that would affect product implementation, consider the following scenario:

> A corporate data processing strategy restricts the type of communications allowed. A workstation is only allowed to send data to a departmental processor, where it will be checked for accuracy before being sent to a corporate processor.

Although the facilities (deployment infrastructure) may be in place to allow other types of interaction, this corporate policy must be followed when the operating characteristics of deployed systems are developed. Failure to do so will result in an unacceptable system even though it operates correctly from a functional point of view.

The different development models all must be able to work with a specific deployment environment if it exists. The discussion in this chapter thus applies to all of the models. However, a robust deployment infrastructure is fundamental to the cost-effective development and use of fourth- and fifth-generation systems. It will be assumed for the remainder of the book that a suitable infrastructure has been designed and put in place. One of the major differences between development process for third-generation systems and those for fourth- and fifth-generation systems is the existence and use of the deployment infrastructure. This part of the development infrastructure must be considered at appropriate places in the development methodology in order to make the most effective use of the infrastructure. Retrofitting the results of a development to an environment in which it was not meant to function is a difficult and resource-intensive operation that should not have to take place except under unusual circumstances (such as when the deployment environment is not known until after the implementation has been completed). A comprehensive discussion of the use of the deployment infrastructure in a development methodology is presented in the companion book, *Information Networks: A Design and Implementation Methodology.*

Implementation Environment The implementation environment provides the tools and management structures used by the development methodology. Although the tools are not part of the development methodology, they are closely associated with it. The specific set of tools that can be used effectively depends in large measure on the methodology chosen. The tools currently are grouped and marketed under the heading of Computer Aided Software Engineering (CASE) tools. Because of their complexity, these tools cannot be discussed in detail here.

The management structures include personnel organization, project management, contractual requirements, etc. Personnel organization is considered in chapter 7, which discusses the business dynamics necessary for a technology-oriented enterprise. The other aspects of the implementation environment are outside the scope of this book and will be deferred to future publications.

In general, each of the models will require an implementation environment that is specific to the needs of that model and the organization using it. Because a large number of variables for each individual enterprise must be known before this topic can be considered adequately, no general treatment can be provided. As indicated above, however, some aspects of these topics will be considered later.

Although much of the development infrastructure is currently implemented through manual activities, significant progress toward automation is being made with the aid of the fifth-generation techniques discussed in chapter 2.

Because development based on the custom shop model has been adopted for the remainder of the book, the domain knowledge (architecture) and available products (standard components) elements of the support infrastructure are examined in additional detail in this chapter. In addition, necessary characteristics of the development methodology are also considered.

System Architecture As defined earlier in the chapter, the purpose of a system architecture is to provide the domain knowledge necessary for the implementation of network systems when using the custom shop model. This information must be represented in such a way that it can be utilized by personnel not having the degree of experience and knowledge that the architecture represents.

Although there are many usable representation forms, one

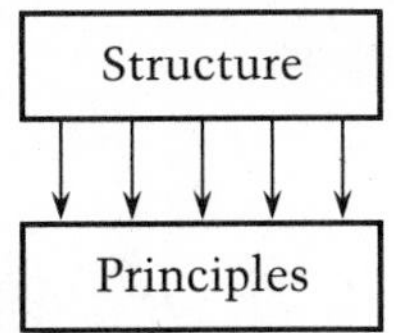

FIGURE 3.11 ARCHITECTURE KNOWLEDGE REPRESENTATION FORM

of the most widely used ones is shown in figure 3.11. This representation format consists of two fundamental parts: structure and principles. The structure organizes the knowledge, and the principles, which are derived from the structure, are used in the development methodology to guide the formation of the system.

The amount of knowledge contained in an architecture designed for large, complex systems is usually quite large. This requires that the two basic parts of the architecture be decomposed into smaller pieces so that the complexity can be managed effectively. The first partition level defines the principles in terms of strategies, standards, guidelines, and rules. Strategy principles are general statements that indicate overall development directions. Standards principles define the internal and external standards that will be used in the development process. Guideline principles cover broad areas and indicate desired results. Rule principles are required to be followed exactly. Exceptions to the rule principles must be severely limited and must be approved at a high level in the organization. For very large architectures, each of these principle types can be further subdivided. Division into architectural, design, and operations principles is often useful for this second-level partition.

The structure partitioning is governed by many environmental factors, including the type of systems being developed, the needs of the business, and areas in which specific emphasis is needed. One partitioning that is suitable for architectures guiding the development of network systems is shown in figure 3.12. There are seven partitions, called subarchitec-

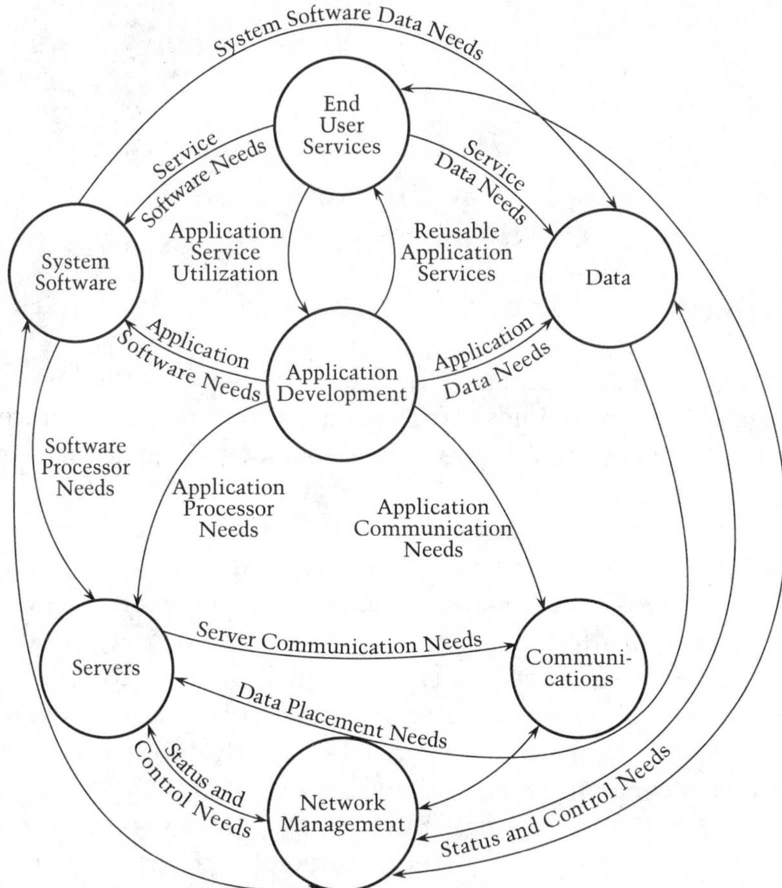

FIGURE 3.12 NETWORK SYSTEM ARCHITECTURE STRUCTURE

tures, each of which relate to a specific aspect of network system implementation and operation. The names of the subarchitectures are descriptive enough to provide a high-level understanding of the range of each of the subarchitectures. Further discussion of the specification and structure of each of these subarchitectures is beyond the scope of this book.

Because the architecture must act as an integrated whole, the relationships between the subarchitectures must be carefully defined. These high-level relationships are also indicated in figure 3.12.

TABLE 3.1 EXAMPLE ARCHITECTURAL PRINCIPLES END USER SERVICES SUBARCHITECTURE

Type of Strategy	*Example*
Architectural	All end user interfaces will be based on intelligent workstations containing at least one user-accessible processor. Only one physical workstation will be provided per end user. All necessary functions must be available on that workstation.
Design	A single end user system will be designed and used for all network functions. Changes to the end user system may be made as required for new systems. The "look and feel" of all functions should be identical.
Operational	All workstations will be connected to a physical or virtual LAN through direct coupling or via a remote access facility. Gateways will be utilized for access to other networks. All network functions should have 100% availability.

Type of Rule	*Example*
Architectural	The end user system will have the same interface regardless of the physical device or system software on which it is resident.
Design	The coupling devices, entry/presentation format and access procedures components shall be resident on the workstation.

Some examples of the type and scope of the principle statements are shown in table 3.1 for the user services subarchitecture. Keep in mind that these principles are part of a much larger set and that by themselves they do not convey much information.

With the use of the custom shop model, the need for an architecture is critical, because all of the standard components must work together effectively to produce the desired results.

The architecture must not only define areas in which standard components can be useful but also provide the principles that are to be used in assembling the standard components. The architecture helps ensure that this will be accomplished in a predefined way regardless of the number of people or organizations involved in the implementation of the system. This standardization is accomplished through the methodology. The relationship between the architecture and methodology is discussed later in this chapter. The companion book, *Network System Architecture,* contains a much more detailed discussion of the design and implementation process for a system architecture. In addition, the book defines an example architecture along with a comprehensive set of principles.

Standard Components Two distinct methods exist for using the standard components required by the custom shop development model. The first is static utilization, in which the standard components are assimilated into the final product and lose their individual identities. The second is dynamic utilization, in which the components remain as separate entities whose use is coordinated by a control mechanism associated with the product being developed. A useful analogy would be the difference between macros and run-time subroutines in classical software development. Macros that are used in a program lose their separate identity as soon as the entire program is converted to machine code. Run-time subroutines always retain a separate identity from the programs that use them.

Macros and run-time subroutines are a useful analog in the above discussion, but they are not necessarily standard components. The definition of standard components is much broader, even though the functions can include those of macros and run-time routines. The differences between macros and run-time subroutines and standard components are manifested in three ways: intent, scope, and implementation.

The intent of standard components is to serve as the main building blocks of a network or network-based system. Macros are generally designed for use within a specific program or set of programs to make the coding job easier. Run-time subroutines are intended for use as optimally coded algorithms that serve more than one system but that are not intended to make up more than a small portion of a program's processing need.

Both macros and run-time subroutines are limited in scope. They are generally thought of in terms of individual programs or modules. Standard components are thought of as building blocks for systems, and they themselves may consist of smaller systems. In addition, standard components need not be limited to software. They can include methodologies and associated procedures such as test suites. Characteristics of standard components are discussed in more detail in the companion books, *Network System Architecture*, and *Information Networks: A Design and Development Methodology.*

The final difference is in terms of implementation. Macros and run-time subroutines are linked to the main program through the use of calling sequences consisting of <name parameter> formats. Their execution is tightly integrated with the main program. Standard components may use this type of coupling but are also permitted to be called via a general message format and are allowed to execute asynchronously with the main program if desired. In addition, standard components may exist anywhere on the network as appropriate. Macros and run-time routines run on the same processor as the calling program.

The detail of the preceding discussion was necessary in order to present standard components as entirely different building blocks than those used in classical software development. Without this characterization, the whole approach to software development contained in the custom shop model will fail.

Standard components must be administered with the same attention as any other asset of the business. A process must be in place to decide when new components are necessary and what their function and environment should be. Their availability must be made known to developers so that maximum use of the components can be made. Finally, they must be retired when their usefulness is over.

Because of the importance of this administrative process to the effective utilization of standard components, a brief discussion of one of the aspects of the administration process is presented here. Although not the most complex, this aspect — the support provided for the individual system components — is one of the most visible because of the interface with the system implementors. Some of the ways in which this support can be provided effectively are presented. Various levels of support can be defined, depending on the overall importance of the standard component to the product development cycle and the degree of definition that is attainable. These levels of support are shown in table 3.2. All of these levels of support probably will be needed in a viable and robust standard component administration function.

The overall administration process is a complex and resource-intensive function. Because of space limitations, it will not be possible to discuss this topic in more detail than is presented here. Current literature may be examined to obtain more information on this aspect of the support infrastructure of the custom shop model (see the bibliography).

Earlier in this section, a distinction was made between standard components and macros and run-time routines. In order to further develop standard components as specific entities, they must be defined in terms of their attributes and values. Major ones are listed in table 3.3. The attributes are generally common to all system components, whereas the values are specific to standard components.

These characteristics generally reflect the view that system components are separate and distinct from the systems in which they are used. Their requirements and specifications

TABLE 3.2 STANDARD COMPONENT ADMINISTRATION SUPPORT LEVELS

Support Level	*Functions*
Full service	This is the level with the most support; it consists of development, consulting, acquisition, maintenance, distribution, and training in the use of the asset.
Central acquisition	This level provides for direct maintenance, distribution, and training by personnel dedicated toward the asset administration function. This is a lower level of support than would be provided under the full service level. However, a great deal of help in the utilization of the asset is still available to the potential user.
User group	This level of support is usually associated with a user group dedicated to a particular asset or set of assets. Support is usually accomplished through a published catalog of available offerings with instructions on how to obtain them. Meetings of the members of the user group are also used to inform others about these assets on an informal basis. Although there is documentation, it tends to be rather brief and little help is given in the way of utilization or employment of the assets.
Bulletin board	The last level of support is basically distribution only. Distribution is based on the bulletin board concept, where the asset and whatever documentation is available can be obtained on an "as is" basis. Generally, no support organization or individual is available to help in the event difficulties are encountered. However, a great deal of software is distributed successfully by this method.

TABLE 3.3 MAJOR STANDARD COMPONENT ATTRIBUTES AND VALUES

Attribute/Value	*Comments*
Control	Controlled by the development organization, not the market
Timing	Definition and development must be a continuous process
Management	Managed separately from product development
Implementation	Based upon a genuine business need, including a return on investment analysis
Procurement	By several methods, including purchasing, developing internally, developing on a contract basis, and/or a combination of the above
Classes	Hardware, software, and methodologies alone or in combination; anything that can be reused and leveraged across many products

must be obtained using criteria optimized to their specific needs.

If a robust enough set of dynamic standard components is available, system implementation can be reduced to the task of developing a "script" that controls the use of these components. A further refinement can be made if these scripts are considered to be knowledge bases to an artificial intelligence system, so that control is based on heuristics instead of algorithms. Research toward this possibility is currently in progress.

Development Methodology

The final part of the system development process is the specification of the development methodology. This methodology must be defined such that it is consistent with the development model and infrastructure. For any set of development conditions (model, infrastructure), a large number of effective methodologies usually could be defined and implemented.

Different methodologies may optimize specific criteria, such as cost, elapsed time, or personnel requirements. Others emphasize documentation (usually government-connected), adherence to certain standards (ANSI, CCITT), or use of specific concepts (packet transmission).

Methodology Requirements Before a methodology can be specified, all of the nonprocedural requirements of the methodology must be determined. Requirements of this type surface as a result of development process used, specific business or technology needs, or the characteristics of previously developed systems. Any methodology must consider the installed base when new systems must interwork with those already deployed.

There is usually no single "right" methodology, but there are plenty of wrong ones. The goal is to identify at least one of the set of usable methodologies. A brief discussion of how this can be accomplished is presented below. The companion book, *Information Networks: A Design and Implementation Methodology*, presents this subject in much greater detail.

As stated above, any development methodology must start with a basic set of requirements. For example, a development methodology may utilize the set shown in the following list:

- Modular framework
- Architecture based
- User validated
- Prototype driven
- Integrated deployment infrastructure
- Life cycle view

These particular requirements result from the assumption that the development will use fourth- and fifth-generation methods, the custom shop model, and development in the large. Experience with the advantages and disadvantages of several development methodologies, and an appreciation for the need to increase the productivity of the development process by at least an order of magnitude from that which currently exists, also contribute to the list.

The concepts of modularity and life cycle view are well known and need not be more thoroughly explored at this time. Architecturally based, user-validated, prototype-driven, and integrated-deployment infrastructure concepts are not as well understood and need some further explanation.

A methodology that is architecturally based requires that each step in the methodology directly utilize the architecture constructs and principles as defined earlier in the chapter. Because the methodologies of interest are to be utilized with the custom shop model and development infrastructure, this is a necessary requirement. Also implicit in this statement is a requirement to rely on standard components (assets) as a fundamental part of the methodology. The reliance on fundamental architectural considerations is explicit in each step of the methodology.

To ensure that the final system will meet the needs of the users, regardless of the implementation period, the example methodology requires that the users examine the results of each methodology step. The validity of the design in meeting the needs of the users is thus made a continuous part of the methodology. Under no circumstances can the implementation of the system proceed to the next step of the methodology unless the users have approved the results of the current step. In addition, this approval must be based on sufficient supporting evidence. This will usually involve some type of system embodiment that can be accessed and understood by the user, as discussed above.

The output of each step of the methodology contains one or more elements — called *prototypes* — that users can examine to determine whether or not the results of that step are in accordance with their needs and desires. The requirement for a prototype as an output from each step is necessary to identify potential problems as soon as possible. The longer the problem is hidden, the costlier it is to correct. This aspect will be discussed further in chapter 6, which deals with the economics of the development process.

Integrating the deployment infrastructure into methodology requires that the design process be oriented toward the eventual assignment of functionality and data to elements of the infrastructure. Because the infrastructure is generally designed independently of any specific system, the addition of this detail is accomplished by an assignment method, as discussed earlier in the chapter. Assignment must be accomplished in several steps of the methodology, and it represents one of the fundamental differences between methodologies designed for network systems and those designed for single-computer implementation. Single-computer development methodologies do not include an infrastructure assignment process.

Methodology Steps The management of complexity requires that the methodology be partitioned into a series of steps. Each step has been defined with the same basic framework. This common structure is shown in figure 3.13. and is used to ensure that each step will meet the requirements of the methodology.

Each step has two input streams. One is the accumulated output of each of the previous steps. Although a given step may not use all of the available information, that information is nevertheless available. The second input comes from the architecture. A specific part of the architecture, directly applicable to that step, is identified explicitly. However, all of the architecture results (structure and principles) are available if they are needed by the step process.

Each step also contains a specific procedure that is unique to that step. This procedure provides the required step functionality as well as an embodiment of the system (prototype) using the detail developed through the application of that step. This system embodiment is the means by which the user determines if the results of the development — through

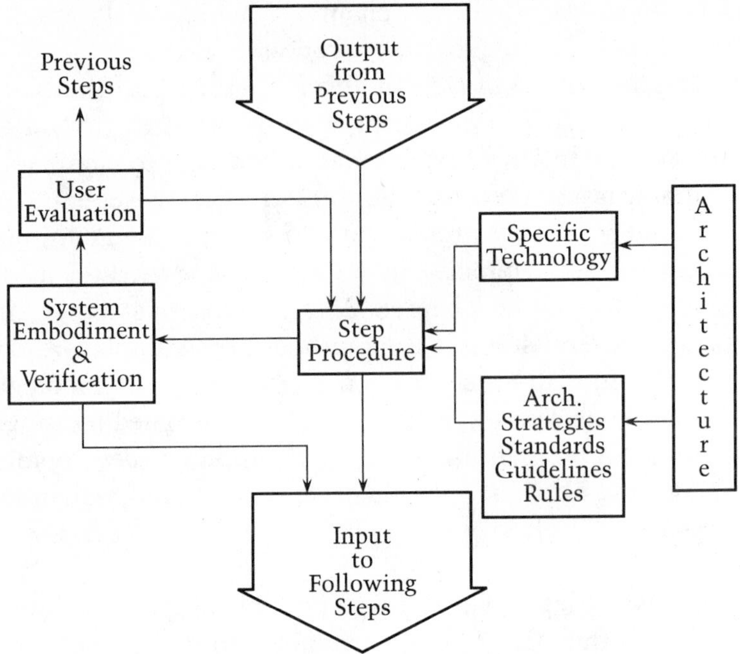

FIGURE 3.13 COMMON STEP STRUCTURE

the current step — remain in conformity with the business needs.

Overall Methodology The complete example methodology is shown in figure 3.14. The process starts with user needs and proceeds through eight steps. As is also indicated in the figure, each of these steps has an output to the user, and the user has an implicit input back to the step. In addition, one or more specific architectural considerations are defined for each step. Each of the step names is descriptive enough to provide a high-level understanding of the function of the step. Further expansion of the methodology definition and construction is beyond the scope of this chapter.

Although only the major inputs to a step are shown in this figure, to avoid undue complexity, the input to every step is considered to be the aggregate of all previous steps. For ex-

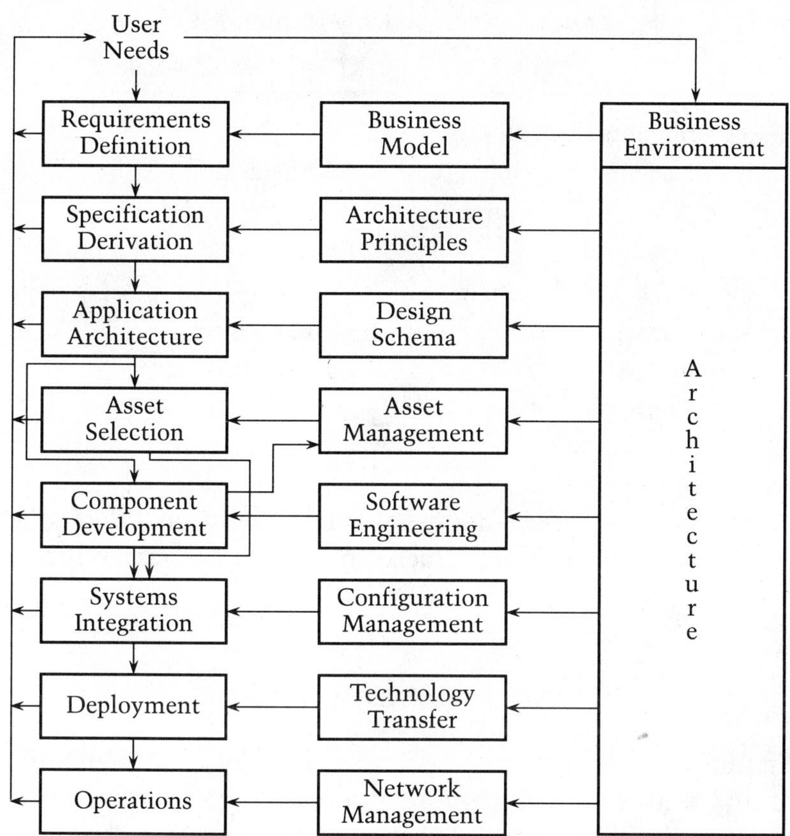

FIGURE 3.14 COMPLETE METHODOLOGY STRUCTURE

ample, the input to the functional development step consists of the outputs of the requirements development, specification development, and asset selection steps. Although the output from any given step may not be utilized explicitly in a later step, it is necessary to make this assumption to assure that each step has access to all of the information available.

As defined earlier in the chapter, the type of detail that must be added at each step should be defined explicitly. This is shown in table 3.4 for the example methodology. For every method that is not a decomposition process, information in addition to that available from the previous steps must be provided. The diversity shown is characteristic of a network

TABLE 3.4 STEP DETAIL PROCESS

Step	*Detail Process*
1. Requirements determination	
2. Specification derivation	Augmentation
3. Application architecture	Assignment & decomposition
4. Asset selection	Discovery & augmentation
5. Component development	Decomposition
6. System integration	Assignment
7. Deployment	Assignment
8. Operations	

system design methodology. Except for functional decomposition, however, the detail addition process is rarely identified.

PROCESS DETERMINATION

The specific development process used by an organization results from two major influences: the characteristics of the enterprise and the characteristics of the project to be developed. This relationship is depicted in figure 3.15. An enterprise might use only one process for all projects or might tailor the process to the project. Organizations do not usually choose a development process explicitly; it develops over time as a result of experiences gained from a number of developments — successful and unsuccessful. In such cases, the enterprise cannot use the process to its advantage. It is stuck with what exists. By explicitly choosing one or more processes, the enterprise can tailor the characteristics of the processes to the needs of the organization and the products it develops.

A change in process can occur in one or more of the elements. The model might change from a job shop to a custom shop. In a custom shop model multiple architectures might

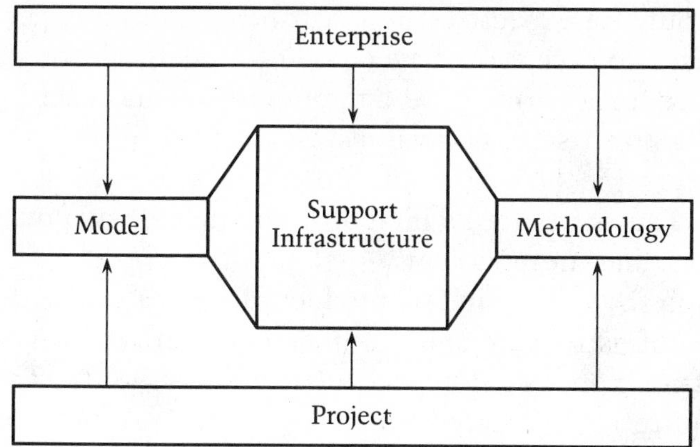

FIGURE 3.15 DEVELOPMENT PROCESS DETERMINATION

be used, depending on the product to be developed as well as the intended market. If the model and infrastructure remain the same, an organization may rely on two different methodologies that are used for different-sized projects. The number of possibilities is quite large. As with any process, the development process should be continuously monitored for effectiveness, and changes should be instituted when appropriate.

Enterprise View

The enterprise must consider a number of attributes before deciding on the development processes that will be used. Some of these attributes are listed below:

- Financial resources
- Number of development personnel
- Depth of technical expertise
- Amount of experience
- Previous development process use
- Project diversification
- Management depth
- Size of customer base
- Customer expectations

As would be expected, these attributes form a superset of those used to define the development models, although they are stated in a form more appropriate for an enterprise to answer about itself. The values assigned to these attributes will determine how the enterprise can structure a process that best suits its needs, including the model, support infrastructure, and methodology.

The job shop and standard product models, along with their support infrastructure and methodologies, are the easiest for an organization to define and utilize successfully. They do not require sophisticated financing or large support organizations and can be implemented effectively with simple methodologies.

Once established in an organization, these processes are hard to eliminate in favor of more complex ones, because of the amount of perceived "nonproductive" support work that must be performed before the new process can be used. A great deal of management time must be expended to effect a successful changeover.

The custom shop model requires a sophisticated organization with relatively good capitalization, a support organization large enough and with enough expertise to develop and maintain a comprehensive architecture and catalog of standard components, and a culture that will allow this type of process to occur. A rather complex methodology is also necessary to use all of the infrastructure information.

Project View

The main characteristics of a particular project that will influence the development process selection are scope, complexity, uniqueness, and phase. This latter characteristic is important in the case of a mature product that needs new development or modifications. If the needs of a project indicate that a specific development process is appropriate but the organization does not or cannot use that process, a development mismatch will occur. If the organization does not reject the project, the resulting development will be too expensive, late, of low quality, or otherwise unsatisfactory. No amount of effort or dedication on the part of the developing organization will be able to overcome the process deficiency.

The scope of the project is usually reflected in the development infrastructure, where it will influence the personnel organization aspect of the implementation environment. The methodology will also be affected to a significant extent. The complexity, uniqueness, and phase of a project will for the most part be reflected in the model selected.

Development Scope Although the size of a development can vary continuously from very small to extremely large, developments are usually partitioned into two scope classes: development in the small and development in the large. The classification into one partition or the other is only indirectly a function of development size. The classification directly depends on the organization that must be put into place in order to accomplish the development. If the development can be performed by one person or at most a small group of people, it is defined to be development in the small. If the development requires a large organization, with the attendant overhead and formal communications structure, the development is referred to as development in the large. One of the areas of on-going research is the development of organizations that would increase the project size that could be addressed by development in the small.

Development in the Small Development in the small utilizes one person, or at the most a small number of people (typically five or fewer). The procedures are mostly informal, and no approvals from outside the group are necessary. Because all development knowledge is contained within this small group, decisions can be made quickly and implemented without a great deal of documentation or communication. Systems can be constructed and deployed quickly if this type of organization can be used. The deficiencies, however, are significant: testing is usually inadequate, as is documentation; decisions concerning interfaces and software structure are not sufficiently discussed or reviewed; little attention is given to training and support; and the effects of future changes are not usually taken into account.

The chief programmer team concept of the 1970s was an attempt to use the advantages of development in the small while minimizing the deficiencies. It was a method of formalizing a methodology suited to a small number of developers. Of course, small ad hoc teams have been developing software and systems since the beginning of computers. To some extent, it has worked, but its success has depended in large measure on the particular people involved. Because of the difficulty in deciding if a particular team was appropriate (a psychological and sociological question rather than an engineering one) this type of organization has fallen into disuse. The concept, however, is still valid. More research needs to be done on the selection and utilization of the teams before it will again become an accepted method of system development.

Development in the Large Development of most network system products requires development in the large because of the sheer size involved. Organizations of significant size are used, and the resultant systems are complex and large enough so that no one person, or even a small group of people, understands all of the system. Most of the systems that classical management information systems (MIS) addresses are in this class. The goal in this area is to develop methodologies that allow systems of this magnitude to be developed effectively by reducing the overhead and inefficiencies usually associated with this type of organization.

On the plus side, it should be noted that development in the large usually produces systems that undergo rigorous quality control in terms of testing, documentation, and training programs. Entire teams of people are typically assigned to these functions, and in many cases a negative result from their efforts can stop the entire development until the problem is resolved. To some extent, because of the large number of people in separate organizations involved with development in the large, enough separation of "powers" occurs to ensure that all needs are met.

The inefficiencies inherent in this type of organization, unfortunately, are usually the reason most large-scale software and systems development projects result in long delays, cost overruns, and user dissatisfaction with the delivered product. Most network developments tend to be complex and large. Thus, the emphasis of this book concentrates on effective methods for development in the large. This is not intended to downplay the usefulness and effectiveness of development in the small where it is appropriate, but only to recognize the realities of today's large-scale development needs.

Project Type The complexity, uniqueness, and phase of a project (project type) indicate the model that should be used for an optimum development process. Complex projects generally require the custom shop approach, because they need the discipline of an architecture and the availability of standard components to eliminate as much of the complexity as possible. Unique projects benefit from a job shop approach, because very little previous work can be reused and no future project can take advantage of the current effort. Projects that are in the maintenance phase of their life cycle could best use the standard product model for development, as long as the modifications were not of the same magnitude as the original product.

The above approach does not eliminate the need for experience and judgment in the selection process. For example, a unique project could also be complex, and different models may be indicated. The decision as to the most effective model would have to weigh the characteristics of the project against the characteristics of each model to determine the best fit. This is also true for all of the other elements of the process.

The determination of the "best" development process for a given project and organization remains a somewhat subjective procedure. This is not a contraindication of the usefulness of this explicit decision process. Useful insight into the needs of the enterprise and project and the possible deficiencies of the approach adopted can be gained through this approach. Through the use of knowledge-based systems, it may be possible to automate much of the selection process by using appropriate optimization criteria.

Development Conflict

Use of different development processes can lead to a number of conflict situations within and between organizations. These usually arise when an organization acquires software from another organization and incorrectly assumes that the development process used in the development of that software is in agreement with the ones used internally. Two scenarios will be presented to illustrate the problem.

Scenario 1

An organization has defined a network application that they wish to have developed. The organization sends out a detailed Request for Proposal (RFP) to a number of development organizations. Two proposals are received. The first proposes a development of six months for a cost of $100,000. The second proposes a development of two years for a cost of $1,000,000.

This is an obvious conflict in proposals between a development in the small versus a development in the large. Which one should the organization choose? The expertise of the sponsoring organization must make the required value judgment and decision. The outcome should depend on the experience with previous developments and the specific needs of the current request. However, the temptation is great to make the decision purely on a cost and time basis, which may not reflect the true requirements of the development. The result may then be an inappropriate system that cannot be deployed effectively because it does not contain the required quality or functionality.

Scenario 2

> An organization contracts for a materials management system from another organization because of a lack of internal resources. A comprehensive set of requirements and specifications designed to provide consistency with the other manufacturing software produced internally was made available to the development organization. The development organization produced a system consistent with all of the given information and the system was accepted and installed.

When the system was installed it was found that the users avoided use of the package and tried to find ways of using the previous software to provide the required functions. Upon investigation it was found that the architecture used by the developers was not consistent with the internal architecture. One of the resultant incompatibilities was in the human interface to the system. The developers used an industry standard graphics package, and the using organization used a proprietary package. Although the standard package met all of the given requirements and specifications, there were enough differences in operation between the two to confuse the users and cause them to reject the new system.

To prevent this type of problem, the contracting organization would have to specify the use of its development process to the developing organization. This may or may not be practical, because the contracting organization may hold its process to be a competitive advantage and therefore proprietary, and the development organization may not be capable of utilizing a process imposed from the outside. As with the previous scenario, organizations requiring this type of outside development must recognize the dangers and be prepared to address the problem.

SUMMARY

Because the discussion in this chapter consolidates the information presented previously and forms the basis for the material presented in the remainder of the book, a short recap of the main points will be useful.

- An explicit knowledge of the development process is necessary for the process to provide an advantage to the enterprise. The process must be matched to the characteristics of the enterprise and the products being developed. This knowledge is required whether the products are being developed internally or by an outside supplier.
- By definition, network systems are fourth and/or fifth generation. This requires the use of an extensive deployment infrastructure. The use of this infrastructure is one of the main requirements for the development methodology.
- Most network system developments are large and complex. This necessitates a custom shop approach for their initial implementation. Development in the large is also a requirement for the same reasons.
- The specification of a comprehensive architecture and associated development methodology is crucial to the success of the development effort. Although not directly discussed in this chapter, the effective management of standard products, including assets, is also critical to a successful development process.

The remainder of this book assumes the use of a fourth/fifth generation, custom shop development process using development in the large. This has technical and business implications that will become evident as the discussion proceeds.

Before the business issues and their interrelationship with the technical aspects of development can be presented, an understanding must be gained of the specific technologies involved in the development process. A discussion of these technologies is the subject of the next chapter, which will complete the discussion of the technical portion of the development process. The business-oriented issues will be addressed in the remaining chapters.

FOUR

INFORMATION TECHNOLOGIES

INTRODUCTION

Network systems require many technologies in their design and development. A working knowledge of the capabilities of the major technologies and the most likely directions of their future evolution is necessary to (1) understand what is capable of being accomplished by network systems and (2) how they can be used effectively to enhance the performance of the enterprise. The purpose of this chapter is to present the major technologies that influence the design and implementation of networks and resident systems (information technologies) so that their impact on the development process can be evaluated.

Obviously, this type of discussion represents only a slice of time. To be useful, the information must be updated continually to reflect the addition of new technologies, the obsolescence of others, and the changing nature of the ones that remain. The discussion is intended as background material for the remainder of the book and by necessity must remain at the overview level with an emphasis on the dominant future directions. More detailed discussions of any of these technology areas can be obtained from numerous publications and books, as listed in the bibliography.

In addition to the discussion of individual technologies, this chapter will also address the integration of these technologies. Integration has the potential of providing a higher order of capability than that associated with the individual technologies. Technology integration has the potential of providing the greatest source of new capabilities for network systems. This will be discussed in more detail later in the chapter.

If you are already familiar with one or more of the technologies presented in this chapter, you may skip or skim those sections as desired. However, the technology integration example presented at the end of the chapter is recommended even if you know the rest of the information in the chapter.

APPLICATION OF TECHNOLOGY

The elements of a development process and the characteristics of the products produced as a result of that process must of necessity depend on the technologies utilized. As the capabilities of the technologies improve, so should the capabilities of the products. Currently, however, the tendency in the development of network systems is to use only proven technology in order to avoid reliance on research or advanced development. Unfortunately, the state of the art of all of the required technologies is moving so fast that, when current system developments are completed, the technology utilized is far out of date. Clearly a middle position must be taken. It is probably wise to avoid high-risk technology but foolish to require no-risk technology.

Many organizations have resorted to the use of formal technology management procedures to guide them in the optimum application of technology in their current and future products. One approach to this type of planning is presented in chapter 5. It relies on the concept of strategic technology areas (STAs). These STAs are defined to be those areas of technology which the organization needs to meet the competition and/or provide a competitive advantage in its marketplace. The technologies described in this chapter could be defined to be STAs for an enterprise that produces networks and associated applications and systems. In fact, this will be assumed in examples presented in chapter 5 as part of the network management discussion.

TECHNOLOGY INTEGRATION

Up to the present time, the creation, evolution, and application of technology has focused on individual areas with little thought being given to exploiting the integration of these technologies. This is especially true in the software and network areas, where a number of technologies, such as artificial intelligence, network management, communications, presentation technology (human factors), database systems, etc., have each started and matured as independent entities. Although individually they have produced enormous gains in the effectiveness of network systems, the effect of their integration will be at least as large.

Combining artificial intelligence with human factors technology, for example, will enable humans to have a much greater degree of efficiency in making use of network resources. The major effect of this particular integration is to enable the developer to tailor the network access to the individual characteristics of the human user instead of trying to design an access that is usable in some form by the largest number of people possible. For example, the artificial intelligence component of the human interface should be able to identify the skill level of the user in specific access circumstances and adjust the interface accordingly (such as change from a command-driven interface to a menu-driven interface). It is also possible to imagine an interface that could sense when the user was fatigued at the end of a long day and that could adjust the interface accordingly by increasing the size of the characters on the screen. Although this example may not be practical, the capabilities possible in this merging of technology are enormous.

Unfortunately, the integration of complex technologies is an even more complex undertaking that must be managed carefully through use of a suitable development process. As has been seen, however, the opportunities for innovative systems are worth the effort. A detailed example of a number of technologies integrated together in a network service will be presented later in this chapter. This example will illustrate the complexities and opportunities in the integration process.

TECHNOLOGY DESCRIPTIONS

The information technologies discussed in this section will provide the basic knowledge needed for later discussions. The technologies presented are shown in the following list and, as stated previously, may be considered to be the strategic technical areas for an enterprise performing network based development:

- Cooperative processing/data
- Network design
- Communications
- Presentation technology
- Software engineering
- Modeling and simulation
- Artificial intelligence
- Advanced architecture computers
- Database management systems

To facilitate the discussions, each technology presentation will contain the following elements, although the order may vary with each technology:

- Definition
- History
- Current status
- Future directions

These items are sometimes grouped under the heading of "technology assessment and forecast," which forms an integral part of the technology management process mentioned previously. As such, emphasis will be placed on the specific

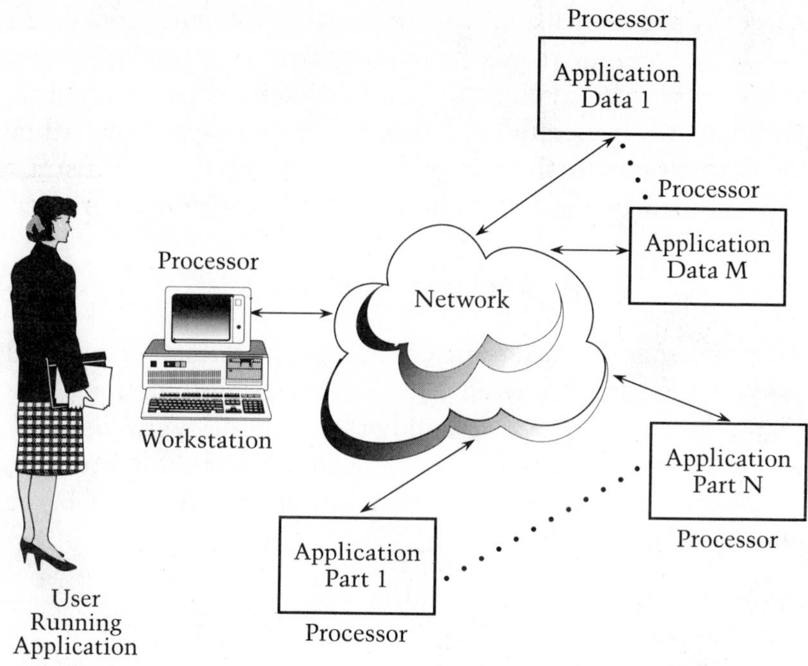

FIGURE 4.1 COOPERATIVE PROCESSING/DATA

characteristics of the technology that are most likely to cause changes in future development projects.

Cooperative Processing/Data

Cooperative processing and/or data is the technology that allows application functionality and data to be decomposed into two or more parts such that each part may be resident on different nodes in the network. The application may be designed so that the different parts operate asynchronously or synchronously with respect to one another. This concept is illustrated in figure 4.1. The major current use for cooperative processing is to split the processing between a personal computer or workstation and the mainframe.

Cooperative processing is not the same as distributed processing, although the two terms are similar and are often confused or used as synonyms for each other. *Distributed processing* is generally used to refer to one of two cases, as illustrated in the following examples. An application with functionality and data that is resident on a single network node but that can be moved from one node to another for execution is an example of distributed processing/data. This fits the classical use of a network for load balancing, one of the early uses for a computer network. Either static or dynamic load balancing may be considered under this definition, but there are still many unsolved problems in providing a completely dynamic load-balancing function.

The ability of a user to access different nodes of a network on a one-at-a-time basis in order to obtain the functions and/or data resident on that node is another example of distributed processing. In this case, the network merely acts as a transport mechanism to enable the user to obtain self-contained services from one of a number of network nodes. The main effect of this type of access is the use of one terminal on a desk instead of many.

The design and development of systems for either of these cases of distributed processing are not much different than those used for systems that reside on a single computer. Cooperative processing requires a completely different approach to system development because of the complexity of the assignment process (which functionality will be assigned to which processors). This approach was discussed briefly in chapter 3 and is presented in considerably more detail in the companion volumes *Network System Architecture* and *Information Networks: A Design and Implementation Methodology*.

Cooperative processing/data is effective when the characteristics of specific nodes are matched to the characteristics of the component parts of an application. If part of an application requires the inferencing capability of a knowledge-based system, a node that has a computer optimized to this type of processing could make the application more efficient. Matching of function to node type would hold true for applications that require large databases, bit-mapped graphics, document distribution, human intervention, etc. The specific characteristic of the network node optimized for an application part could be location, size, computer architecture, or other feature.

Because cooperative processing/data requires a network for implementation, its history begins with the advent of computer networks in the early to mid 1970s. These early networks were used for distributed processing/data. In fact, even now, with the exception of the split of functionality between the workstation and mainframe as mentioned above, little cooperative processing/data is being performed.

However, the design and implementation of many networks contain the inherent capabilities to support distribution. The lack of cooperative processing systems has occurred because current development processes do not contain the architectures, standard components, and methodologies that would allow the necessary decomposition and assignment to take place. The architecture and methodology defined in chapter 3 are based on the concept of cooperative processing/data and as such represent an advance over most of the development processes in current use.

Another factor in the slow development of cooperative processing systems is the lack of network systems software (such as a network operating system, or NOS) that would be required for system control. Because different parts of the system run on different nodes, the control of the overall process as well as error detection and correction become critical issues. Several approaches to this problem are currently being investigated, but the solution to the general distribution problem has not yet been obtained. Distribution in some specific cases has been accomplished with the network control software tailored for the application system.

Because of the growing power of workstations, the proliferation of LANs, and the need to access and utilize efficiently many different types of processors for specific computational

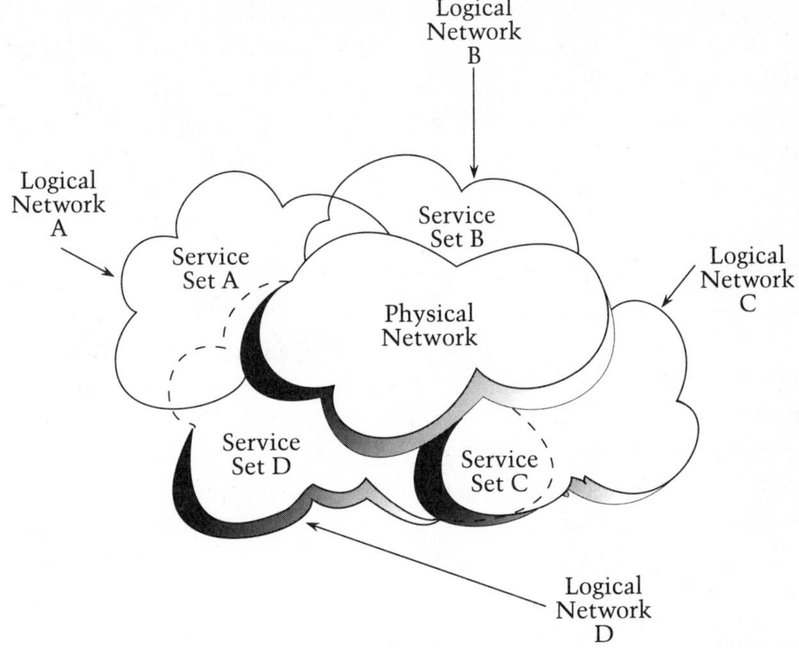

FIGURE 4.2 NETWORK TECHNOLOGY PARTITIONS

needs, the network orientation and culture is growing in a large number of educational institutions and industrial corporations. As this culture becomes ingrained, cooperative processing/data will become a more acceptable way to implement applications. The necessary support infrastructures will then be produced to make this type of development feasible and routine.

Network Design

In terms of overall technology, a network can be considered in two ways, as illustrated in figure 4.2. The first way views networks as a strictly physical mechanism for the transport of information from one node location to another. Up until recently this has been the dominant way of considering networks. The second view considers networks as logical entities that contain a number of embedded services. A logical network that is part of an overall business system can be considered to be a service network, as will be discussed shortly. Bowing to history, physical network technology will be discussed first.

Physical Network Design The design of the physical network is usually accomplished independently of the logical structure. Many issues, such as tariffs, government regulations, available products, and communication standards, must be considered in provisioning a cost-effective network, in addition to choosing among the basic technologies that are available. The network must also accommodate the expected traffic within the bounds of the specified delay and error characteristics. As discussed in chapter 3, the logical network, which is functionality-based, is specified independently of the physical network. The elements of the logical network will be assigned to the physical network elements using the architecture rules.

As suggested above, many attributes can be used to define the structure of a physical network. Examples of some of the major ones are listed below.

- Interconnection matrix
- Link capacity
- Link delay
- Node types
- Subnetworks contained
- Addressing schemes
- Communication protocols
- Owner (public/private)
- Cost per network element
- Traffic expected

A number of interrelated technologies influence the network design. Changing from copper wire to fiber optics increases the capacity of a link several orders of magnitude. Larger networks can be created from independently defined subnetworks through sophisticated gateway nodes. New communication protocols (discussed in the next section) allow for more uniform transmission, better security, and improved control. As the underlying technologies advance, so can the design and capability of the physical network structure.

Initially, networks consisted of asynchronous links between terminals and a computer. As traffic volumes increased, synchronous transmission was utilized. Concentrators of various types were used to reduce the number and lengths of these links between terminal and computer. As capabilities grew, processors were linked together, forming a different subnetwork. When these processors were workstations in a limited geographical area, the resulting subnetworks were labeled *local area networks* (LANs). A subnetwork containing mainframe processors in a limited geographical area was labeled a *"back-end" network*. A subnetwork containing mainframe processors in a wide geographical area was labeled a *"backbone" network*. Finally, networks of processors (of either type) were linked together to form larger networks. Because each defined subnetwork could have different values for the attributes given above, different software technology was necessary to allow the subnetworks to be developed and to operate together.

Most early physical networks were implemented using private dedicated facilities because of the deficiencies of the voice lines utilized in the public telephone network. Public "data-only" networks, such as Telenet, were created to address those deficiencies, but their use imposed other constraints and difficulties (such as delay). Thus, most large-scale physical information networks are still being implemented using private facilities. New advances in telecommunications network technology, such as the Integrated Services Digital Network (ISDN) will allow information network implementation to evolve away from private facilities to the public telecommunications network. On this network, economies of scale can be utilized to lower costs and increase capabilities while still allowing most of the benefits of private facilities (such as control). Some of this migration is currently taking place.

Almost all information networks started as data only. As the information needs of the enterprise increased and the economics and technology employed in the implementation of the network allowed, other forms of information were accommodated on the network through the use of various types of multiplexers. Initial additions were usually voice, but some networks also included video for teleconferencing and other uses. Sophisticated coding algorithms can be used to reduce the bandwidth demands of these non-data services.

It is anticipated that network structures will evolve greatly in the future in order to provide more efficient mechanisms for cooperative processing/data along with more fully integrated voice/data/image information forms.

Logical (Service) Network Design A logical network is usually defined with respect to one or more functions or services that are provided to an application system utilizing the network. The logical network is independent of the physical network discussed in the previous section and may have several physical embodiments depending on the technology and economics required. A logical network may be defined on many levels of abstraction. The highest logical level is called a *service network* to distinguish it from networks with lower logical levels, which are more function-oriented. An example of a service network would be an electronic document interchange network (EDI Network). An example of a lower logical level network would be a LAN. The technologies of interest in any logical network are concerned with the utilization of the resident functions/services by the systems needing them. In the following discussion, the word *feature* will be defined to mean either a service or a function. Some of the attributes defining a logical network are as follows:

- Features provided
- Feature access method
- Feature interfaces
- Feature costs
- Feature stability
- Feature provider
- Network system software
- User domain

Service instability may result when a number of networks are interconnected to obtain a needed service without an overall plan for the service. Under certain conditions (not necessarily faults), the number of messages sent by elements of the service can paralyze the network. Consider the following scenario, based on the EDI service network.

> Assume that Company A and Company B decide to connect their proprietary networks together in order to make the transfer of orders and invoices easier and faster. Now suppose that Company B and Company C, along with a number of other companies, also agree to interconnect their networks for the same purpose.
>
> Company A orders 10,000 widgets from Company B through the network. Company B has an inventory program that takes an incoming order, calculates the amount of raw material involved and automatically places orders for the material from its suppliers (for example, Company C). Those suppliers, in turn, perform the same process with their suppliers. Orders begin flying throughout the network.
>
> Company B cannot fill the order of Company A until it makes more widgets and quickly sends out the appropriate orders for materials. Company Q, somewhere in the procurement chain, needs material from Company A, which cannot supply it until it receives all of its order from Company B. Messages begin flowing over the network, ordering, back-ordering, looking for alternate sources until the service network becomes totally

clogged or reaches a deadlock. Everyone reaches for the aspirin!

The problem is the near instantaneous processing of each step in the chain. There is none of the delay that was present in the manual and non-network automation of the process. In addition, because all of the connections are autonomous, no overall plan exists for the behavior of the service system. Without sufficient delay and the presence of feedback loops, control theory predicts that the system can become unstable.

Although a service network may be implemented on a large number of logical and physical networks, a new class of network is emerging that will make the implementation of service networks more efficient. This type of network is called an *intelligent network*, and its attributes and characteristics are now being defined by the telecommunications industry. This term is usually reserved for networks that provide a great deal of functionality, possibly augmented by the use of artificial intelligence. These networks are easy to use and have enough network system software to provide for cooperative processing without a great deal of domain-specific software development. An intelligent network is another example of a logical network with its own set of features.

Communications

Most activity in data communications has been and still is concerned with the definition and implementation of reference models, associated architectures, and protocols that define the communication activity. Layered reference models are used exclusively as the basic definition of communications. The two most widely used models are Systems Network Architecture (SNA) and Open Systems Interconnect (OSI). Each model has seven layers, although the definitions of the layers vary between the two.

SNA was developed in the early to mid 1970s by IBM and was used initially to standardize and control the terminal-to-processor communication links. Although the SNA architecture is quite general and comprehensive, initial protocol definition and implementation follows a "master-slave" orientation that would be expected from its early application. A great deal of work has been expended to broaden SNA into a peer-to-peer orientation. Because of the amount of history and the implementation of current SNA networks, this extension is going slowly and will not be accomplished easily.

OSI is the result of international standards activities, and, to a larger extent than many people would admit, is based on the IBM work on SNA. OSI has the same number of layers as SNA, and there are probably more similarities than differences between them. OSI did have the advantage of coming later than SNA and was able to take advantage of operational experience with SNA. In addition, the need for peer-to-peer type networks was becoming evident during the discussion of the OSI standard, and the resulting architecture and protocols accommodated and emphasized this type of communication.

Other communication models have been defined and extensively utilized. Most of these have been designed by computer or network vendors and implemented in their proprietary products. The most significant of these are DECNET, developed by Digital Equipment Corporation, EXPAND, developed by Tandem Computers, and TCP/IP developed for the pioneering ARPANET packet network. These particular models have fewer than seven layers (DECNET has since evolved to be OSI compatible) but include more functions per layer than OSI or SNA. These products are almost entirely peer-to-peer oriented.

Figure 4.3 compares some of the reference models discussed so far and illustrates the differences and similarities among them. In examining these models, remember that all communication functions must be accommodated. The packaging is an implementation decision.

As the communications technology matures, the OSI model will emerge as the dominant standard because of the

OSI	SNA (IBM)	TCP / IP	EXPAND (Tandem)
Application	End User	Application	User
Presentation	NAU Service Management		Encompass
Session	Data Flow Cont.	Transport (TCP)	File System
Transport	Transmission Control		
Network	Path Control	Internet (IP)	
Data Link	Data Link Control	Network Interface	Message System
Physical	Physical	Physical	Physical

FIGURE 4.3 REFERENCE MODEL COMPARISONS (APPROXIMATE)

need to connect the products and services of many vendors. This can be accomplished only by a model and associated implementation that is independent of any specific vendor. The only major model that can provide this independence is OSI.

The OSI communications model is not a static entity but is evolving and changing as the technology matures. As an example, additional layers above layer 7 are beginning to be defined to accommodate functions such as electronic document interchange (EDI). These high-layer functions use multiple applications and require protocols and interfaces that are in addition to those defined for the applications of layer 7.

In addition, new protocols needed to accommodate changes in transmission technology are being defined and are currently working their way through the standards bodies. These include the Synchronous Optical Network (SONET) protocol specifically designed for fiber optic links and the Asynchronous Transfer Mode (ATM) protocol designed for broadband networks. The ATM protocol is designed to accommodate any data type (text, voice, image, video, etc.) in a uniform way. As an indication of the current confusion and overlapping directions in the communications industry, it should be pointed out that the interaction between SONET and ATM has not yet been defined.

The development of more efficient transmission protocols and the specification of additional OSI layers with their associated features will be the major change factors in communications technology in the foreseeable future.

Presentation Technology

The concept of presentation technologies has evolved from and has started to supplant the technology of human factors. Human factors technology was originally motivated by a need to design equipment so that it could be utilized by a large number of people without the design or operation of the equipment having to be changed. Although each person using the equipment has a unique set of needs and desires, all users had to adapt themselves to the requirements of the machine once it was implemented. Because of the limited computing power available, it was easier and more cost effective to require human adaptation even though the efficiency of the human interface was sacrificed to a sometimes large extent.

Presentation technology inverts this process and places the burden of change on the non-human part of the interface. The operation of the workstation is expected to change to meet the needs of the individual user. Historically, this tailoring has been accomplished to meet the needs of handicapped individuals so that they could be productive as system users. To this end, workstations have been designed to accommodate blind, palsied, and paraplegic handicaps, among others. This tailoring, however, has been accomplished manually and, once altered, the operation of the workstation does not change.

Presentation technology is defined to accommodate the

characteristics of individuals with the above handicaps, as well as persons who are not usually considered to be handicapped. Left-handedness would be such a characteristic. In addition, other attributes of individual taste, such as preferred colors, type fonts, character size, graphical or text display, etc. are under the control of the individual operator. The most significant difference between presentation technology and human factors technology, however, is that presentation technology allows some characteristic changes to occur automatically without intervention of the operator. These could include different entry methods depending on the skill level or the fatigue condition of the operator. An AI knowledge-based system may be used to determine when a change in the operating characteristics of the workstation or system is necessary and to define what the new mode should be.

The design attributes and characteristics of workstations and systems that can accommodate the type of changes required by presentation technology are currently in the definition process. Sufficient computing power and systems software functionality exist in the current generation of workstations to provide an adequate environment to accomplish the processing needed on a timely basis. Designs for the necessary software are currently being researched, and the adaptive workstation and system are becoming realities. Chapter 2 of the companion volume, *Network System Architecture,* which is concerned with the end user architecture, will consider the architectural impact of this technology as it concerns the end user.

Software Engineering

As discussed to some extent in previous chapters, development of software was initially considered to be an "art," and the programmer was the artist. As larger and more complex software systems became feasible and were developed, this outlook quickly became unsatisfactory, and ways were investigated to make the development of software an engineering discipline similar to those of the classical engineering fields of electrical, mechanical, and civil engineering. In order to accomplish this engineering approach, software had to draw on related scientific information that was arranged so that it could be used in practical design situations. Although this idea is not quite correct, the necessary base scientific data can be thought of as coming from computer science. The design methodologies using this base information then form the discipline of software engineering.

Unfortunately, computer science does not reveal basic physical information in the same way that physics, chemistry, or mechanics does. Computer science provides information that is dependent on the particular computing technology in use, and its "facts" are therefore subject to change. For this reason, computer science is often referred to as a "soft" science as compared to the others mentioned. The commonality between the hard and soft sciences is the use of mathematics to describe the phenomena of interest and to provide a model of the process. Because of this commonality, an engineering discipline can be defined and utilized in the design of software.

Computer science did not become a recognized entity until the mid to late 1960s, and software engineering did not emerge until the 1970s. Thus, as an engineering discipline, it is still in its infancy. In addition, the use of an engineering discipline requires an engineer. In this context an engineer is a person who not only is an expert in a specific area but is trained to approach the design problem in an engineering fashion. It can safely be said that there are far more people who understand the basics of programming technology than there are who can approach it from an engineering point of view. This has resulted from the way in which software technology (programming) began and matured, and it has to a great extent resulted in slow advancement of the technology.

Because of the increasing costs of software development, as well as the increasing complexity of the systems produced, a great deal of pressure is building for software development to reflect the engineering approach. It is anticipated that this type of approach will be needed to keep projects within budget and time constraints. This approach will become more prevalent as trained software engineers become available in the numbers required and as the necessary tools and techniques are developed and deployed.

Modeling and Simulation

Modeling and simulation are used to determine characteristics about a software system when the real system, or a suitable prototype, is unavailable or not usable for that purpose. This will be the usual case when the system has not yet been implemented. It can also occur because of a need to obtain information about the internal state of the system, which may not be measurable. In that sense, modeling and simulation perform the same function for software systems as they do for physical systems.

Historically, the use of modeling and simulation has been limited because the effort necessary to model and simulate a software system has not been considered to be economically justified. With the advent of new tools and software engineering techniques, along with an increased need to understand the implications of large network systems before they are fully implemented, this attitude is changing somewhat. It is becoming possible to obtain a great deal of information through the use of simple models and simulations and to use that information to design better systems. These systems will be better in terms of meeting user needs and utilizing the correct types of processor and network resources for more cost-effective operation.

In addition to more use of modeling and simulation in this classical context, modeling and simulation techniques are beginning to be used in a totally different sense. As an example of this new type of use, consider the following scenario:

> A complex system has been designed and deployed for a number of years. During this time it has undergone many changes and additions, in terms of both functionality and technology. Through some amount of study it has been determined that more efficient use can be made of the system if it is placed under positive control by externally controlling the values of certain parameters in near real time. Depending on the dynamic operating characteristics of the system, these parameters will be changed so as to improve the efficiency of system operation. Because of the complexity and changing nature of the system, the relationship between the observed characteristics and the parameter values is nonlinear and complex, and it has many degrees of freedom. A methodology must be developed to determine the correct set of parameter values for each observed set of operational characteristics.

One way to accomplish this determination is through the use of a model and real-time simulation that can accept the observed operational characteristics and produce a set of parameter values that can optimize the operation of the system according to the desired metrics. The model should be as simple as possible while still being able to produce credible parameter values. Determination time is important, because the simulation is used as a component in a closed control loop. A model and simulation used in this manner is called an *animator,* because it can be considered to be alive in the same sense that the actual system is alive. The use of an animator for system control is shown in figure 4.4.

At the current time, animators are difficult to design and use because the basic techniques are still under development. One of the first applications of this technique will be in network management and control. The example given above was abstracted from this application, and practical animators for certain network types, such as SNA data networks, packet

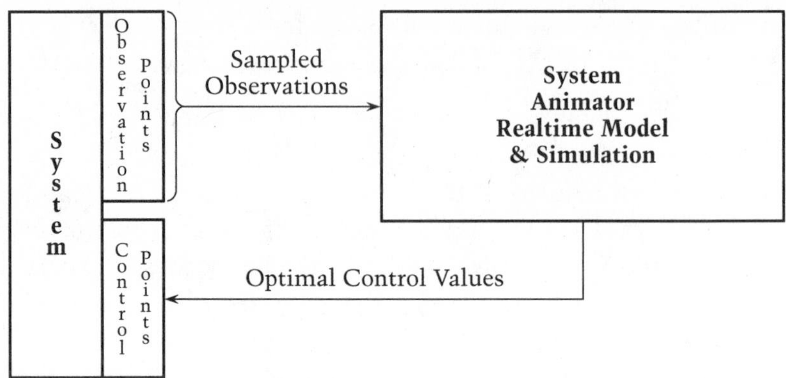

FIGURE 4.4 ANIMATOR USAGE

data networks, and the public switched telephone network, will be the first to be deployed.

Artificial Intelligence

Artificial intelligence (AI) started as an attempt to model the way in which the human brain and thought process work. When computers were relatively new and the computational limitations were not thoroughly understood, this seemed like a plausible goal to reach. A great deal of effort was put into this research, but the goal remained as elusive as ever. Because of the lack of hoped-for results, the field fell into disfavor. As more is discovered about the theory of computation and the workings of the thought process, this lack of progress does not now seem unusual.

In the mid 1970s, some researchers decided to take a somewhat different direction while still remaining under the AI umbrella. Because they could not model the human thought process, they decided to determine what the technology could accomplish. In the process, the definition of AI was changed to the one that is in use currently: The simulation of the process, in a very narrow domain, by which a human would solve a problem. In this context, it is not necessary that the simulation utilize the same mechanism used by the human.

TABLE 4.1 AI AREAS OF HUMAN ACTIVITY DOMAINS

AI Area	*Human Activity*
Expert systems	Problem solving
Speech recognition	Hearing
Natural Language	Understanding
Voice processing	Talking
Robotics	Movement
Image processing	Seeing Pattern recognition

It is only necessary that the output produced by an input condition be the same as a human would provide under the same circumstances. To use the terminology discussed in chapter 1, this type of system would be defined to be a synthetic process or an emulation.

Because of the need to limit the domain in order to make practical use of the concepts, a number of subareas of AI have been defined. Each of these addresses a specific application of human-oriented skills. Table 4.1 lists the major subareas along with the human skill being emulated.

Although AI is being used to emulate the actions of a human to obtain solutions to problems previously considered intractable, it is currently being extended in a way more suitable to its machine implementation environment than its human roots. This extension allows the emulation technique to be used in circumstances that would overwhelm a human and prevent him/her from reaching a suitable conclusion. The extension takes two major forms. The first is needed when the number of inputs that must be considered in real-time or pseudo-real-time is too great for a human to process. The second occurs when the data required to reach a conclusion is too voluminous for a human to consider adequately, regardless of the time available for the task. Because these conditions are suitable for machine consideration, they can be addressed, and in essence a "super-human" can be created in the specific domain in question.

Another type of extension occurs when a humanlike approach is necessary but no human is available to emulate. In these circumstances, a human model is constructed from the available information and the model is then used to provide a machine implementation. This indirect step increases the complexity of the solution, but in many cases there is no other way of solving the problem. This approach is most often referred to as *model-based reasoning*.

To understand AI technology, you must remember that the methodologies and techniques that have become a part of the current definition and the emerging extensions discussed above merely represent another tool in the software engineer's "bag of tricks" and an additional entry in the handbook of design techniques. They are available for use as required and are neither more nor less important than the other software development tools, such as decision tables and object-oriented design.

New Architecture Computers

This is the only technology of the strategic technical areas (STAs) defined in this chapter that is not software-based. It must be included because software technology is useless without a vehicle to execute the logic contained in its structures. Although some software technology is certainly independent of the execution mechanism, others are not, and a change in computer technology will almost certainly influence the evolution of the software technology.

Computer architecture technology is not concerned solely with the processing power of a particular processor or processor complex. It is more concerned with the way in which processing occurs, especially when the software required to take advantage of the architecture or processing method must be altered somehow from the classical approach defined by the von Neumann model. Of course, the major objective behind changing the architecture of a processor is to increase the computing power it is able to deliver for a given cost.

This technology is also not concerned with the computer power that is obtainable through the usual kinds of networking. Networks imply multiple nodes, and this technology implies the computing power at a single node. In saying this, it is necessary to state that the definition of a node is relative. Most modern computers of any architecture really contain several processors, each of which has a specified function or functions to perform. These processors are connected via links of various types, which could certainly be considered to be a network in the true sense of the word. As a matter of fact these networks can be considered to be computer area networks (CANs) — pun intended — and they require an approach similar to other networks, such as LANs and WANs. For the purpose of this technology, however, a computer or CAN will be defined to be a single entity, and its architecture is the area of concern. As the technology evolves, however, this fuzzy distinction between a network and a computer is bound to become even fuzzier.

Architectures of current computers may be classified into one or a combination of major connectivity types (processors in this list may be either fixed- or floating-point):

- Functionally assigned monoprocessors (a monoprocessor is a processor in the von Neumann sense)
- Loosely coupled monoprocessors (*Loosely coupled* implies dedicated memory to each processor and communications via message passing. Depending on the network characteristics connecting the loosely coupled processors, several different configurations can be obtained.)
- Tightly coupled monoprocessors (*Tightly coupled* implies shared memory and high-speed communications busses.)
- Array monoprocessors (Each processor performs the same operation at the same time using a different array element.)
- Pipelined processors
- Very Long Instruction Word processors

It is possible to produce computers that use several of these techniques, and most modern computer architectures contain multiple configuration types. No attempt will be made to relate power or programming complexity to each of these architecture types except to say that in general both are higher than in the classical von Neumann architecture.

It is anticipated that the rapid change in semiconductor technology and the emergence of ever more powerful microprocessors and cheaper memory will make possible all sorts of new ways of combining processing elements. The test of the marketplace will determine which of these become useful standards and which become laboratory curiosities. This is an area that is ripe for elegant approaches to computing. Unfortunately, many of these approaches become solutions desperately searching for problems that they can solve.

Up to this time, the term *supercomputer* has been used to indicate a computer that contains nontraditional architectures, usually in the form of array processors or tightly coupled parallel processors, where each processor operates on floating point numbers. I prefer the term *new generation computer architectures* because of the diversity of the available architectures and the fact that the raw power of a particular architecture is dependent on the components used to implement it. We currently have supercomputers, mini supercomputers, super minicomputers, etc. This terminology is outmoded and confusing and should be dropped.

Database Management Systems

Data storage began as main-memory-only storage for temporary values. The need for storing larger amounts of data occurred as computing matured and addressed more complex problems. This need for "mass" storage was initially met by the use of punched cards or tape. Data stored in this fashion required considerable manual handling and intervention in order to be used by application programs. Advances in technology eventually allowed the use of magnetic media, starting with tape and advancing to rotating disks and drums.

Early methods of storage gave rise to the concept of a file or dataset, which was defined to be a collection of data. Files were usually subdivided into records and fields, but the master unit of storage was the file. The sequential nature of tape and cards produced sequential access methods, and the logic of programs using this data was designed around this type of access. Requests to access this data were handled manually by loading the deck of cards or mounting the tape. This need for manual intervention before the data could be used resulted in the term *off-line* being applied to this type of storage.

The use of rotating magnetic storage allowed the use of large amounts of data without manual intervention, hence the name *on-line* storage. Initially, this media was used in the same fashion as off-line media — for the storage of sequential files. Access was then broadened by using random access techniques whereby a record in a file could be accessed directly without all of the records ahead of it in the file having to be read. However, the file concept did not fundamentally change in the transition. Regardless of whether they are on-line or off-line, files suffer from a number of problems:

- They are closely associated with application code
- They are difficult to maintain
- They offer little access security
- They are inefficient for large amounts of data
- The coordination of multiple files is difficult
- They provide a single level of data dependency

The solution to these problems came in the form of database management systems (DBMSs), which were initially deployed and used in the early 1970s. These systems were designed to allow the management of data independently from the application code that required it. Data integrity, security, efficiency, and multiple user access were all addressed by these systems. Initial DBMS implementations utilized a hierarchical or tree structure that allowed several levels of data dependency. Later designs generalized this to a network structure in which a child record could have more than one parent record.

These early DBMS techniques also have some disadvantages, although they are considerably better than files, especially for large amounts of data. Access is generally limited to predefined paths, making ad hoc queries almost impossible and often requiring lengthy access time for data located deep in the structure. Distributing data across a network is also difficult with these DBMS types.

A new technique for DBMS design called relational storage was developed in the mid 1970s. Relational storage had the potential to overcome the deficiencies of hierarchical and network storage. However, because of implementation problems and the eventual large installed base of earlier DBMS types, relational DBMSs did not achieve widespread deployment until the mid to late 1980s. Relational techniques support random queries and allow data to be distributed. These features make relational storage useful for management support system applications and other office services.

Because of the simplicity of the storage definition, which uses a single-level table format, the efficient implementation of a relational system is easier than that of either of the other two earlier formats. Access time has tended to be longer than earlier formats, but the difference is rapidly being eliminated. The relational format allows the use of parallel operations in many retrievals, and it may be implemented efficiently on specialized machines known as *database machines*. These are computers with the single function of providing database services. Because of the economics involved, they have not yet seen widespread deployment. This may change in the future as specialized network processors become the rule rather than the exception.

Relational formats also have some deficiencies, such as the difficulty in defining complex data types such as those needed in systems that utilize multiple media (voice, text, image). New organizations such as object-oriented databases and intelligent databases are being proposed to deal with these deficiencies. The latter technique integrates database technology with artificial intelligence techniques to allow access using incomplete or inaccurate search conditions. This technique will also allow the determination of complex data interrelationships that are unknown at the time of data generation. The first commercial products using object-oriented techniques are now beginning to emerge. Commercial implementations of intelligent databases are some time away.

Currently most large computer users and many minicomputer users employ a DBMS of some type. These are usually hierarchical or network-based, although a significant number of relational systems are beginning to be deployed. Several relational DBMS implementations are also available at the microcomputer level. Most specifications of new DBMSs are for relational systems because of the greater flexibility and network orientation. Eventually, relational systems will dominate.

Research into more advanced organizations will continue, and commercial products will probably emerge in the mid to late 1990s. Deployment of new products with new organizations is likely to remain slow because of the installed base and the reluctance of most large system developers and operators to employ advanced techniques.

INTEGRATION EXAMPLE

Consider the following common scenario:

> A homeowner puts his trash out by the curb in the late evening for a scheduled early morning pick-up. When he arises the next day the trash is still there. No pick-up has been made. The irate homeowner picks up the phone to complain to city hall (assuming that the municipality provides the trash pick-up service).
>
> The scene shifts to include city hall, as depicted by figure 4.5. The client (homeowner) communicates with

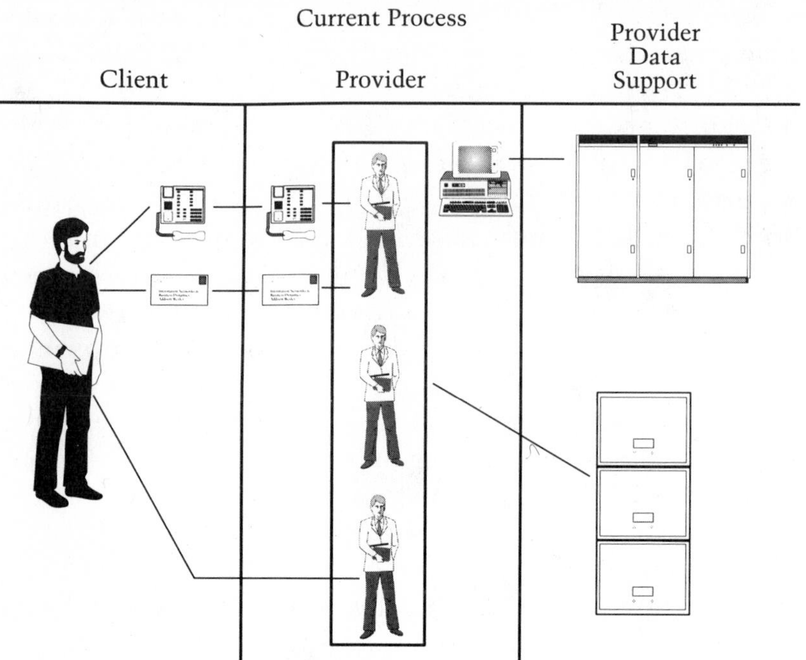

FIGURE 4.5 CLIENT-PROVIDER INTERACTION (NOW)

a person who represents the service provider (municipality). The communication could also have been implemented using other means, such as the postal service or face-to-face conversation.

The provider may or may not have immediate knowledge concerning the client's problem. More than likely, the provider would have to research the reason for the lack of pickup by contacting other provider personnel, accessing a computer database, or looking in a manual file. This assumes that the original person contacted is willing to help the client. In many cases the client is shuffled from provider person to provider person before someone is found who is willing to help.

Because of the complexity of the research that must be done to provide a complete answer to the client's problem, the usual result is an unsatisfactory explanation to the client and a lost opportunity to improve service and maintain effective control over the service. Some of the questions that should be answered during the investigation are listed below:

- Commercial or residential contract?
- Bill paid or service suspended for nonpayment?
- Was the day in question a scheduled pick-up day for the address?
- Did the truck have mechanical problems or other difficulty?
- Was the volume of the trash more than allowed for a single pick-up (10 bags)?
- Was some material placed for pick-up of a kind not allowed (large tree sections or furniture)?
- Did hazardous conditions exist at the pick-up site (mean dog or flooded lot)?

Note that these questions include both on-site as well as contractual conditions. If the provider representative cannot address these questions effectively, there will be no satisfactory ending to the client's problem.

In addition to the problem-solving aspect of the investigation, there is also an opportunity to provide additional services (at possible increased cost) to meet the client's needs and improve the efficiency of the provider. Some of the possibilities are listed below:

- Improve grade of service (more frequent pick-up, more bags per pick-up, or move from residential to commercial type)
- Arrange bill payment schedule
- Arrange different pick-up schedule
- Arrange for special pick-up of large material
- Notify proper department concerning hazardous conditions

Unless the provider representative is an accomplished salesman or trained in public relations, this opportunity is lost.

In order to deal with this type of situation effectively, a service network may be defined. The domain of the service network is complaint reconciliation. A value chain is imple-

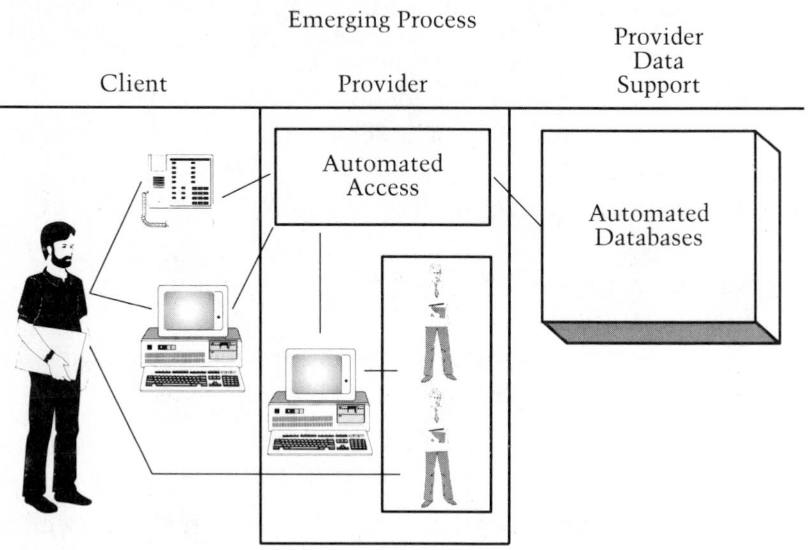

FIGURE 4.6 CLIENT-PROVIDER INTERACTION (EMERGING)

mented such that the client may interact directly with the city hall system containing the information needed to resolve the complaint. The technology areas that must be integrated in order to provide the necessary functionality are listed below:

- Networking
- Artificial intelligence
  - Expert systems
  - Voice processing
  - Natural language
- Presentation technology
- Distributed processing/data
- Software engineering

These technologies are utilized in a system structure shown in figure 4.6.

In this emerging service network concept, the scenario proceeds as follows:

> The client picks up the phone to complain as in the previous case. The client could also have used a computer terminal (personal computer), but to keep some similarities with the previous resolution process a phone contact will be assumed. Instead of a human answering the call, the provider response is given by an automated system under control of an artificial intelligence system using a digitized voice response unit.
>
> By asking simple questions and interpreting the tone response (eventually a voice-recognition system coupled with a natural language facility could be used, but this is some years away) the AI access system interrogates the databases to determine the source of the problem and so inform the client. The enhanced services mentioned earlier could also be sold depending on the results of the client interaction.
>
> In order to make this work, some type of intelligence would have to be placed on the trash collection truck so that the operators could enter the reasons for any trash collection location that produced problems. Operational problems with the collection equipment would also be entered. This information could be sent back to the required databases immediately or stored locally on the truck and transferred to the databases upon returning to the garage.
>
> Of course, if desired, a client could elect at any time during the dialog to talk to a human associated with the provider. That person would then use the system in order to answer the client's request. Additional consultation with other provider personnel should not be necessary.

This type of scenario could be extended to a large number of customer service situations. There are benefits to both the client and the provider, as listed in table 4.2. Additional ben-

TABLE 4.2 SERVICE SCENARIO

Client Benefits	*Provider Benefits*
Faster response to the complaint	Greater control over the entire process
Better resolution to the problem	Improved cost efficiency
Higher confidence in the solution	Greater consistency of responses
Greater accessibility to information	Automatic audits
	Automatic enquiry statistics
	Higher degree of service

efits will be found as this type of network is deployed and utilized by a large number of clients and their providers.

The key result of the discussion is that technology integration is required for this type of function to be specified, developed and eventually deployed. Systems of this type will help illustrate the advantages of technology integration and ease the path for the development of other advanced systems.

SUMMARY

Many technologies are required in the implementation of an information network and systems. To achieve the maximum effect from the use of these technologies, they must be considered as an integrated group. Considering a technology as an isolated entity will not provide the total range of capabilities that can be achieved.

Some risk in the selection of technologies and capabilities is necessary or the resultant deployed system will contain obsolete technology. The length of time required for most large system development, relative to the technology change rate, requires some specification of currently unproven technology. Although this increases the development risk, it can also greatly increase the useful life of the system. This is especially important in large-scale systems that must have a long life to return the investment that was necessary for their creation.

Although important, technology is still only an enabler. Other parts of the process must be considered and combined with the technological aspects to form a complete picture of the needs of the enterprise in the development process.

Toward this goal, the remainder of this book will consider the business-oriented aspects of the development process. Specific business needs will be defined and integrated with the technology concepts previously presented. This will be accomplished gradually to keep a high degree of continuity in the presentation.

FIVE

TECHNOLOGY MANAGEMENT

INTRODUCTION

In any enterprise that utilizes technology as an integral part of its activities, the management of that technology is crucial to the health of the organization. Without proper management, inappropriate application of technology will result in a less efficient business at best and a totally ineffective one at worst. Development of network systems that are competitive and economically viable is particularly dependent on the close management of the applicable technologies. No discussion of network-based system development can be complete without a thorough presentation of this topic. This chapter, therefore, examines the major underlying principles, along with some analysis techniques that can be used to manage technology effectively without placing unnecessary constraints on the operation of the business. Emphasis is placed on the quantitative and procedural aspects of the process that can be measured and evaluated for effectiveness. Without this type of foundation, it will not be possible to utilize the rapidly advancing technologies in the most effective and efficient manner possible. No matter how effective and well managed the development process, the products produced generally will not stand the test of the market unless the technologies employed have been managed well.

Technology management cannot be examined without also considering the business aspects as an integral part of the process. The suitability of a given technology for a specific product can be determined only through the context of the business environment. Technology management thus becomes one of the major interfaces between technical and business issues.

Technology-oriented Enterprise

In order to examine the management of technology as it relates to a given enterprise, two difficult questions have to be posed and addressed:

- What is technology?
- What is a technology-oriented enterprise?

In order for technology to be managed, it must be defined and understood to a level sufficient for the implementation of the necessary management procedures and metrics. Although many definitions have been proposed and used for various purposes, the following is particularly suited for the discussions of this chapter.

Technology is any area of endeavor that requires for utilization:

- Knowledge based on scientific principles
- Knowledge that is not universally known
- Experience in the application of this knowledge
- Tools designed specifically for the endeavor

This concept of technology addresses a wide range of fields, from engineering to medicine to agriculture. A given enterprise will generally utilize only a fraction of all of the technologies available. For the purposes of this discussion, only those technologies which are applicable to the design and implementation of information networks and systems need be considered. Many of these technologies were discussed in the previous chapter, although others certainly could fall into the category of interest. Because the remainder of the discussion is restricted to the limited class of network technologies, for convenience the word *technology* will be assumed to represent this class.

A significant variation exists in the range of knowledge, experience, and tools that may be applied to a particular endeavor. The terms *high tech(nology)* and *low tech(nology)* have emerged to signify large and small amounts, respectively, of the above quantities as being necessary to utilize the technology in the context of the enterprise. *No tech(nology)* would also be a valid classification.

The concept of a technology-oriented enterprise is necessary because these organizations are the only ones for which the management of technology is necessary. If an organization is not technology-oriented there is obviously no need to manage a technological component, which would of necessity be quite small. The definition and identification of a technology-oriented enterprise is at best a subjective process. However, as an aid in the effort, a number of attributes and associated value domains can be identified and used to characterize and classify individual enterprises. These attributes and values are shown in table 5.1.

Depending on the specific values for these attributes, a given enterprise can be subjectively classified as technology-oriented or not technology-oriented. As an example, consider the attributes and values of table 5.1 for three types of enterprises, as shown in tables 5.2 to 5.4. Although these examples represent fairly obvious classifications, changing a few of the attribute values would make the class determination more difficult and subjective.

The remainder of this discussion assumes that the enterprise of interest is oriented toward a "high tech" characterization even though it might not be as strong as that shown in table 5.2. Organizations that do not fit this type of profile will probably not be able to make cost-effective use of the level of planning presented in this chapter. Remember, how-

TABLE 5.1 TECHNOLOGY-ORIENTATION ATTRIBUTES AND VALUE RANGES

Attribute	*Value Domain*
Level of use	Low, medium, high tech
Extent of use	Little, moderate, heavy
Rate of change	Low, medium, high
How used	Product/service component, development, strategy determination
Number used	One, few, many
Knowledge required	Little, moderate, expert
How obtained	Purchased, developed internally
R&D capability	None, little, moderate, large
Technical personnel	None, some, many

ever, that the characterization of "high tech" is a level of technology involvement, not of organization size or technology utilized in a product. Many organizations that sell or are otherwise indirectly associated with products containing a

TABLE 5.2 HIGH-TECH ORGANIZATION CHARACTERIZATION

Attribute	*Value*
Level of use	High tech
Extent of use	Heavy
Rate of change	High
How used	Product/service component, development, strategy determination
Number used	Many
Knowledge required	Expert
How obtained	Developed internally
R&D capability	Large
Technical personnel	Many

TABLE 5.3 LOW-TECH ORGANIZATION CHARACTERIZATION

Attribute	*Value*
Level of use	Low, medium
Extent of use	Little, moderate
Rate of change	Low
How used	Product/service component, limited development
Number used	One, few
Knowledge required	Little, moderate
How obtained	Purchased
R&D capability	None, little
Technical personnel	None, some

large technological component consider themselves to be "high-tech" companies when in fact they are not. Only a small understanding of these technologies is required in the operation of the business.

TABLE 5.4 NON-TECHNICAL ORGANIZATION CHARACTERIZATION

Attribute	*Value*
Level of use	Low
Extent of use	Little
Rate of change	Low
How used	Product/service component
Number used	None, one
Knowledge required	Little
How obtained	Purchased
R&D capability	None
Technical personnel	None

Definition and Purpose

Technology management is a process that uses a specific methodology for technology-related coordination, planning, and decision-making. The major purpose is to use the proper technologies at the proper time:

- In the products and services produced by the enterprise
- In the tools and methodologies used to develop those products and services

If technology management is emphasized and utilized effectively, the enterprise becomes the master of its technology rather than its slave. This latter condition unfortunately holds for too many technology-oriented companies.

Although a specific methodology is defined and discussed in this chapter, it should be recognized that many possible methodologies can be effective in the technology management process. Each organization must determine what procedures will work with its particular culture, marketplace, and industry. However, the basic principles and objectives will remain the same.

Methodology

The technology management methodology that will be defined and discussed as one example of the required process is shown in figure 5.1. The inputs to the methodology come from the major areas that influence the activities of the enterprise:

- Current technical environment
- Sources of technology
- Business strategies of the enterprise
- Products and services produced by the enterprise
- Market and competitive environment

These inputs include the two views of technology that are necessary for a comprehensive technology management pro-

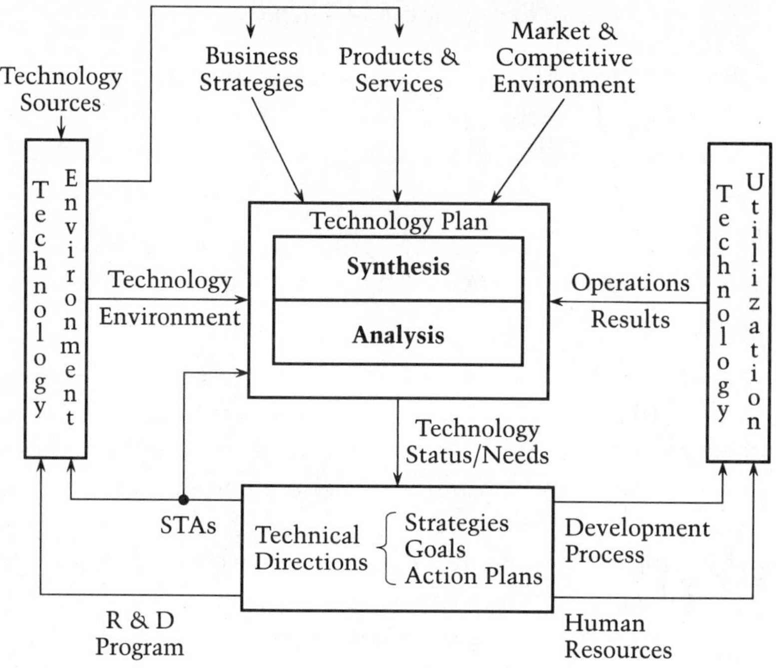

FIGURE 5.1 TECHNOLOGY MANAGEMENT METHODOLOGY

cess. The first is a technology-based view as to what the technology is capable of providing. The available technology may then influence changes to the enterprise products and services and/or the fundamental strategies that the business follows. The second is a business-based view as to what the enterprise needs from technology. This will influence the specific technologies of interest and the manner in which the technologies are made available.

The outputs of the process are not all indicated explicitly in the figure because of their large number and diffused nature. Outputs occur at every step of the process and in many cases represent "soft" rather than "hard" information. The knowledge of the state of the art of a given technology may cause a specific product to be altered slightly with far-reaching results, or nothing specific may immediately occur. It is difficult to predict what the outcome of the knowledge may be. The major "hard" outputs occur as a result of the technical action plans whereby the enterprise defines specific steps to be taken to better utilize the technology available.

The process forms a closed loop that usually completes a cycle in about one calendar year. Although the timing could be changed, experience has taught that this planning period is quite acceptable and fits in with the natural planning cycle of most organizations.

There are four major activities in the technology management methodology:

- Technology plan development
- Development of technical strategies, goals, and action plans
- Technology environment determination
- Technology utilization

Each of these activities is crucial to the technology management process and will be discussed in some detail.

TECHNOLOGY PLAN DEVELOPMENT

The technology plan is central to the technology management process. It forms the central database through which the enterprise can assess its uses and needs for technology and make appropriate decisions as to future directions. The technology plan consists of two stages: synthesis and analysis. The activities of the synthesis stage are designed to present the input data in a form suitable for making the required comparisons. The analysis stage utilizes the data from the synthesis stage to develop a set of charts that contain the data in a form that can be used for developing required action plans. The major components of each stage are presented in figure 5.2.

The following discussion uses a series of examples to illustrate the components of the technology plan. These examples are consistent with one another and with the strategic technology areas (STAs) developed in the previous chapter. As such, they represent the data that would be obtained from a large enterprise that produces network systems and associ-

Synthesis

- Identify Product/Service Categories
- Identify Enterprise Strategies
- Identify Technologies of Interest
- Using a Matrix of Product/Service Categories and
  - —Strategies; Indicate High and Medium Relationships
  - —Technologies; Indicate High and Medium Impact
  - —Technologies; Indicate Resources Applied

Analysis

- Find Correlations for Each Product Service Category Among Strategies, Impact, and Funding
- Identify Inconsistencies, Gaps, Misplaced Resources, Strengths, and Opportunities in the Application of Technology
- Identify Technologies That Must Be Added, Deleted or Redefined from the STA List

FIGURE 5.2 TECHNOLOGY PLAN METHODOLOGY

ated products and services. The development of a technology plan for smaller "high-tech" companies is also of significant value but the number of products and services would be much smaller and the process somewhat simpler.

Synthesis Stage

The synthesis stage is used to develop a set of four matrices that summarize the application of technology to the needs of the business: the strategy impact matrix, STA impact matrix, STA financial impact matrix, and the STA human resource impact matrix. These matrices are based on two basic forms: the product/strategy form and the product/STA form.

The synthesis stage begins with a list of the products and services of the enterprise, grouped into appropriate categories. One such list for an enterprise that produces network systems and associated products and services is shown in figure 5.3. Because this list will be used as one side of a matrix it is shown in that form. Although categories are used as the basic elements in this example, if information needs to be produced

Consulting				Data Processing								Network								
				Systems Development				Facilities Mgmt.				Transport			Services					
Training & Education	Expert Testimony	Technology Planning & Evaluation	Organization Planning & Evaluation	Turnkey Systems	Requirements & Specifications	Quality Control	Maintenance	Purchased Product Customization	Data Center Management	Capacity Planning & Other Support Services	Time Sharing	Network Control	Network Planning & Engineering	Network Construction & Deployment	Service Network Design	Service Control	Service Design & Development	Voicemail	Electronic Document Interchange	

FIGURE 5.3 PRODUCT/SERVICE CATEGORIES

at an increased level of detail, it is possible to carry the process along by using actual products and services.

Product/Strategy Form The next step in the synthesis stage is to list the fundamental business strategies of the enterprise and form them into a matrix with the product and service categories discussed earlier. The resultant form is shown in figure 5.4. If the enterprise has not developed a set of guiding business strategies, it must do so before the technology plan can be continued. Without a set of business strategies, the impact of various technological alternatives cannot be determined. An old adage (updated for the present circumstance) then holds: If the business doesn't know where it is going, any old technology will get it there.

The product/strategy form is used to develop the strategy impact matrix, which shows the product and service category impact on the business strategies. An example of this matrix is shown in figure 5.5. The impact of a product/service category on meeting the strategies of the enterprise is classified into three levels, (H)igh, (M)edium, and Low. For purposes of clarity, the Low levels are not entered explicitly. This matrix could be used for many purposes, such as deciding which products/services to continue and/or emphasize. However,

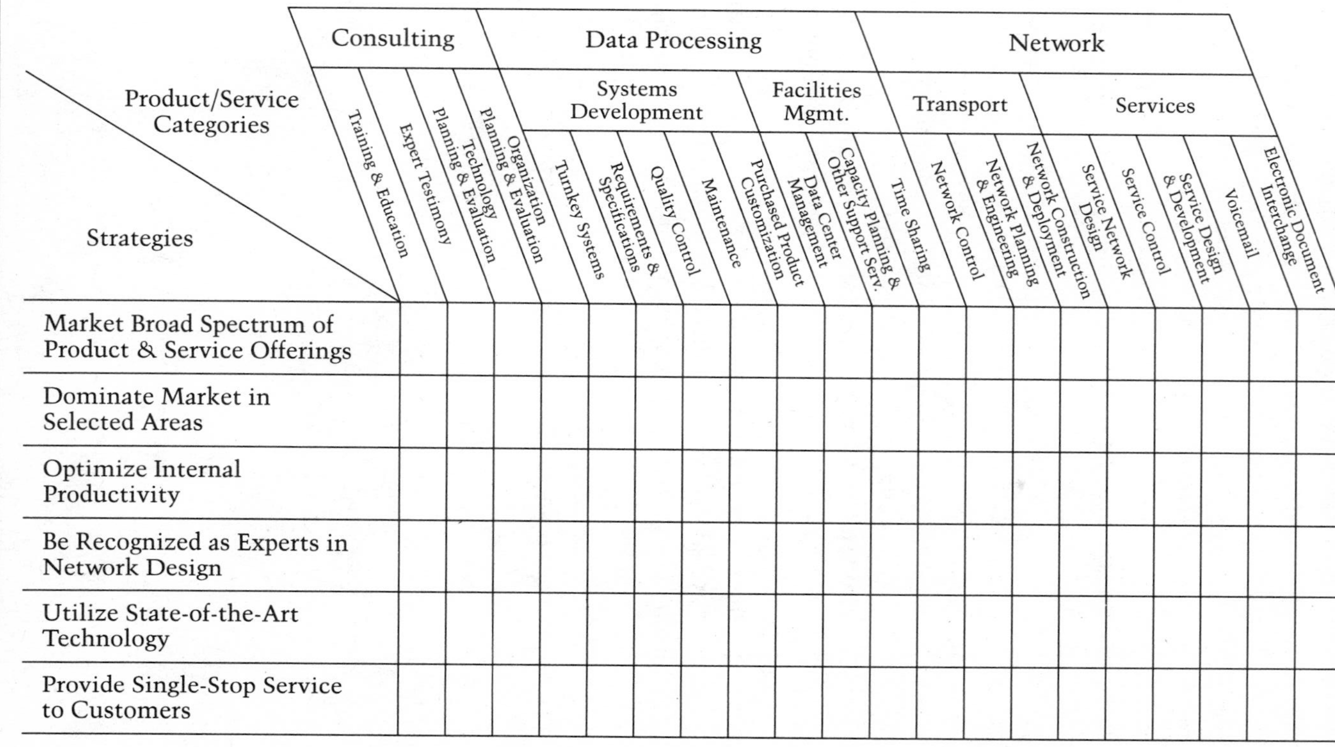

FIGURE 5.4 PRODUCT/STRATEGY FORM

Product/Service Categories	Consulting				Data Processing								Network							
					Systems Development				Facilities Mgmt.				Transport			Services				
Strategies	Training & Education	Expert Testimony	Technology Planning & Evaluation	Organization Planning & Evaluation	Turnkey Systems	Requirements & Specifications	Quality Control	Maintenance	Purchased Product Customization	Data Center Management	Capacity Planning & Other Support Serv.	Time Sharing	Network Control	Network Planning & Engineering	Network Construction & Deployment	Service Network Design	Service Control	Service Design & Development	Voicemail	Electronic Document Interchange
Market Broad Spectrum of Product & Service Offerings		H		M												H	H	H		
Dominate Market In Selected Areas													M	M	M	H	H	H	M	M
Optimize Internal Productivity					H				H					M		M				
Be Recognized as Experts in Network Design					M								H	H	H	M				
Utilize State-of-the-Art Technology					H					M			H					H	M	M
Provide Single-Stop Service to Customers	H				H					H			M	H	M	H	M	H		
Totals*	2	2		1	7				2	3			6	6	4	8	5	8	2	2

*H = 2, M = 1

FIGURE 5.5 STRATEGY IMPACT MATRIX

the discussion in this section will be confined to its use in the technology plan development process.

If you assign a number to the High and Medium entries, the total impact of each product and service to meeting the enterprise objectives can be determined. This information will eventually be combined with the amount of technology applied to each product/service category to determine the impact technology is having on the business strategies.

Although a quantitative result is obtained, the impact matrix substantially results from a subjective analysis. This is important to note because a great deal of business expertise and experience is necessary to produce the values placed in the matrix. Be careful not to place more faith than warranted in the result just because quantitative values are presented.

Product/STA Form The product/services categories are now formed into a matrix with the current strategic technical areas (STAs) of the enterprise. This form, shown in figure 5.6, will be used in the development of three matrices that contain the impact of company technical resources on each of the product/service categories. The first of these is the STA impact matrix, which quantifies the influence a specific STA has on each of the product/service categories. An example of this matrix is shown in figure 5.7, which is quantified to three levels — High, Medium, and Low, with Low again represented by spaces for increased clarity.

The amount of each impact must be developed from an integration of two views of technology as applied to a product/service category. The first is concerned with the level of a technology being used as compared with those used by the competition. The second comes from an analysis of the innate capabilities of the technology that can be utilized in further improving the products and services of the category. This latter view is required because there is no guarantee that increasing the level of a technology will automatically result in better products/services as perceived by the marketplace. The combination of the two views then provides the data for

Product/Service Categories			Distributed Processing/Data	Network Design	Communications	Presentation Technology	Software Engineering	Modeling & Simulation	Artificial Intelligence	Adv. Architecture Computers	Database Mgmt. Systems	
Consulting		Training & Education										
		Expert Testimony										
		Technology Planning & Evaluation										
		Organization Planning & Evaluation										
Data Processing	Systems Development	Turnkey Systems										
		Requirements & Specifications										
		Quality Control										
		Maintenance										
	Facilities Mgmt.	Purchased Product Customization										
		Data Center Management										
		Capacity Planning & Other Support Serv.										
		Time Sharing										
Network	Transport	Network Control										
		Network Planning & Engineering										
		Network Construction & Deployment										
	Services	Service Network Design										
		Service Control										
		Service Design & Development										
		Voicemail										
		Electronic Document Interchange										

Strategic Technical Areas

FIGURE 5.6 PRODUCT/STA FORM

Product/Service Categories / Strategic Technical Areas	Consulting				Data Processing							Network									Totals*
					Systems Development				Facilities Mgmt.			Transport			Services						
	Training & Education	Expert Testimony	Technology Planning & Evaluation	Organization Planning & Evaluation	Turnkey Systems	Requirements & Specifications	Quality Control	Maintenance	Purchased Product Customization	Data Center Management	Capacity Planning & Other Support Serv.	Time Sharing	Network Control	Network Planning & Engineering	Network Construction & Deployment	Service Network Design	Service Control	Service Design & Development	Voicemail	Electronic Document Interchange	
Distributed Processing/Data	M				M					M										M	4
Network Design						M								H						M	4
Communications		M														H	H	H			7
Presentation Technology					M									H			H	H			7
Software Engineering					M																1
Modeling & Simulation												M		M			M				3
Artificial Intelligence		M				H				H			H	H			H	H	H		15
Adv. Architecture Computers					M	M						H				M					5
Database Mgmt. Systems	M	M																	M		3
Totals*	2	3			4	4				3		3	2	7		3	7	6	3	2	

*H = 2, M = 1

FIGURE 5.7 STA IMPACT MATRIX

TABLE 5.5 COMPETITIVE TECHNOLOGY STATES

State	*Meaning*
Evolutionary	Application of proven technology (may be strongly entrenched in the organization)
Competitor	Adoption of a competitor's level of technology to improve competitive position (may be accomplished by reverse engineering)
Innovative	Development and exploitation of advanced state-of-the-art technology (requires R&D capabilities and advanced engineering personnel)

determining the best way to use the technology in the products and services of the enterprise.

Unfortunately, this is a complex and highly subjective determination that involves a large number of technical and business variables. However, because of its importance in the development of the technology plan, a structured approach to the analysis is presented here to provide a framework for the process and discuss some of the major nuances.

The competitive comparison may be quantified into three levels, or states of technology use, as shown in table 5.5. A more detailed scoring system could be used if the benefits are felt to be worth the increased effort. Figure 5.8 shows a way of determining this competitive technology state if the levels

Enterprise Technology Level \ Competition Technology Level	L	M	H
L	C	E	E
M	I	C	E
H	I	I	C

FIGURE 5.8 COMPETITIVE IMPACT DETERMINATION

	Impact of Using Current Technology	Impact of Using Advanced Technology
Current Product/ Service Category	L	M
Enhanced/ Replacement Product/ Service Category	M	H

FIGURE 5.9 TECHNOLOGY IMPACT POTENTIAL

of technology applied by the enterprise and its competitors can be estimated. The entry in each box represents an estimate of the technology state of the enterprise. When competitors are using little technology, there could be a big impact on the enterprise in applying technology to that category and achieving a competitive advantage. If the competition is applying a great deal of technology to the category of interest, the impact may again be large but from a "catch-up" perspective. Whether or not the application of technology in either of these situations will be of use depends on the innate capabilities of the technology in achieving improved or replacement product/services in the category.

One way of performing this latter analysis for a specific technology and product/service category is through the diagram shown in figure 5.9. This diagram categorizes the impact of technology on the current and projected product/service offerings of the enterprise. This categorization is required to assure that the future product/service directions of the enterprise are considered during the analysis. Into each box is entered the projected impact using a High, Medium, or Low indication.

In the example shown, the current technology level is being exploited to its maximum for the products/services in the category. Using an advanced technology level would have only a medium impact on the current products/services in

Competitive State \ Capability Projection	H	M	L
E	E, L C, [M - H] I, H	E, L C, M I, H	E, L C, L I, L
C	C, L I, [M - H]	C, L I, [L, M]	C, L I, L
I	I, L	I, L	I, L

FIGURE 5.10 OVERALL TECHNOLOGY IMPACT DETERMINATION

the category, as would using the current technology to develop new versions of the products/services. The only high-impact action is to develop new products/services using an advanced level of technology. This is a typical situation for a mature product set that has been available for a significant period of time but is still well accepted in the marketplace. For a new, recently introduced product there might be a high impact in each case. For a product/service category that is becoming obsolete, there might be a low impact in each case. The results produced from the analysis will depend on the particular situation involved.

The results from both views of the technology and product/service interaction must be integrated and analyzed to determine each impact value. The diagram presented in figure 5.10, which is a form of state table, presents one method of performing this integration. Each box represents one combination of a competitive view (state) and an innate capability view (input). The results of the individual technology view analyses will thus consist of a state and input value. Each entry will contain the new state and an output (s,o), which is the overall impact. The difference between this diagram and a normal state table is that each state-input combination may have more than one possible result. This occurs because enterprise management has the option of choosing more than one possible result.

As one example of the use of this diagram, assume that for a given product/service category the current competitive state of the enterprise is "E," the application of proven technology. Further assume that the innate capabilities of the technology for further improvement are high. There are three possible transitions from this state:

- Stay in the present competitive state — low impact
- Go to the competitor technology state — medium to high impact
- Go to an innovative technology state — high impact

The enterprise must decide what action is appropriate from a business standpoint before the overall impact of the technology to the product/service category can be determined and entered in the STA product matrix.

Two other matrices are needed to complete the synthesis phase of the technology plan. These are also developed using the product/STA form and contain actual operational results from technology activities of the enterprise over the planning period (usually one year). The first contains, by STA, the dollar amount spent for other than direct personnel-related expenses in each of the product/service categories. These amounts include equipment, education, travel, and similar expense areas. The second contains direct personnel expenses and is presented by the number of personnel assigned rather than by actual cost. The conversion can of course be made by using an average cost per technical staff member. These two matrices are shown in figures 5.11 and 5.12, respectively, using the form structure of figure 5.6.

The information necessary for the analysis phase is now available in a suitable format. Although the information contained in the synthesis section matrices can be used for other management processes, as indicated previously, the present discussion is limited to their use as an input to the analysis section.

Strategic Technical Areas \ Product/Service Categories	Consulting				Data Processing							Network									
					Systems Development				Facilities Mgmt.			Transport			Services						
	Training & Education	Expert Testimony	Technology Planning & Evaluation	Organization Planning & Evaluation	Turnkey Systems	Requirements & Specifications	Quality Control	Maintenance	Purchased Product Customization	Data Center Management	Capacity Planning & Other Support Serv.	Time Sharing	Network Control	Network Planning & Engineering	Network Construction & Deployment	Service Network Design	Service Control	Service Design & Development	Voicemail	Electronic Document Interchange	Totals*
Distributed Processing/Data						.2				.3						.1					.6
Network Design	.3											.1	.3								1.9
Communications		.1										.7		1.2							.7
Presentation Technology					.4	.2															.6
Software Engineering					.1	.1	.4														.6
Modeling & Simulation														.8							.8
Artificial Intelligence	1.3																				1.3
Adv. Architecture Computers											.1							.2			.3
Database Mgmt. Systems												4.1									4.1
Totals*	1.6	.1			.5	.5	.4			.3	.1	4.9	.3	2.0		.1		.2			

*In Millions

FIGURE 5.11 STA FINANCIAL APPLICATION MATRIX

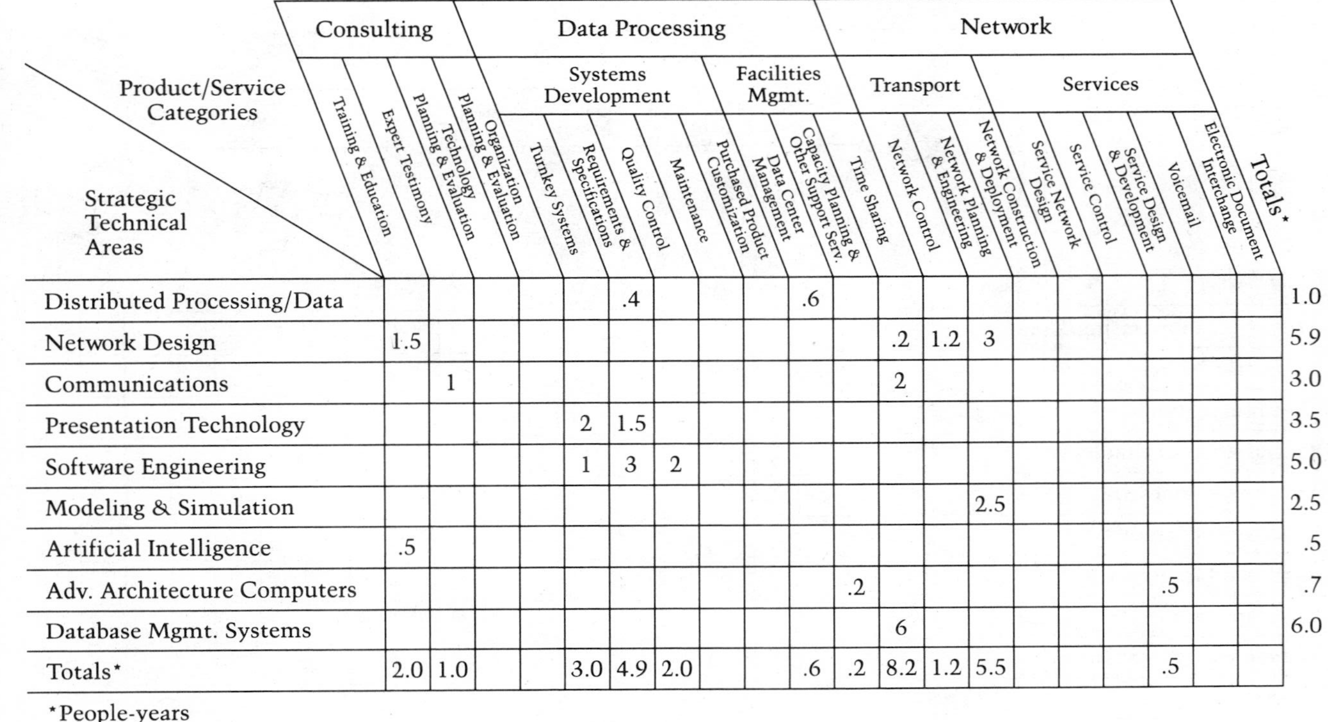

Strategic Technical Areas \ Product/Service Categories	Consulting				Data Processing							Network									
					Systems Development					Facilities Mgmt.		Transport				Services					
	Training & Education	Expert Testimony	Technology Planning & Evaluation	Organization Planning & Evaluation	Turnkey Systems	Requirements & Specifications	Quality Control	Maintenance	Purchased Product Customization	Data Center Management	Capacity Planning & Other Support Serv.	Time Sharing	Network Control	Network Planning & Engineering	Network Construction & Deployment	Service Network Design	Service Control	Service Design & Development	Voicemail	Electronic Document Interchange	Totals*
Distributed Processing/Data						.4				.6											1.0
Network Design	1.5											.2	1.2	3							5.9
Communications		1										2									3.0
Presentation Technology					2	1.5															3.5
Software Engineering					1	3	2														5.0
Modeling & Simulation														2.5							2.5
Artificial Intelligence	.5																				.5
Adv. Architecture Computers											.2							.5			.7
Database Mgmt. Systems												6									6.0
Totals*	2.0	1.0			3.0	4.9	2.0			.6	.2	8.2	1.2	5.5				.5			

*People-years

FIGURE 5.12 STA HUMAN RESOURCE APPLICATION MATRIX

Product/Service Category	Strategy Impact	STA Impact	$ Applied	Personnel Applied
Network Services	25	21	.3	.5
Network Transport	16	9	2.3	6.7
Systems Development	9	8	1.4	9.9
Consulting	4	5	1.7	3.0
Facilities Management	3	6	5.3	9.0

FIGURE 5.13 STRATEGY IMPACT CHART

Analysis Phase

The analysis phase consists of the development of three charts from the matrices produced in the synthesis phase. These consist of the strategy impact chart, the STA impact chart, and the STA resource goal chart. They summarize the overall impact of technology on the enterprise in the previous planning period and outline the technology-related goals for the next planning period. The technology goals will be used to formulate action plans for the organization to follow in meeting those goals.

Strategy Impact Chart The strategy impact chart is designed to summarize by major product/service category the results of the synthesis phase in a format that will allow the various pieces of information to be correlated. An example of this chart, using the previously developed data, is presented in figure 5.13. The product/service categories are listed in order of their impact on the business strategies. The column values are calculated from the matrices produced in the synthesis phase. The strategy impact column entries are found by summing the numerical column-total values over each category in the strategy impact matrix. This provides a relative indicator as to the impact of each product/service category on the business strategies.

The STA impact column values are found by performing

the same sum as described above using the STA impact matrix instead of the strategy impact matrix. This provides an overall indication of the current STA influence on the products and services. The dollars applied and personnel applied column values are found by the same summing procedure using the STA financial application matrix and the STA human resource application matrix, respectively. These provide an indication of the amount of available technical resources applied to each product/service category.

The following conclusions can be drawn from an analysis of the example depicted in this chart:

The potential impact of the STAs on the product/service categories is in approximate proportion to the categories impact on the business strategies. (Ways to increase network transport STA influence may have to be investigated, however.) This agreement between strategy and STA impact would indicate that the current set of STAs is close to optimum for the enterprise. If this condition were not true, a reexamination of the STAs would be in order. Some technologies may need replacing with other more appropriate ones.

The resources (dollars and personnel) are not allocated to the STAs in the same proportion as the STAs' potential impact on the strategies. This would suggest that the funding mechanism needs to be altered and personnel assignments changed.

Any proposed changes to the STA list would have to be resolved before the analysis phase continues. This is required because the remainder of the process uses a list of STAs to form a base for the analysis of the necessary resources. Changes to the STA list would also require a reworking of the synthesis phase to list all of the technologies under investigation (both current and proposed). Because the current STA set for the example company seems to be appropriate as listed, no changes will be made during this plan cycle.

STA Impact Chart In order to obtain sufficient detail, by STA, as to the types of changes needed, two more charts are required. The first presents the results of technical resource

STA	Weight	$ Applied (1)	Personnel Applied
Artificial Intelligence	15	1.3	.5
Communications	7	.7	3.0
Presentation Technology	7	.6	3.5
Advanced Architecture Computers	5	.3	.7
Distributed Processing/Data	4	.6	1.0
Network Design	4	1.9	5.9
Modeling & Simulation	3	.8	2.5
Database Management Systems	3	4.1	6.0
Software Engineering	1	.6	5.0

(1) Millions

FIGURE 5.14 STA IMPACT CHART

application in the last planning period by STA across all products and services. Included are relative rankings of the potential of each STA (weight), expenses incurred for each STA except those for direct personnel, and direct personnel expenses. This STA impact chart is shown in figure 5.14 and is arranged in order of STA weight. The STA weight is the total for each STA in the STA impact matrix.

A quick analysis of the values contained in this chart shows that the resources currently being applied to technology do not support the possible impact of the technologies. The amount of the direct personnel and other expenses are not in the same proportion to the potential impact of the STAs that have the greatest potential for meeting the business strategies.

STA Resource Goal Chart The next chart presents an ideal value for the application of technology resources to each STA. The STA goal chart shown in figure 5.15 has the same columns as the previous chart, but the values represent a different set of conditions, as discussed below. The raw STA weight is a combination of the strategy impact and STA impact by product/service category and is calculated as follows:

STA	Weight (Normalized)	$ (Millions)	Personnel
Artificial Intelligence	31	3.4	8.7
Communications	20	2.2	5.6
Presentation Technology	18	2.0	5.2
Advanced Architecture Computers	6	.7	1.7
Distributed Processing/Data	5	.6	1.4
Network Design	9	.9	2.5
Modeling & Simulation	6	.7	1.7
Database Management Systems	4	.4	1.2
Software Engineering	1	.1	.3

FIGURE 5.15 STA RESOURCE GOAL CHART

$$\underset{\text{(raw)}}{\text{STA WEIGHT}} = \sum_{\substack{\text{all} \\ \text{categories}}} \begin{matrix}\text{category} \\ \text{strategy} \\ \text{impact sum}\end{matrix} * \begin{matrix}\text{category} \\ \text{STA} \\ \text{impact sum}\end{matrix}$$

The category strategy and STA impact sums are obtained from the strategy and STA impact matrices, respectively. Mathematically, this is a form of convolution and is used to accentuate the effect of similar values of the two impacts at the expense of dissimilar ones. The weight value shown in the STA goal chart is normalized to the total of all raw weights for convenience in comparing the relative weights.

In order to determine goals for resource allocation in the coming planning period it is necessary to determine the total amount of each resource that will be available. This can be determined in a number of ways but is usually found by taking the previous amount and increasing it by an inflation factor or some other factor. In the case of the continuing example, it will be assumed that the total resources available in the next period will be the same as that available in the previous period. This total is then allocated to each STA in the same proportion as the normalized weights.

The difference between this idealized resource allocation

and the current allocation forms the basis for determining the required change. Usually, as a practical matter, only a small portion of the difference can be redirected during any given planning period. This is discussed further in the next section, where the development of specific action plans is presented.

Plan Integration

In many large organizations, individual departments or other subdivisions develop their own technology plans, which are designed to meet their own unique needs. The parent organization usually needs an overall picture of the use and application of technology throughout the organization. This requires that the individual technology plans must be combined into an overall plan. This can be done by taking into account the relative sizes of each of the contributing organizations as well as their technology status and intensity. Because the integrated plan is not the result of a single cohesive organization, care must be taken in interpreting and using the results.

TECHNICAL DIRECTIONS GENERATION

The information developed in the technology plan — which in a sense represents the technology status and needs of the enterprise — is now used to formulate technical directions that will provide more effective use of the available technical resources. This technical directions generation process is used to define the technical strategies for the enterprise and to develop associated goals and action plans that will implement those strategies. One methodology for accomplishing this task is shown in figure 5.16.

The inputs to the directions-formulation process are the

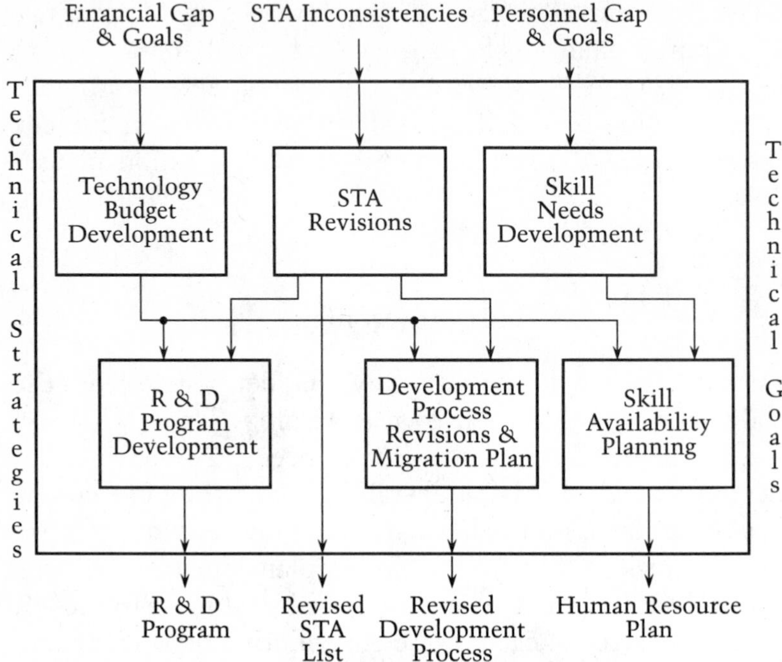

FIGURE 5.16 TECHNICAL DIRECTIONS GENERATION

STA resource gaps and any proposed changes to the STA list. The STA resource gaps are found by subtracting the values in the STA impact chart from those in the STA resource goal chart. Positive values indicate that more resources are needed, and negative values indicate that too many resources are being expended.

The four outputs are the R&D program, revised STA list, revised development process, and human resource plan. These represent the action plans that will govern the technical activities of the enterprise over the next planning period. The revised development process contains those changes which are deemed necessary to use the appropriate technologies in new products and services developed by the organization as well as in the development process itself.

The aggregate outputs of the action parts of direction generation represent the technical strategies of the enterprise.

These outputs also contain the goals that have been defined to meet those strategies. The strategies and goals are a diverse mixture, including funding, skill requirements, technology standards, required investigations, methodologies, and others as appropriate.

Technical direction generation requires input and active participation from most areas of the organization, including finance, human resources, engineering, sales and marketing, and all levels of management. Without this comprehensive contribution to the process, the result will not meet its intended goal of driving the organization toward optimum technology usage.

Technology Budget Development

The development of the enterprise technology budget is crucial to the other parts of directions development. The budget must determine the total amount available for technology-oriented activities and also determine the relative amounts available for R&D, changes to internal procedures (such as purchase or development of new tools), and acquisition of needed human skills. Because they do not go through the technology management process, many organizations emphasize R&D funding without considering the funds needed to utilize the results of R&D and/or provide a staff with the proper skill level to understand and put the technologies to use in the organization.

A commonly held belief among enterprises that do not have technology management programs is that funding for R&D, development process changes, and training/education is a luxury overhead item that can be cut or eliminated at the first sign of an economic downturn. As can be seen from the discussion in this section, that viewpoint is simply not true. All of the technology management activities are vital to the continuing viability of the enterprise in producing products/services for a competitive market.

STA Revisions

As discussed previously, the need for revising the enterprise list of strategic technology areas can be determined from the strategy impact matrix. If the current list does not support the strategies of the enterprise adequately, the technologies must be changed until there is a reasonable match. Unfortunately, there is no algorithmic procedure to follow in accomplishing this change. The revisions to the STA list must utilize all of the technical and managerial strengths of the organization and may take several planning periods to accomplish effectively. This will almost certainly be the case when new technologies must be investigated to determine their capabilities and usefulness to the enterprise. If the enterprise devotes sufficient attention and resources to the planning process, the need for radical changes in the list will usually be small.

Changes in the STA list will be felt throughout the organization. As mentioned previously, the R&D program may need to investigate the properties and capabilities of new technologies in order to determine their place in the organization. New technical skills may be necessary and must be obtained at a sufficient level to produce the desired results. Finally, and probably most importantly, the methods, policies, and procedures of the enterprise must be changed to accommodate the new technologies in an efficient and effective manner. If this latter step is not accomplished well, all of the new technical capability will be wasted.

Skill Needs Development

The STA resources chart contains the idealized personnel needs by STA. Indirectly this data also determines the ideal skill set of the technical organization. Changes to the current set of available skills can be inferred by comparing this chart with the STA impact chart. Because of the inherent inertia in any organization and the long lead time usually associated with personnel changes, it is usually not possible to achieve the new set of skills in a single planning period. In fact, it is probably not desirable even if it were possible. Because the values in the analysis charts are not exact quantities and may vary considerably from the absolute ideal (which cannot be determined), a deliberate approach to changes is warranted. Personnel changes take a considerable length of time to accomplish, and additional alterations to the STA list may occur during the transition period. This process then becomes a continuous one that must be monitored and managed carefully.

Once the skill needs for the coming planning period have been determined, taking into consideration all of the constraints discussed above, means for achieving this goal must be developed. This is the function of the skill availability planning activity, which will be discussed shortly.

R&D Program Development

The purpose of an R&D program is basically twofold. The first is to provide the knowledge necessary to utilize the STAs effectively in the conduct of the business. The second is to provide the background necessary to evaluate changes to the STAs and determine the current or future readiness of new and emerging technologies for inclusion in the technical strategies of the enterprise. The depth of this information is determined by the amount of funding the enterprise is able to provide to this function. Throwing money at an R&D program without first determining the depth to which the resultant technical information is needed and can be assimilated by the enterprise will result in an inefficient process. In addition, the morale of the R&D people is likely to suffer when the results of their efforts are not fully appreciated or utilized by the development part of the enterprise. It is far better to underfund an R&D effort but utilize the results obtained than it is to overfund it and ignore the information produced.

Another aspect of the R&D program that must be addressed

is the transfer of technology from the research state to the development state. This technology transfer is an integral part of the technology management process and must be considered during the development of the R&D program. A comprehensive treatment of the technology transfer process is presented in chapter 6.

A successful R&D program can be structured in many ways in order to provide the required information. How to best accomplish this for a specific organization, industry, and market is far beyond the scope of this book. For this information, refer to other publications that specifically deal with this subject.

Development Process Revisions

The development process, as discussed in chapter 3, requires the effective use of technology in two ways: in the tools that are used to develop products and services and in the products and services themselves. Although the same technologies may be used in both ways, the characteristics required and the methodologies that apply the technologies may differ considerably. For example, a given technology might be ready for application in a development tool but not yet have sufficient definition for use in a product or service. The technology aspect of the development process must therefore differentiate between these two uses.

The infusion of technology into the development process through the architecture is the major conduit by which the enterprise receives the benefits of new technology. This mechanism must be carefully nurtured and managed to ensure that there is a continuous influx of new technology into the process. The human tendency is to want to stick with techniques and processes that are familiar and that have worked before. Although it is obviously not a good idea to utilize something just because it is new or different, it is at least as bad, if not worse, to reject new things merely because they are new. It should also be remembered that what has worked in the past may not be appropriate for the conditions of the future.

Additional aspects of this topic are presented in chapter 6, where the economics of development are discussed.

Skill Availability Planning

Within the context of the budget available and the skill set needed for the coming planning period, a plan must be developed as to how to meet those needs. A wide variety of possibilities exists, including:

- Retraining existing personnel
- Hiring experienced personnel
- Hiring new graduates
- Using consultants

Each of these alternatives has implications on the organization as a whole and the technical areas in particular. The time of availability, the skill level, the cost per person, and the permanency of the skill are all impacted. The effect on the current employee base would also be a significant factor in any decision made in this area. Depending on the industry and market conditions, the current employee base, and the specific priorities of the enterprise, an optimum mix of alternatives would have to be selected. As circumstances change, the selection of alternatives could be altered. Unless the basic needs of the organization change substantially, however, the initial skill goals would remain intact.

TECHNOLOGY ENVIRONMENT DETERMINATION

Understanding and creating the technical umbrella under which the enterprise operates is the purpose of the technology environment function. This function contains all of the activities designed to provide technology to the enterprise. Some of these activities are listed below:

- Research and development
- Technology transfer
- Technology assessments
- Product/vendor assessments
- Interactions with technology providers
- Technology-driven opportunities

The R&D and technology transfer activities have already been covered in some detail in the previous section, so the discussion will concentrate on the remaining four activities.

Technology Assessments

Technology assessments are detailed analyses of specific technologies that are used to understand the current and probable future states of the technology. These assessments are usually of two types:

- A comprehensive assessment designed to form the basis for further investigation into the technology, to understand the possible impact of the technology on current or proposed products and services, or to determine how a competitor is utilizing the technology in its products.
- A restricted assessment covering only a portion of the information that would be contained in a full assessment and used to answer specific questions about the technology or its intended uses.

The information that would be included in a comprehensive technology assessment is shown in the following list:

- History of the technology
- Current state of the art
- References to current literature
- Major research directions
- Major research organizations
- Current uses
- Possible/probable futures and time frames
- Relationships to other technologies

- Related activities of recognized standards bodies
- Existing standards (advantages/disadvantages)
- Commercial offerings
- Internal capabilities
- Impact potential

For a restricted assessment, only the information of interest would be included. Examples of this type of assessment would be:

- Internal capability assessments
- Impact potential assessments
- Availability assessments

The information that would probably be included in a restricted assessment is shown in the following list:

- Reason for the assessment
- Requested information
- References to current literature
- Possible/probable futures with time lines
- Relationships to other technologies
- Related activities of recognized standards bodies
- Existing standards (advantages/disadvantages)
- Commercial offerings

The scope could easily be expanded or contracted to suit the requesting organization.

Technology assessments may be performed by internal personnel or contracted out to consulting firms or university researchers. In either case, care must be taken to ensure that the information needed is obtained in a format suitable for use.

Product/Vendor Assessments

Another type of assessment is that dealing with a specific product and/or vendor. This type of assessment can be used for a number of reasons, including the following:

- Determine the viability of the product/vendor for use in the enterprise
- Determine the probable evolution of the product so that an optimum purchase time can be found
- Compare the offerings of a number of different vendors to determine the one that best meets the needs of the enterprise
- Determine the probable place for a product in the activities of a competitor
- Determine the characteristics of a product/vendor in direct competition and compare it with yours. (This requires a product/vendor assessment on your own company and product.)

The information that should be contained in a comprehensive assessment is shown in the following list:

- Product descriptions
- Technology base
- History of the product
- History of the vendor
- Major design principles used
- Intended market for the product
- Intended marketplace for the vendor
- Probable evolution of the product
- Possible next generation of the product
- Major advantages of the product
- Major disadvantages of the product
- Major competitive products
- Major competitive vendors
- Vendor technical characteristics
- Vendor business characteristics

As in the case of technology assessments, a restricted version of a product/vendor assessment can also be defined to accommodate a specific need.

Frequently a set of product/vendor assessments is used in conjunction with a technology assessment to obtain a complete picture of a given technology and its embodiment. This set of assessments is also useful to determine possible opportunities for products and services that have not yet been addressed.

Interactions with Technology Providers

Part of the technology environment activities must include the examination and classification of technology information produced by a variety of sources. These include:

- Universities
- Government-sponsored research
- Information from industrial laboratories
- Technical publications
- Conferences and symposia
- Consultants
- Competitors

Each of these sources can be extremely useful if handled properly. Although there is usually a significant overlap in the information received, each source has its own slant, and some amount of data from each source will be unique. The formality and frequency with which each source is utilized will depend on the experience that the organization has had with the source in the past and the particular set of technologies that are being pursued actively.

Entering into cooperative agreements with a university is an excellent way to keep current in a number of technologies and also gain access to comprehensive library facilities. Interactions with faculty members and graduate students on a frequent basis can provide a continuity that is hard to find with other sources for a reasonable expense.

It should also be recognized that other organizations — including competitors — regard your enterprise as a technology provider. Great care must be taken to avoid transferring technology that would put the organization at a disadvantage. Some industry-wide sharing of information is good for all members of the industry, because it allows faster and deeper advances in the state of the art, but caution is certainly advised.

Technology-driven Opportunities

Frequently, in the pursuit of the various activities of the technology environment function, opportunities surface for new and innovative products and services that meet the needs of an identified marketplace. These opportunities are called *technology push* opportunities to distinguish them from the *market pull* opportunities that are determined by the enterprise marketing and sales organizations. Technology push opportunities result from a deep knowledge of the technology and its capabilities along with a general understanding of the competitive situation. As mentioned in the previous section, this type of knowledge can be obtained through a comprehensive technology assessment and associated product/vendor assessments.

Technology push opportunities can prove to be as fruitful as the market pull opportunities. They must, however, follow the same verification path as all other potential opportunities before substantial effort is put into creating a product/service based on the technology. Without this verification step (market surveys, focus groups, etc.), it cannot be determined whether or not a good technical idea will be economically viable in its intended marketplace.

TECHNOLOGY UTILIZATION

Technology utilization performs two basic functions. The first is to monitor the effectiveness of the action plans with respect to the goals and technical strategies of the enterprise. In addition to alerting management to potential problems with the action plans, the utilization function also accumulates the quantitative data required for the start of the next planning period. Without the utilization function to provide feedback to the process, it would be impossible to determine if or how well technology management was performing. Because this function follows the rules and tenets of good management practice, no further discussion of this aspect is provided here. Refer to any of a number of texts on management principles (see the bibliography).

The second function is to effect the transfer of technology to the development process through the architecture. As mentioned previously, this transfer is the major mechanism by which new technology is made available for use in the future products and services of the enterprise. The technology utilization function should be performed on a continuing basis, with full-time personnel assigned to the activity.

A more detailed discussion of this function is given in chapter 1 of the companion book, *Network System Architecture.*

SIX

DEVELOPMENT ECONOMICS

INTRODUCTION

The objective of any business is to make a profit, or as it is now generally called, a return on investment. If the business conducts its day-to-day operations in such a way that it does not generate sufficient return for its owners' investment, it will cease to exist, regardless of the quality and/or demand for its products. An enterprise that has for its business the development of networks and network systems must be able to perform this development in such a manner that the business will generate a suitable return on investment.

Because profit is the difference between the revenue a business obtains and the expenses it incurs, a given profit can be obtained by selling more, raising prices, lowering expenses, or a combination of all three. The amount sold depends on the total industry demand for the type of products and services the enterprise produces and the share of this total market that the enterprise can obtain. Pricing is a complex issue that requires detailed analyses of the marketplace and the intended customers. These two interrelated issues, although important, are beyond the scope of this book. Refer to other sources of information as desired (see the bibliography). This chapter concentrates on the expense aspect of profit determination. It will be assumed that a sufficient market share and price can be obtained to meet the profit requirements if the enterprise can control its costs adequately. If this is not the case, the business is not viable under any circumstances.

Although all aspects of development add cost to the final product/service, certain aspects are especially crucial and must be managed carefully. Some of these, such as software reuse, are discussed elsewhere in this book and in the companion books as an integral part of a related technical presentation. The discussion in this chapter therefore focuses on additional areas that need to be addressed as cost-critical but that do not naturally fit in the context of the technical discussions.

The analyses presented assume some knowledge of elementary economics, which is required to understand the reasoning behind several of the cost curves that illustrate various environmental conditions. Without this background, the reasonableness of the shape of the curves must be taken on faith. Further, it would not be possible for you to extend the analyses to cover topics of interest that are not discussed in this chapter.

The subjects that are presented in this chapter are listed below in the order of discussion. There is no particular substantive significance in the order.

- Technology transfer
- Technology change
- Automation
- Estimation metrics
- Installed base
- Standard products
- Quality assurance
- Deployment infrastructure

These issues fall under the domain of software engineering. All of them must be considered at some time during the system development process. It is these areas, when combined with the purely technical aspects, that make the function of the software engineer so challenging and difficult. To fully perform the actions required in effective system development, the software engineer must have an excellent knowledge of these economically oriented areas as well as direct technical knowledge in system development.

For simplicity and clarity, each topic will be discussed as an isolated entity even though there is considerable overlap and interaction among them. The software engineer must be able to supply the experience and judgment needed to utilize and integrate effectively all of the information required for network system development.

It should be clear from the information in this chapter why the optimum course of action from an enterprise-wide viewpoint is not always the best technical solution. The direction taken must depend on a wide variety of information from business operations and planning as well as that related to technical considerations.

TECHNOLOGY TRANSFER

In the life cycle of a product, the applicable technologies must be transferred successfully among a number of different groups. Although technology transfer has become a common term, there is a great deal of misunderstanding as to what it means and the procedures necessary to accomplish it. If the process is not performed correctly, the resultant inefficiencies can increase the cost to the enterprise considerably.

Technology transfer in various forms is constantly taking place into and out of a technology-oriented enterprise as well as among its organizational components. Figure 6.1 illustrates this transfer in schematic form. The degree and depth of the required transfer varies between entities, as does the time needed for it to occur. This figure is implicitly referenced in the next three sections as the *technology transfer model* and should be referred to during the course of the presentation.

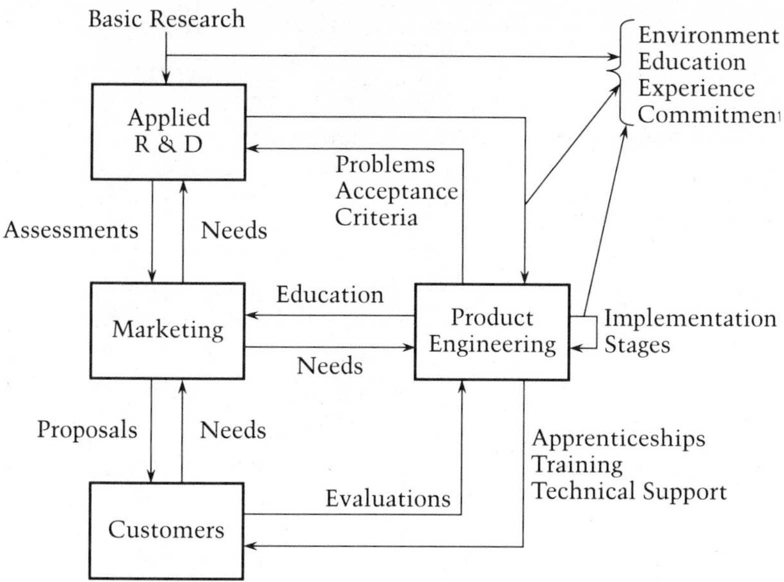

FIGURE 6.1 TECHNOLOGY TRANSFER CYCLE

Technology Transfer Components

A full (or complete) technology transfer is one that enables the receiving organization to independently perform original work in the technology. This type of transfer requires that a number of activities and events be satisfied. A list of these requirements is shown in table 6.1. If all of these occur in a timely manner, a full technology transfer is said to take place. Transfers that involve only a subset of these components are said to result in a partial technology transfer, or, as a special case, a product transfer. Even though they do not transfer independent development capacity, partial technology and product transfers are useful in appropriate circumstances that will be discussed later.

Problems occur, however, when a full transfer is needed but not all of the components are present. This lack of a full technology transfer can result in severe difficulties. Developments that depend on independent capability in that technology may be late, lack functionality, be inefficient, and

TABLE 6.1 TECHNOLOGY TRANSFER COMPONENTS

Area	*Components*
Environment	Equipment Tools Techniques
Education	Assessments Training Technical support Consulting
Experience	Apprenticeships Prototype construction
Commitment	Planning Resource allocation
Needs	Proposed uses Desired characteristics Acceptance criteria

ultimately not meet the needs of the users. Each of the required activities and events of a full transfer are discussed here in enough detail to clarify their definition and their place as a part of the transfer.

During a technology transfer, the environment must be the same at the sending and receiving organization to ensure that no problems occur because of differences. All controllable environmental parameters should be made as identical as possible on both sides of the transfer. This includes equipment, systems software, tools, methodologies, etc. There are usually enough uncontrollable differences to make the transfer a nontrivial process. Even with diligence it is usually impossible to create exactly identical environments. The closer one can come to the ideal, however, the easier it is to track problems to their source. After the transfer has been effected, the receiving organization is free to make changes in the environment to suit its needs. At this time, it is assumed that the receiving organization is self-sufficient and competent to make departures from the original conditions and correct any resultant problems. Some consulting from the sending organization may still be required for some time, however. This need will be discussed further later in the presentation.

Training or education in a technology is most often incorrectly identified as full technology transfer instead of merely one of the components. Further, training is itself only one aspect in a comprehensive education program. Education in the technology must also include a knowledge of the past and future of the technology, its operational behavior, and some of the "tricks" necessary to make use of the technology. Even an excellent education program, however, does not constitute full technology transfer or provide the means to begin independent development and application of the technology. A person who is educated in the technology certainly is aware of the theoretical capabilities and projected uses of that technology. However, without actual experience, proper equipment, and resources there can be no immediate application.

As stated above, experience in a technology is a fundamental requirement to fully transfer a technology. Thus, the receiving organization must obtain personnel with the required experience. This can be accomplished by transferring people along with the technology. In most organizations this tends to be difficult, and other arrangements must be made. Personnel with the required experience can be hired from outside the organization. This has the advantage of providing instant expertise, but the search for the proper persons can consume considerable time and effort. In addition, if the technology is new and perceived by the technical community to be important, people with the requisite skills may be scarce, too costly, or simply not available.

For these reasons, retraining existing personnel remains one of the most popular ways of dealing with the problem. This may be accomplished by the receiving organization sending people to work in the transferring organization early in the process — when it is known that a transfer will take place but significantly in advance of the time when it must be completed. This transfer can take the form of a temporary assignment, a formalized apprenticeship program, or an interdepartmental rotational assignment. The form is not important, but actual hands-on experience is. The transferees must perform the same type of work as the permanent employees in that organization. Just observing will not provide the requisite experience, although it certainly could be considered to be part of the educational component.

The experience component also requires an embodiment of the technology that enables users to understand the applications and limitations of the technology. This embodiment most often takes the form of a prototype that is defined and developed by the transferring organization as part of its initial investigations. As appropriate, the apprentices also work on the design and operation of the prototype and take it (or a copy) with them when they return to the receiving organization. The key point involving this "experience" or "transfer" prototype is that it is not a product! It is merely a convenient method of obtaining the experience component of the technology transfer. In most cases, the "experience" prototype will be discarded after the transfer is complete.

The final component of the technology transfer has little to do with technology as such but instead deals with the commitment of the receiving organization to accept the transfer and make use of the capability. The transferring organization cannot by itself effect the transfer, although there is ample precedent for it trying to do so simply by "throwing it over the wall" at the intended receiving organization. If this intended receiving organization does not want the technology and does not formulate plans to use it effectively, there can be no real transfer regardless of the state of the other transfer components. The receiving organization must plan to incorporate the technology in its work program and products/services as appropriate and must allocate sufficient resources, both financial and human, to the task. This can involve significant effort and is the final true test of the resolve to receive a technology and thereby effect the transfer.

The "needs" component of the transfer differs from the others in that it is mainly a feedback component from the receiving to the sending organization during either a full or partial technology transfer. The transferring organization is usually unaware of the needs of the receiving organization and the uses to which the technology will be put. The needs data in a full transfer can be used to direct the transferring organization in additional work and in tailoring the technology to the requirements of the receiving organization. As a component in a partial technology transfer, the needs component appears in a number of places and again serves as the feedback path for the flow of technology information. This component emphasizes the fact that although the main result of the technology transfer is in one direction, the process itself is iterative and involves a two-way flow of information.

Full Technology Transfers

Three locations in the transfer model require full technology transfer:

- *From the basic research laboratory to the enterprise applied R&D organization.* The basic research laboratory may be either inside or outside of the enterprise. The transfer requirements are the same in either case.
- *From the applied R&D organization to the product engineering organization.* Without an independent development capability, product engineering cannot sufficiently perform its function of developing reliable effective products.
- *Within the product development organization.* This provides all personnel performing development functions, such as design, implementation, and deployment, to have the same level of technology capability. Unless this occurs, the flow of information among these functions will be difficult and will probably result in inefficiencies with the associated increased costs.

Partial Technology Transfers

Technical information flow among other organizations in the model generally reflects more specialized needs that can be met by a partial technology transfer that directly addresses those needs. The actual information present in a partial transfer not only varies with the organizations involved but also may change over time. The key thing to remember about these transfers is that they do not confer on the recipient the ability to perform independent work in the technology.

It must also be recognized that transferring (selling and delivering) a product to a customer is a special form of a partial technology transfer called a *product transfer.* This product transfer requires significant care and attention to provide the customer with the required level of service. Depending on the product and the sophistication of the customer, the amount of information transferred can range from a small amount of training to almost all of the components of a full technology transfer. The determination must be made on a product-by-product basis, taking into account the desires and capabilities of the customer.

The network system development methodology discussion in chapter 3 and the companion book, *Information Networks: A Design and Implementation Methodology,* implicitly assume that the technology transfers described above have taken place and that the information necessary for each stage of design and implementation is available.

TECHNOLOGY CHANGE

Once a technology has been properly transferred and is available for use, the decision must be made as to when new products and services will incorporate the technology — either as a totally new technology or as a replacement for an older one. Either case has significant economic implications, but the decision that requires the most analysis is the one to effect a change in technology. Also, this is usually the most

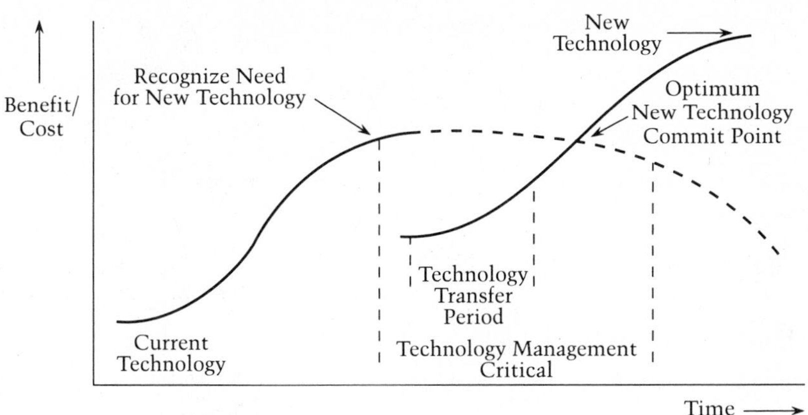

FIGURE 6.2 TECHNOLOGY CHANGE PROCESS

common condition faced in the development process. As a result, the presentation here is limited to that case.

Figure 6.2 presents the change-over decision process and uses what is commonly called the technology "S" curve. The technology "S" curve represents the life cycle of a technology from a benefit/cost perspective. When the technology is young, the benefit/cost is low. There is much to be discovered and extensive experience will be required to understand how to utilize the technology effectively and efficiently. As experience is gained and new information is discovered, the use of technology becomes more efficient, thereby increasing the benefits and lowering the cost. Eventually, the capabilities of the technology are fully utilized and the benefit/cost curve flattens out, reflecting little change in either component. Finally the environment changes to the point that maintaining the technology requires more and more resources (read cost) to make up for those being eliminated by suppliers and vendors as they go on to other technologies. The curve thus reverses and the use of the technology becomes more and more costly.

A replacement technology should have as a potential a higher benefit/cost ratio than that possible with the older technology. If this were not the case, there would be no reason

TABLE 6.2 TECHNOLOGY CHANGE EXAMPLES

Old Technology	*New Technology*
Propeller aircraft	Jet aircraft
Vacuum tubes	Transistors
Transistors	Integrated circuits
Copper wires	Fiber optic light guides
Analog telephone switches	Digital telephone switches
Dumb computer terminals	Intelligent workstations
Assembler language	Compiler languages
Compiler languages	Nonprocedural languages

to consider making a change. In the beginning, however, the actual benefit/cost ratio of the new technology will be lower than that achieved by the old technology. The optimum point at which to change is at the intersection of the old and new curves.

Unfortunately, the locations and shapes of the curves are hard to pinpoint, and finding the exact intersection point is probably impossible. Through the use of a comprehensive technology management program and associated technology transfer activity, it is usually feasible to define a range during which the change can occur and still be close to optimum. The interaction of these technology programs and benefit/cost analyses are also shown in figure 6.2.

Examples of recent and current technology changes are shown in table 6.2.

Many others could have been cited, but this is a reasonable set to illustrate the scope and frequency of occurrence. As a detailed example of the technology change process, consider the change from vacuum tubes to transistors. Tubes were a well-entrenched and well-researched technology, and their cost was low — say on the order of $2 to $3 for a small receiving tube. When transistors first appeared in commercial quantities they were expensive ($50 to $60 for a transistor

TABLE 6.3 TECHNOLOGY CHANGE FAILURES

Old Technology	*Proposed Technology*
Semiconductor memory	Magnetic bubble memory
Voice telephones	Picture telephones
Reciprocating automobile engine	Rotary automobile engine
Paper catalogs	Videotex
Dirt farming	Hydroponics
Homes built "on-site"	Prefabricated homes

that would perform the same function as a tube), but products could be made smaller and more power-efficient. Transistors also tended to last longer. Military product vendors were the first to reach the intersection point because of the premium placed on size and length of use.

As the transistor technology matured and the cost of devices neared the cost of tubes, more vendors reached the intersection point, based on manufacturing economies and customer preference. As the demand for tubes decreased, they became more expensive and their benefit/cost ratio began to decline. Organizations that waited too long to change over began to lose market share, and some met their demise. At this point, tube technology, except for specialized functions (CRTs, high power broadcast), has disappeared, and transistors cost less than a dollar. Interestingly, transistor technology was replaced by integrated circuit technology, which itself has undergone several basic changes in underlying technology.

This analysis is not meant to suggest that every new technology that comes along will replace an older one. There are many examples of new technologies that initially showed great promise but that were never able to replace the then-current technology. Table 6.3 shows some of these failures. One of the most famous of these abortive attempts was bubble memory technology. This technology, which stored bits

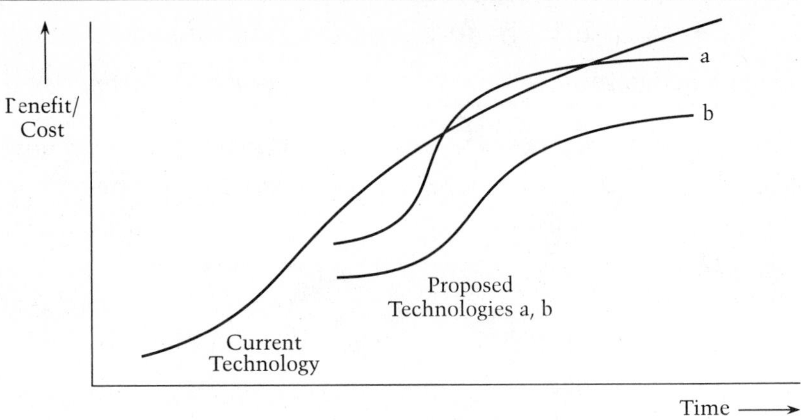

FIGURE 6.3 TECHNOLOGY CHANGE ABORTED (TOO EARLY IN CURRENT TECHNOLOGY)

of information in a magnetic field, was originally thought to be a replacement for semiconductor memory. However, semiconductor memory had not yet reached its benefit/cost peak and continued to rise, eventually passing the peak projected for bubble memory. Semiconductor memory technology was also changing and producing potential benefit/cost ratios far higher than could be forecasted for bubble memory. These two conditions are illustrated in figures 6.3 and 6.4, respec-

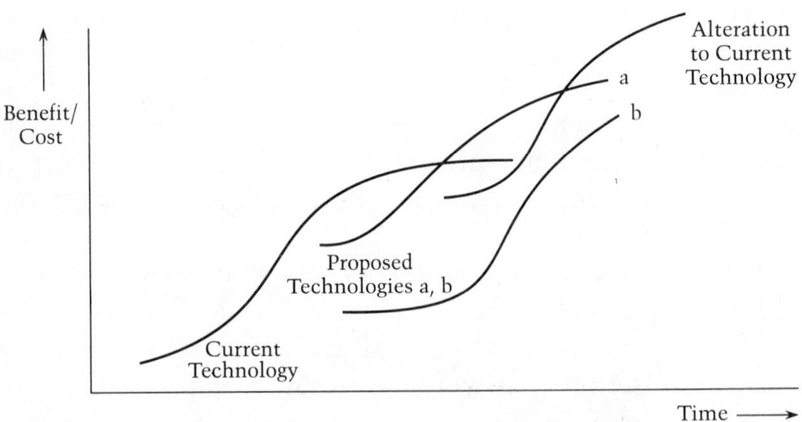

FIGURE 6.4 TECHNOLOGY CHANGE ABORTED (CURRENT TECHNOLOGY ALTERATION)

tively. Determining the approximate shapes of the technology curves is critical and is a major function of the technology management process.

The process continues at an ever-increasing pace. Enterprises must continually monitor the present and new technologies to make sure they are not left behind in the marketplace or make a change at the wrong time or to the wrong technology. The cost of a mistake in deciding when and if to change rises every year.

AUTOMATION

In any discussion of the economics of network and network system development, the subject of automation needs to be considered because of the tremendous potential for reducing costs. *Automation* refers to the replacement of labor costs with equipment costs. Labor costs may be reduced two ways: (1) by making an individual more productive so that the number of units produced by the individual is increased, thus reducing the cost per unit produced by that individual, or (2) by keeping the same output and thereby eliminating the need for as many individuals because of work effort transferred to machines.

The positive economic effect of automation is presented in figure 6.5. This figure illustrates the hoped-for decrease in labor costs made possible through the use of additional equipment. The total cost curve is, of course, the result of adding these two expenses together. The cost with no automation is assumed to be the intersection of the labor and total cost curves with the cost axis. The exact shape of these curves would vary with the specific circumstances involved, and the total costs may or may not reflect the desired results. Notice that there is a range of feasibility (in the short run) where the substitution of equipment for labor is effective. A minimum amount of equipment is necessary to begin an automation program, and the total amount of equipment possible is usu-

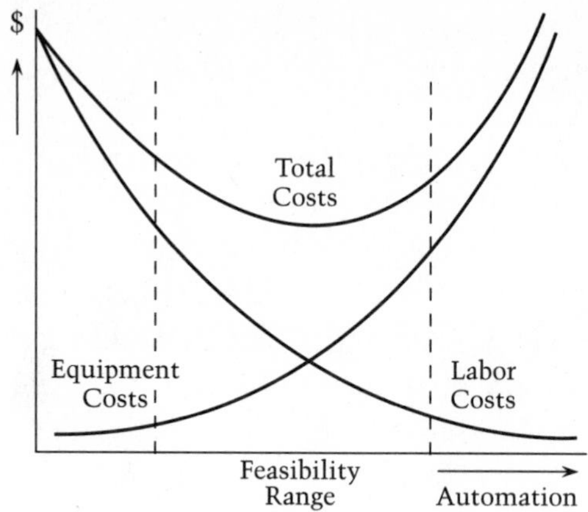

FIGURE 6.5 POSITIVE AUTOMATION EFFECT

ally determined by outside forces, such as space or trained personnel available. Given enough time, all of these constraints, as well as the feasibility range, can change. A constrained feasibility range always exists, however.

Lack of careful planning or failure to use the proper mix of labor and equipment can cause automation actually to increase total costs. This possibility is illustrated in figure 6.6.

One way this can happen is by making individuals more

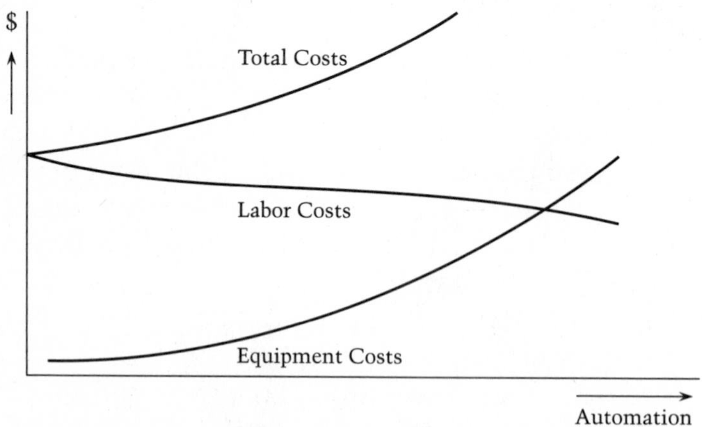

FIGURE 6.6 NEGATIVE AUTOMATION EFFECT

productive without enabling the enterprise to reduce labor costs. This will happen if:

- All current employees must be retained because of their needed skill sets in other areas, and
- The total amount of work available will not increase as capacity increases, thus increasing nonproductive time per individual.

Another way this can happen is when equipment is used that makes the employees' increase in productivity less than the cost of the equipment. Unfortunately, both of these cases occur with great frequency and place the companies involved in some difficulty.

Deciding on the proper amount of automation is important because of the effect it can have in a competitive market. Too much or too little can place the firm at a severe economic disadvantage when competing for business. Many technology-oriented enterprises tend to err on the side of too much equipment because they succumb to their desire to employ the latest technologies and techniques without performing a detailed economic evaluation. This economic evaluation can include intangible as well as tangible benefits but must be made as quantitative as possible for greatest usefulness.

The major form of automation emerging in network and network system development is through the use of computer aided software engineering (CASE) tools. There is a growing number of these tools, with a wide range of sophistication. As with any technology, the use of these tools must be carefully planned in accordance with the presentations in this and other chapters of this book. This planning is complex, but it is necessary for survival.

DEVELOPMENT METRICS

Estimating the characteristics of a proposed development is an economic exercise of great importance. These characteristics include but certainly are not limited to the following: finances required, personnel required, system size, schedule, defects expected, complexity expected. Appropriate metrics must be defined for each of these characteristics so that quantitative data can be calculated and utilized. Defining metrics is not an easy task, and a great deal of research is continuing in this area. The interest in these metrics for the purpose of this chapter is in the economic consequences of their utilization and not in their specification. As a result, further discussion of metric definition must be left to other publications (see the bibliography).

Unless development estimates are performed correctly, the enterprise will be placed at a severe economic disadvantage compared with its competitors. Consider the following scenario:

> A request for proposal (RFP) is received from a prospective client. (The use of the term *client* is meant to imply either an internal or external customer.) Assume further that the RFP is for a fixed-price contract. This type of contract is becoming the norm for system development and is unlikely to change in the near future.
>
> The development characteristics are then estimated, using a set of relevant metrics. The projected cost is added to the required profit in order to develop the bid price for submission to the client. Several possible economic consequences of the bid are now possible and are illustrated in figure 6.7. If the bid is accepted and actual costs far exceed the estimate (curve a through curve b), the enterprise will experience a monetary loss. Too many of these and the enterprise will cease to exist. If the estimate far exceeds actual costs (curve c through curve d), the likelihood of the bid being accepted is considerably reduced. Too many of these and the enterprise will also cease to exist. The estimate must lie between curve b and curve c,

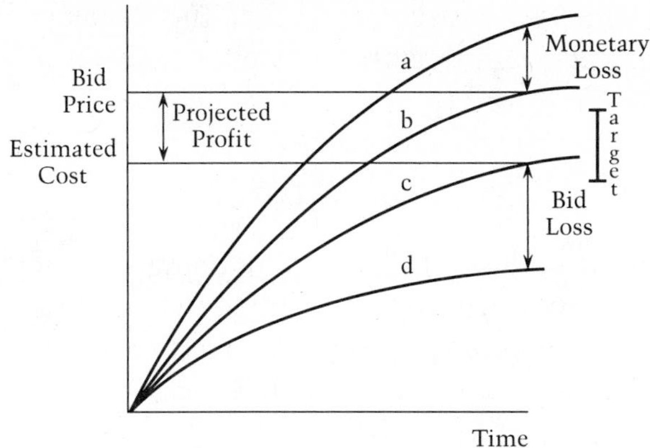

FIGURE 6.7 DEVELOPMENT METRIC DEPENDENCE

and consistently close to curve c, for the enterprise to prosper.

This is admittedly a restricted presentation, and many variables other than cost are involved (such as time), but the scenario presents the essential concepts. This analysis assumes that applying the principles contained in the previous discussions in this chapter have reduced the actual development costs to a minimum and that the products/services produced are of excellent quality from a competitive standpoint. The subject of quality will be discussed in some detail later in the chapter.

Unfortunately, the current state of project estimation technology and the associated metrics continue to be primitive. Reliance on historical data of doubtful consistency (because of the large number of variables involved, which are continuously changing) is the norm. Some enterprises are able to perform this estimation much better than others because of the time and resources committed to the task. These companies recognize the critical economic importance of obtaining the right estimates. They share responsibility for this task among *all* development personnel, because they are the ones who ultimately must ensure that the development follows the estimates and that the enterprise receives a profit.

INSTALLED BASE

A start-up company that is producing and deploying new products/services for the first time or an established company producing an entirely new line is free to adopt for these products/services whatever characteristics are considered optimum for the market. Unless the offerings are intended to interact with products/services from other companies, the design need not be restricted in any way that might be deemed detrimental.

Once an enterprise has deployed products/services, it is in a somewhat different situation. Many customers buy a specific product/service and then spend many times more than the purchase price to make the purchase suitable in the specific situation in which it is applied. Customers in this situation would not be happy if additional offerings from the same company, which provided greater economic benefit along with identical or similar functions, were incompatible with those previously purchased. New offerings, which incorporate advances in technology to reduce costs or improve performance and/or contain functions that meet additional needs, must not obsolete the support environment that has been put in place for the older products/services.

The design problem then becomes much more difficult. This situation is illustrated in figure 6.8 for a variety of circumstances. The figure depicts the increase in development costs as the installed base increases. Curve a represents the case where no attempt is made to accommodate an installed base. This is still possible in some industries, notably the consumer market, which generally does not generate a large product-specific support expense on the part of the user. In fact, some manufacturers deliberately make new products incompatible with the older ones to force even more sales.

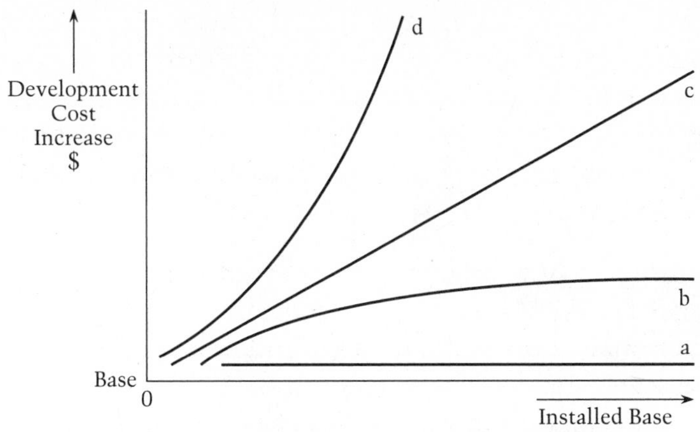

FIGURE 6.8 INSTALLED BASE EFFECTS

This, of course, has been the subject of much debate and concern over the past several years.

The commercial and industrial market is a great deal more sensitive to the issue of installed base. Curves b through d represent the increasing effects of installed base on the development cost of new products/services. The different curves represent varying degrees of difficulty in adapting new designs to accommodate the installed base. This, of course, is highly situational, but the enterprise must know what this curve looks like for its products/services in order to make intelligent decisions concerning replacements and additions. At some point, it may become uneconomic to continue total compatibility, and compromises must be made. Offering conversion products may ease this decision and subsequent effect somewhat. Again, this is an economic decision, not a technical one. Generally the technology exists or can be developed to provide a large number of offerings and design alternatives. The economics will dictate the final choice.

STANDARD PRODUCTS

The development and management of a set of standard products (hardware, software, or a combination) that is used by the enterprise in the operation of the business, both for development and nondevelopment activities, is a growing means of controlling costs while still allowing sufficient flexibility for individual judgment and opinion. A well-controlled set of standard products can reduce costs through the following means:

- Training on new products is kept to a minimum.
- Repair techniques and procedures are well known.
- Functionality of products is well understood (there are no surprises).
- The introduction of new technology is uniform across the enterprise.
- The lowest-cost alternative can be identified and specified.
- Volume discounts can be negotiated with the supplier.
- Qualification of products as meeting minimum corporate standards is reduced to a minimum.

As an example of the selection and use of standard products, the selection of computer workstations is considered here. Because workstations are necessary for general business functions, for design and development activities, and as part of most deployed product/services, they are an ideal vehicle on which to develop the concepts of standard products.

The approach outlined here, however, is easily carried over to other product classes as required for the specific output of the enterprise. The identification of a standard set of workstations from which all selections must be made is a complex issue, and a considerable amount of usage analysis and technology forecasting is required to make a suitable decision. If a formalized procedure is used, however, the process can be made quite manageable. One such procedure is outlined in this section.

The identification process is as follows:

1. Develop a set of attributes for the standard product set which can be used to characterize the specific needs of the enterprise in this area.

2. Using the values for these attributes, develop criteria for identifying all products that meet the minimum requirements of the enterprise. These will then form the candidate list from which the final set will be selected.

3. Develop a set of principles that will allow the selection of the final set of standard products.

4. Apply the first three steps to the product class of interest.

A set of attributes that is suitable for the workstation standard product set example is listed below:

- Projected uses of the workstation
- Specific system requirements
- State of the technology
- Financial requirements
- Replacement or new equipment
- End user requirements
- Information network architecture
- Local conditions
- Depreciation schedule allowed
- Vendor reliability

Other attributes could be utilized if desired. Likewise, some of those listed could be deleted, depending on the individual circumstances of the enterprise. For each intended use of a workstation, a set of values for the attributes must be identified. The standard product set must provide at least one workstation that will meet the needs inherent in each set of values. If that coverage does not occur, the requirements of at least one application will not be met and the standard list will have to be updated. Additional uses that occur after the standard list has been developed may also require additions or changes to the list. It is desirable to change the standard product list as little as possible because of the costs involved in adding new entries to the list. The initial list, therefore, must be developed with considerable care.

Restriction Criteria

Although there is a growing number of workstations available on the market, the selection set can be restricted as indicated by the following conditions:

- Workstations of a type that already are in use in the enterprise
- Workstations specifically required by a system and/or equipment necessary to run a particular application being installed
- Workstations that are capable of performing all current applications and projected future applications
- Workstations that are designed to accommodate significant changes in technology
- Workstations that best accommodate the characteristics required based on the attributes defined in the previous section
- Workstations that are consistent with the information network architecture (as defined earlier in this book)
- Workstations that meet the minimum qualification standards of the organization

This restriction criteria will be used to narrow the set of all possible workstations to a candidate set from which the final standard set of products will be selected. This candidate set, or *short list,* as it is sometimes called, consists of all workstations that meet the minimum requirements for use in the systems developed by the enterprise.

Selection of the final set will require additional guidelines, as discussed in the next section.

Final Selection Principles

After the allowable set of workstations has been reduced in accordance with the discussion of the previous section, several general principles can be used to select the final set of standard workstations. Some of the major principles are listed below:

- Keep the number of workstation types to a minimum (3 or 4).
- Keep the number of workstation vendors to a minimum (3 or 4).
- Keep the number of similar alternatives to a minimum (1 or 2).
- Consistent with future projections of use within the equipment life, choose the lowest cost alternatives.
- Select the alternative with the most flexibility.
- Select function-compatible and/or plug-compatible alternatives with caution. Problems may occur when new functions or applications become available but cannot be utilized with the supposedly compatible alternative equipment.
- Use products from unknown or unproven vendors with extreme caution.

After these principles have been applied and the initial standard set of workstations have been identified, an audit must be performed to be sure that this set covers all of the combinations of characteristics that were defined for projected applications.

Although all of the considerations given so far seem easy enough to state, implementing them is much more difficult because of the problems involved in projecting future uses, predicting the useful practical life of a workstation under rapidly changing technology, prioritizing the sometimes-conflicting selection criteria, and deciding when an additional workstation or workstation type is justified. Removing a workstation or workstation type from the standard product list is also an event of significant importance. This action must utilize most of the same analysis process as that required for additions. There is always great pressure to define a larger set than absolutely necessary.

Tight controls must be maintained in order to reap the full economic benefit of the standard product concept.

It should be remembered that approaches such as those discussed here can bound the problem and provide insight into the relevant considerations, but the actual decision is basically a subjective one that will result from engineering and financial judgment. Although not mentioned previously, significant intangible considerations also must be taken into account (such as a desire to maintain a good relationship with a particular supplier).

A detailed discussion of the initial selection process and follow-up management methodology for standard product administration is beyond the scope of this discussion and will not be pursued. However, this is an important area in the total development process and must be addressed effectively if a development organization is to remain economically viable.

Because of the rapid changes in technology and the relatively short lifetimes of current products, specific vendor offerings are not named as part of the example in this chapter. Doing so would result unnecessarily in the premature obsolescence of at least that part of the discussion, and by implication, other parts that would still be valid.

QUALITY ASSURANCE

Because of the increasingly global nature of competition and the customer's ability to choose from a wide variety of products, there has been increased recent emphasis on providing quality products. This is seen as giving a competitive edge in a crowded market. Unfortunately, even with all of the increased emphasis on quality, much still needs to be done, especially in the area of software and systems technology.

Quality assurance in hardware technology has a long and well-defined history and approach. It is possible to define and calculate such meaningful quantities as "mean time between failures" (MTBF) for systems and the failure rate of individual components. No such analog exists for software and system technology, although a great deal of effort has been expended in the search. Although "mean time to failure," or MTTF, is sometimes used for software in the same way that MTBF is used for hardware, the mathematical underpinnings for MTTF are not nearly as well understood or defined as those for MTBF. Innovative approaches to producing quality software systems need to be developed.

The main thrust of this section is that quality, like any other component of the system, needs to be engineered. Overengineering or underengineering this component, as well as any of the others, can result in significant problems for the enterprise and the customer.

Three Quality Myths

Part of the problem with obtaining large advances in quality assurance for software systems has been the existence of three myths that keep getting renewed and reinforced to the point that they are assumed to be true. The first is that we know what quality is. The truth is that there is no uniform definition of quality or means to measure it. Facetiously, quality can be compared to goodness:

- Everyone is for it.
- Everyone has his own definition as to what it is.
- Others seem to cheat a little when no one else is looking.

Discussions of quality and its definition take on the same characteristics as the story of "The Blind Man and the Elephant." The result achieved depends on the perspective of the participants and the particular problem at hand.

The second myth is that quality is free. You always get at least as much back as you put into it. Unfortunately, this is also not true, especially in a situation in which all of the competitors are putting money into some form of quality assurance program. Part of the understanding of quality is knowing how much you can afford in a given situation and the most productive way to utilize and leverage those resources by proper engineering.

The third myth is that quality is a technical problem. In fact, a great number of techniques exist to increase the quality of software regardless of the definition. In reality, as alluded to above, quality is an economic problem, not a technical one. You can get as much as you are willing to pay for. In some cases, more is purchased than can be afforded.

With these myths in mind, an analytical approach to software and system quality can now be developed. The technique will be to present and at least partially answer the following series of questions:

- What definition of a quality system should be used?
- After one is picked, how is the quality measured?
- Assuming it can be measured, what procedures can be used to make it happen?
- If a quality system can be developed, how much will it cost to do so?

What Is a Quality System?

Many definitions of a quality system have been proposed. Some of the more well-known ones are shown in table 6.4. Although this definition is not listed, it is safe to say that the ultimate quality goal is to meet the customers' definition of quality. That is, unfortunately, not the same as definition 1 in the table. The customer in many cases expects an inferior product and is not disappointed when it arrives. The customer may have been unwilling to pay more for a system of higher quality. The customer got what was expected — but don't believe for a second that this equates with quality in the customer's mind. Just ask someone who bought a cheap used car because it was the only thing he could afford. He will probably say he got what he expected but I doubt if it would be considered a quality purchase.

Most customers probably do not have a conscious opinion

TABLE 6.4 DEFINITIONS OF A QUALITY SYSTEM

It meets or exceeds the customers' expectations.

It conforms to the requirements and specifications.

It contains no errors.

It conforms to the "ilities":

- Reliability
- Usability
- Maintainability
- Flexibility
- Testability
- Portability
- Auditability
- Reusability
- Interoperability
- Securability
- Data commonality
- Expandability
- Traceability

It is better than the competition.

as to what their definition of a quality product or system is, but they will know it when they see it (and vice versa). This lack of articulation as to what a customer expects in a quality system is what makes creating one difficult, if not impossible. To this problem must be added the increased difficulty in meeting multiple customers' definitions of quality, each of which may be different from the others. All of this does not mean that the job should not be attempted, just that it is wise to be prepared for less than perfect results.

Because the goal of meeting the customer's definition of quality cannot be directly attacked, the next best thing would seem to be to meet *all* of the other definitions of quality as presented in table 6.4. This is not as impossible a task as it first seems, because techniques exist that focus on satisfying one or more of these definitions.

Quality Metrics

The general management principle that "You can't control it if you can't measure it" has made it imperative that some metric be defined that provides a quantitative measure of how well a system meets the defined quality standards. The only one that has achieved widespread acceptance is "defects per life cycle phase per lines of code." As discussed previously in the chapter, this is a development metric that must be estimated, usually from historical data. This is then compared to actual experience to determine if the quality (as measured by this metric) meets expectations. Unfortunately, this metric leaves a great deal to be desired, but because it is widely used, an examination of its characteristics is necessary.

The word *defects* implies that only errors in the classical sense are counted. In actuality, software problems encompass a much larger set of difficulties. The use of another word, such as *exception,* to indicate this much larger class of problems would increase the value of the metric. Some of the more common exception sources are shown in the following list:

- Incorrect requirements
- A difference between the way the software operates and the
    - initial requirements
    - initial specifications
    - documentation
- Invalid assumptions
- Design deficiencies
- Interface mismatches
- Inconsistencies
- Requirements changes
- Technology changes
- Operating personnel difficulties
- Expectations greater than warranted

When this wide variety of exception sources is included, many of the quality definitions in table 6.4 can be partially addressed. The use of *defects* restricts this quality measure to the third and part of the fourth definition in table 6.4.

There are other problems with the metric as originally defined that must be at least indicated, if not resolved. The

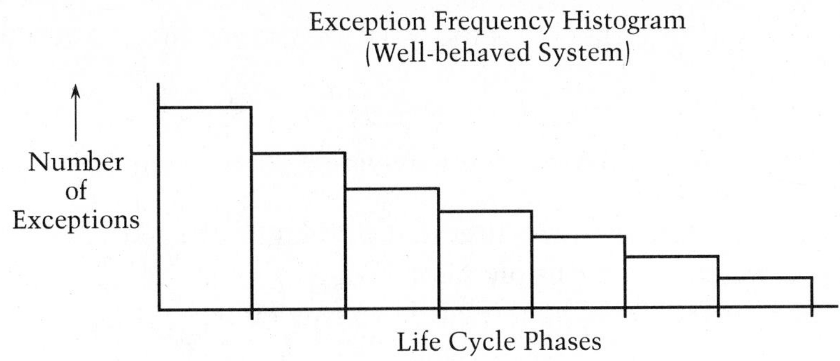

FIGURE 6.9 EXCEPTION FREQUENCY HISTOGRAM (WELL-BEHAVED SYSTEM)

metric is ambiguous as to when an exception will be counted — in the phase in which it originally occurred or in the phase in which it is finally discovered. The use of "lines of code" is a specific measure of the size of a program that may or may not be highly correlated with the defect rate. The complexity of the system and/or design technique is certainly a factor, as is the development methodology being utilized. The following exception characteristics are not considered.

- Exception severity
- Time and effort required to resolve
- Effect on the customer
- Effect on development time and cost

It is possible that a system that has ten minor exceptions that are quickly and easily resolved can be a higher-quality system than one with a single catastrophic failure.

Using this metric (assuming exceptions instead of defects), a quality system would be considered to be one that followed the histogram of figure 6.9, having large numbers of exceptions in the early development phases and few after deployment of the system. Although this is certainly a desirable result, it is far from the whole story, as indicated above. These issues must also be addressed in a comprehensive system quality metric. Work is continuing on identifying such an entity, but as yet no agreement exists as to a suitable definition.

Philosophies of Quality System Development

Assuming that the measurement problem has been resolved, the next task is to implement a quality system. There are three basic philosophies relating to this effort:

1. Eliminate all software exceptions
2. Design the system to tolerate software errors and exceptions
3. Design the system to reduce the effect of software errors and exceptions

The difference between 2 and 3 is as follows. A system that will tolerate errors works correctly under error conditions. A system that reduces the effects of errors detects and prevents the propagation of the error. Although the system does not work entirely correctly in the latter case, the effects of the error are minimized. An example of 2 would be a majority voting system that calculated a given result three different ways. The majority result would be chosen as correct if any of the three differed. Although the error may persist, the system would still work correctly. An example of 3 would be a system with an audit program that continuously checked the validity of data. If any wrong data was found the audit would try to correct it or flag it as bad to prevent its being used in further processing.

Most approaches to a quality software system rely almost totally on philosophy 1. This may or may not be appropriate depending on the project and the customer. One change to this philosophy that is sometimes considered is to find the worst exceptions and eliminate those. The difficulty is in defining the attributes and characteristics of the "worst" exceptions and in assuming that procedures can be defined that will accomplish the desired result.

Later in this discussion, some techniques applicable to phi-

TABLE 6.5 APPROACHES TO QUALITY SYSTEM IMPLEMENTATION

Approach	*Philosophy Supported*
Construction	Eliminate errors
Testing	Eliminate errors
Analysis	Eliminate errors
Design	Tolerate errors
Operations	Reduce error effect

losophies 2 and 3 will be presented. When all of the philosophies are used simultaneously, a lower-cost result that has the same or higher quality may be obtained.

Approaches to Quality System Implementation

Depending on the philosophies adopted, several approaches can be used to implement a quality software system. These are shown in table 6.5, along with the development philosophy each supports. It should be emphasized at this point that all of these approaches require continuous attention to the quality component of the system throughout the development process. Assigning quality assurance to a single phase or milestone during the later part of a development methodology will not provide the depth and coverage necessary. A formal review of the results of the quality aspects of the development is always appropriate and may be used near the end of a development to determine how well the quality process performed and to suggest ways for its improvement.

The construction and testing approaches are methodology-based approaches to eliminating all sources of exceptions. Although it is probably impossible to eliminate all exceptions using these techniques, their proper application can eliminate the majority of potential problems.

In the design approach, probable sources of exceptions are

identified and a system design is constructed that will allow the system to function correctly in spite of the presence of these errors. Check values and alternate evaluation algorithms are among the techniques that can be used.

The operations approach tries to reduce the effect of errors that occur during operation of the system. Additional functions are added that monitor the operation of the system and alert repair routines or human operators to the existence of a problem. The use of Abnormal End (ABEND) functions that simply abort the operation of the system without attempting a recovery is highly discouraged. This approach relies on real-time checks and associated corrections during operation of the system to prevent error results from spreading.

Construction Techniques Four techniques can be used for constructing a quality system:

- Prototype-based methodology
- Technical reviews
- Technical inspections
- Formal deployment program

Each of these addresses a specific aspect of eliminating potential errors and exceptions. The prototype-based methodology is designed to eliminate conflicts with the requirements and specifications and to provide the users with continuous feedback during the development process; this feedback is especially important in the initial phases. Major characteristics of this type of methodology are shown in the following list:

- A system embodiment always exists.
- The customer is always aware of the current and projected system capabilities.
- Quality is evaluated at every step.
- There is little room for any surprises at the end of the project.

Changes in this list certainly can be made in keeping with the desires and practices of individual organizations as long as the basic philosophy remains intact.

Technical reviews are designed to encourage frequent developer-level interactions that not only examine the system designs for conformance with the requirements, specifications, and design guidelines but also share information and, in general, increase the level of communications among the personnel directly involved in the implementation process. It is hoped that the increased communications will provide a more uniform product. The major characteristics of the technical reviews are presented in the following list:

- At least one review for every step of the methodology for each module or larger-sized system component
- 3 to 5 people attending, including responsible individuals (all peers)
- No management personnel attending
- No longer than 1/2 day
- Enough advance preparation to ensure participants are familiar with material to be reviewed. (Because peers only are involved, they should be generally familiar with the subject material.)
- Nonadversarial atmosphere

As with the review procedures, each organization can tailor the exact format and parameters to those which will provide the most quality assurance in its environment.

Technical inspections are a more intense form of control than technical reviews. The purpose of an inspection is much more managerial in nature; such inspections are designed to ensure that all efforts follow the proper practices and policies of the organization. The major characteristics of a technical inspection are shown in the following list:

- At least one per major methodology phase for each major system component

- 10 to 12 attendees, including responsible individuals
- Management participation required. (Two levels are recommended.)
- May last 1 to 2 days
- Thorough preparation on the part of each attendee
- Adversarial atmosphere possible although not encouraged

Technical inspections are a rather new quality assurance device but the purpose and structure is much in alignment with the goal of constructing an exception free system.

A formal deployment program is an integral part of the system implementation methodology. Its major purpose is to avoid exceptions due to customer misunderstandings and lack of knowledge required for proper operation. Such a program is necessary to ensure successful operation under realistic conditions. The major components of a formal deployment program are shown in the following list:

- Physical network assignment
- Training program
- Field trial (Alpha test)
- Pilot (Beta test)
- Production installation
- Cutover
- Initial production operation

Only those specifically oriented toward the elimination of customer-originated exceptions are discussed here. The others are covered in the companion book *Information Networks: A Design and Implementation Methodology*.

The training program is used to educate the users of the system as to its proper operation. In addition, it is used to familiarize the users with the support structures available in case difficulties develop. Users can be trained in many different ways:

- Formal training courses
- Books and manuals
- On-line instruction and help facilities (CAI)

- One-on-one demonstrations
- Recorded instructions (videotape/audiotape)
- Trial and error

These methods may be used singly or in combinations. Which method is employed in a particular situation depends on the characteristics of the system as well as the users.

Although trial and error is listed as a training method, it obviously should never be used in practice. Unfortunately, too many systems are deployed that train their users by this process. The user may eventually learn to use the system in some fashion but rarely will be able to learn all of the necessary aspects efficiently.

Another aspect of training that must be addressed is the tendency to use training to make up for poor human interface design. It is sometimes thought that a complex, inconsistent, or plain "hard-to-use" interface can be made palatable by training. This is rarely the case, and the attempt usually results in spectacular failure. For example, this is one of the major reasons that advanced services such as call forwarding, conferencing, and speed calling, which are enabled through the telephone, are rarely used once the newness wears off. The telephone instrument is a difficult human interface when it is used for other purposes than placing a voice telephone call. Training does not and cannot make up for having to remember combinations such as *4 or #9 to invoke various options. Interpreting the sometimes strange noises that are supposed to signal various conditions to the user is not easy either.

The field trial is used to insure that the basic design of the system is correct and that no major deficiencies exist in the system design. It is also possible at this time to determine whether there are areas that have not been addressed by the system capabilities but that are necessary in day-to-day operation. The field trial is also used to begin the technology transfer of the system technology from the development group to the operations group. Without an adequate job of technology transfer between these groups, the system could encounter severe difficulties once it has been deployed and the development personnel have, in effect, disengaged themselves from the system.

The field trial, by its very nature, is limited in scope and time and therefore usually has a defined beginning and end. Its major purpose is to provide operational experience to the major users and assigned operations personnel, as well as to provide an early indication of any problems that would arise in operational use.

The next stage of deployment is called the *pilot stage* (or *Beta test*) and is designed to introduce the user community to the system on an operational basis. The only difference between the pilot and full deployment of the system is that the pilot generally is restricted to a relatively small cross-section of the intended user community. This is done in order to manage the complexity of introducing the system and as a further way of determining whether there are any deficiencies that require additions or changes to the system. If the pilot is successful (the users like it and are willing to pay the cost of its operation), it is generally assumed that the system will be made continuously available to them. This, of course, differs from the field trial, in which no guarantee is made as to the system's continued availability.

The pilot also affords the opportunity to further pursue the technology transfer from the developing organization to the operations personnel. The pilot is really aimed at evaluating the operation of the system from a business standpoint, rather than the technical standpoint on which the evaluation of the field trial is based.

Testing Approaches The purpose of testing is to discover if the system is behaving as expected for the input that is presented. Although valuable, testing has some severe limitations:

- Only a fraction of all possible system states can be tested because of time and cost considerations.
- Testing under simulated operations conditions cannot completely reproduce operational conditions.
- The exact expected behavior for each test must be known.

In spite of these limitations, testing remains the most used technique in the development of quality systems. If done properly with an understanding as to the weaknesses, testing is a valuable approach to reducing errors.

Tests generally fall into one of two classes: user-oriented tests and developer-oriented tests. User-oriented tests treat the system as a user would and do not assume a knowledge of the internal construction of the system. Test suites consist of entries that a user could make, although not necessarily ones that are expected in the normal course of operation. Developer-oriented tests assume a detailed knowledge of system construction. Test suites are designed to force the system into certain states in order to test each major system path and function. When these two test types are combined, a significant reduction in errors can be achieved. However, the most important point to remember about testing is that unless the tests are almost exhaustive in scope there is no guarantee that all errors have been eliminated. In fact, the ones remaining will usually be difficult to correct; significant resources may be required to determine their source and resolution. Testing helps considerably, but it is only one tool of many.

Analysis Approaches The general approach to quality by analysis is through "proof of correctness" algorithms. Although a great deal of research has been performed on this technique, it remains limited to small programs of well-defined structure. Even in these cases, the proofs are complex and in many cases amount to recoding the algorithm in a

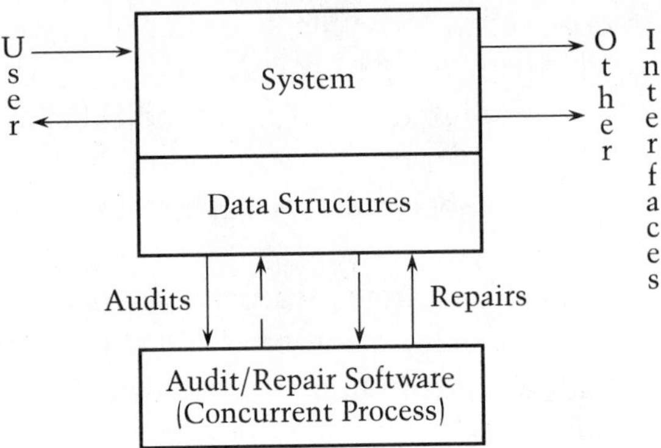

FIGURE 6.10 AUDIT/REPAIR PROCESS

different way. This, in effect, changes the problem to a design diversity approach, which was discussed previously.

Quality by analysis has been and undoubtedly will remain a sought-after goal. Significant research efforts are continuing because of the tremendous savings that would be possible using a practical analysis technique. However, the current state of the art seems to indicate that any analysis approaches to software quality for systems of significant size are many years away and will require fundamental breakthroughs to accomplish.

Operations Approaches In some systems, especially those which receive inputs from processes that cannot be completely characterized or specified, quality requires approaches other than those described so far. Examples of such systems are process control and network control. If a system of this type has internal data and data structures that can be completely specified, operational approaches to maintaining quality can be used. The first approach, depicted in figure 6.10 uses concurrent audits and associated repair procedures to keep the internal data and structures "clean."

If the system must remain operational on a continuous basis, one other technique pioneered by telephone switching systems is useful. This is a phased recovery process that

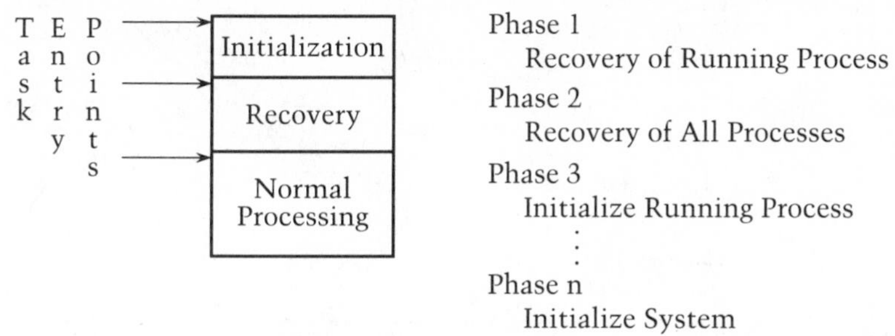

FIGURE 6.11 PHASED RECOVERY

attempts in a systematic and well-structured fashion, to recover a system that has failed as a result of hardware or software problems. This type of recovery requires that each software task have two sections in addition to that which performs normal processing, as shown schematically in figure 6.11. The additional sections perform a recovery function that attempts to return the task to a known state and an initialization function that returns the task to an initial state. These functions are usually performed by manipulating data that is local to the task. Global data may be changed only when it is common to all tasks being recovered or initialized.

When an error is discovered that prevents a continuation of normal processing, the "phasing" subsystem examines the state of the software system at the time of error discovery (which may be later than the time at which the error actually occurred) and takes a minimal step toward resuming operations (Phase 1). As shown in the figure, this step could be as simple as running the recovery routine of the process that was executing at the time of error detection. The processing system is then restarted and monitored by the phasing subsystem for a period of time to determine if the system has returned to normal operation. If normal operation has resumed, the phasing subsystem is terminated. If problems still exist, an additional recovery phase is started. Subsequent phases recover additional modules and begin initializing modules depending on the definition of each phase. Ultimately,

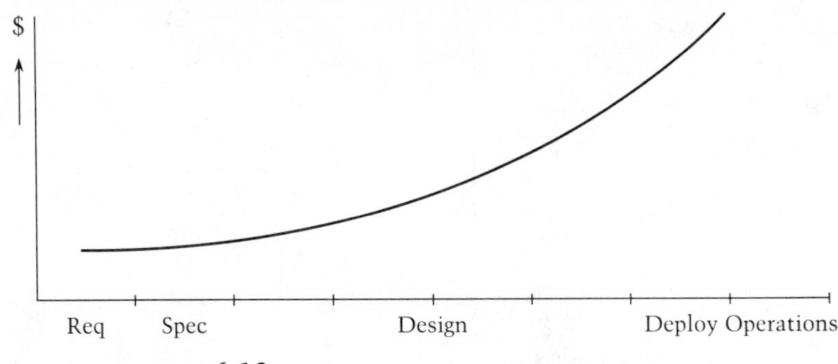

FIGURE 6.12 COST OF SOFTWARE EXCEPTIONS

when the final phase is reached, all modules are initialized and the system is started from the beginning.

The Cost of Quality

The costs incurred because of exceptions reported for the system fall into two categories, tangible and intangible. Tangible costs are those which can be quantitatively measured. They generally consist of the resources expended to diagnose and correct exceptions or to overcome any development delays that result. Intangible costs are those attributed to areas such as increased customer dissatisfaction and diminished corporate image, which eventually could lead to loss of market share. These are real and potentially large but hard to measure.

In most discussions concerning quality assurance, there is almost total emphasis on intangible costs and a close to mystical quality is imparted to them. From an economic viewpoint, however, these costs, for analysis purposes, act in the same way as direct costs, and must be considered similarly. Balance between the tangible and intangible costs is important, and a large portion of the following presentation is devoted to ways of achieving that balance.

Discussions concerning the cost of exceptions generally show a graph similar to that given in figure 6.12. This graph presents the cost of an exception as reflected by the amount

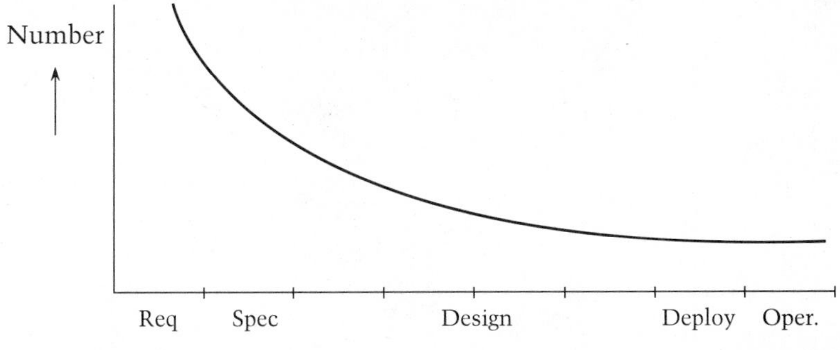

FIGURE 6.13 NUMBER OF SOFTWARE EXCEPTIONS

of time (as measured in phases) that elapses from the time the exception occurs to the time that it is found. Thus, if an exception is found in the same phase in which it occurs, the cost to fix it remains low. As the number of phases between occurrence and detection grows larger, the cost to fix the exception increases dramatically. In the worst case, when a requirements exception is not found until the system has reached operational status, the cost to fix an exception can be 1,000 times more than if it were detected and fixed during the requirements phase of the development. This curve is presented only for illustration purposes. The reader is referred to various studies which have attempted to quantify the increase in repair cost for specific classes of exceptions.

This cost graph must be tempered with the results obtained from other studies that tend to indicate that the number of exceptions found in the various development phases occurs as depicted in figure 6.13. This latter piece of information is necessary in order to determine a total cost for all of the exceptions discovered in all of the development phases. The shape of this "total exception cost" graph is dependent on the individual slopes of the cost per exception and exception number graphs. Possible results are presented in figure 6.14. Total cost is the area under the curve found by integrating the curve over all of the development phases. For convenience, continuous curves are shown, although the process is inherently discrete.

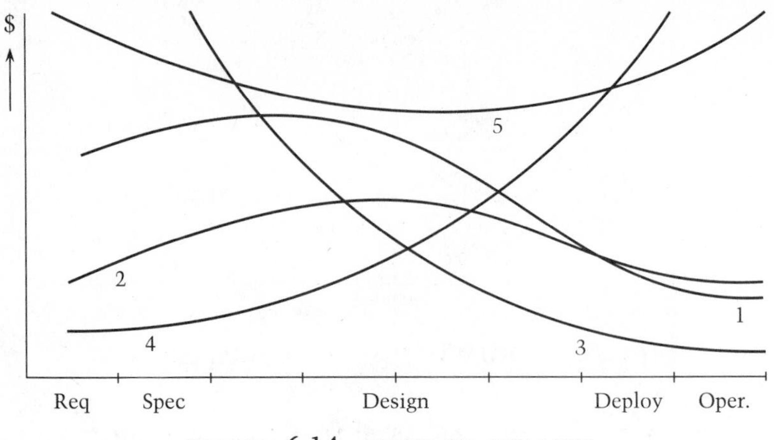

FIGURE 6.14 COST OF QUALITY

Two general types of cost curves are shown in figure 6.14 — those that exhibit a large slope at one or both ends of the development cycle and those that remain relatively flat. Curve 3 has a high slope in the early phases of the life cycle and reflects the philosophy of "eliminating all exceptions before delivery." The high initial amount shows the effect of a large number of exceptions found at a relatively high cost. Trying (unsuccessfully) to get that last 5 percent can be expensive. Curve 4 reflects the philosophy of "let the customer debug the system." (This definitely is not a quality-oriented philosophy.) A significant number of exceptions remain after operational status has been achieved, and they must be corrected at high cost (both tangible and intangible costs). Curve 5 reflects paranoia about the whole process and allocates enormous resources to the exception-elimination program at both ends of the life cycle.

Curves 1 and 2 show a more balanced approach to the quality assurance process. As many exceptions as possible are eliminated in early stages, consistent with a reasonable amount of resources assigned to the task. This will leave a small number of exceptions that are not found until deployment. Although the cost per exception will be high, the relatively small number of exceptions will keep the total costs consistent with those of the other phases.

There will always be specific cases in which each of the philosophies and approaches are appropriate, and the costs involved *must* be incurred. In order to maintain a viable business, however, an enterprise must remember that whatever the costs of the quality assurance process, they must be recovered — from the customer or from elsewhere. If this does not or cannot happen, the business is in danger of failing, no matter how good the final product may be. There are no easy answers in quality assurance and certainly no magic slogans or algorithms. Quality assurance must be engineered along with all other aspects that are concerned with the final product.

DEPLOYMENT INFRASTRUCTURE

The deployment environment was introduced in chapter 3 as a part of the development infrastructure. The deployment infrastructure consists of all of the shared facilities that are available for use by the deployed application system. These would include the following:

- Networks
- Network processors
- Network functions
- Network management

The existence of a significant amount of infrastructure will have a considerable impact on the economics of building a new system. This impact may have both positive and negative aspects.

If a large set of infrastructure facilities exists and can be used with or without modification for deployment of the new system, considerable savings can be obtained. This occurs for a number of reasons:

- The total amount of new development is reduced.
- In-place resources will be thoroughly tested.
- Economies of scale can be realized.
- Maintenance resources will be reduced.

Even if only part of the current infrastructure is suitable, that part can still provide significant benefits. When other facilities needed for the newly developed system are added, they can become part of the total infrastructure and can be made available for future use by other systems.

The initial design and implementation of a suitable infrastructure may be quite costly, however, because many facilities have to be developed and put in place before revenue producing systems can be made available. This requires a considerable investment based on the promise of future benefit. Many enterprises are not prepared for this commitment and are therefore unable to reap the future efficiencies and other benefits. This may put them at a competitive disadvantage relative to their competitors. Conversely, having a good deployment infrastructure may provide the edge necessary to obtain a large market share.

A poor infrastructure design or implementation may result in the need to modify products adversely in order to be able to make use of the infrastructure. The resultant systems may not meet the needs of the marketplace or may be more expensive than their competition.

Infrastructures have characteristics that are similar in nature to standard components:

- Conformity to the architecture must be maintained.
- Obsolete parts must be eliminated.
- New technology must continuously be infused.

In addition, the infrastructure has other unique characteristics:

- It behaves as if it has mass and inertia. It is not easily altered and considerable resources are needed to do so.

- It provides a barrier to entry for competitors, because they must provide a similar structure with all of the attendant costs or incur the penalty to provide the functions on a system-by-system basis.
- Capacity planning and performance monitoring must be continuous and thorough. Otherwise, the equivalent of "rush-hour" bottlenecks will occur, reducing the effectiveness of all systems that use the infrastructure.

As stated in the beginning of this section, all of these characteristics have a significant economic impact on the development. The key is to manage the infrastructure in such a manner that its potential considerable benefits outweigh its possible deficiencies.

There is always a question as to which functions are best implemented as infrastructure and which are best implemented as system-specific. As stated under similar circumstances in other discussions, this requires engineering judgment, which will eventually be supported or refuted through experience. Corrections can always be made. If a large adjustment is necessary, however, the cost can be high.

From an economic viewpoint, the worst mistake that can be made is to have an infrastructure in place and then not use it for system deployment. This occurs when the custom shop model is the nominal choice for development but is not being used effectively. This can easily result in existing facilities being ignored or underused throughout the entire development process, including the deployment aspects under consideration here.

SEVEN

BUSINESS DYNAMICS

INTRODUCTION AND PURPOSE

Throughout the latter part of this book there has been a gradual migration away from purely technical considerations toward the business aspects of the network design and implementation process. This chapter completes that migration by concentrating almost entirely on business-related issues. This type of knowledge is essential for a full understanding of the technology-dominated processes of the enterprise. The close interrelationships between technical and business functions demand that decisions consider both types of issues.

The purpose of this discussion is to complete the general understanding of the operation of the technology-oriented enterprise, specifically its development function. As such, the presentation will necessarily be limited to those areas that have a direct bearing in this regard. Other functions, such as general management, human resources, finance, and accounting, although vital to the survival of the enterprise, will not be covered. In addition, the chapter will provide only an overview of the business functions that are addressed. For further depth and/or breadth of coverage, see any of a number of publications in general business administration or any of the specialized topics therein. Remember, however, that business texts, with rare exceptions, do not discuss the interrelationships with technical functions and issues. Refer to the principles discussed in this chapter for best understanding.

The discussion in this chapter differs in many respects from that contained in classical approaches to business organization and function. This was done for two reasons:

- To emphasize the close interaction needed between the technical and business aspects of an enterprise in order to provide a successful business unit.
- To show that alternative structures can be utilized to accomplish this interaction and to create an efficient and effective "high-tech" enterprise.

Global markets and competition require that businesses restructure themselves to utilize more fully the vast amount of information available and to reduce the internal friction that produces inefficiencies in the development process. This discussion is dedicated toward facilitating that change process.

It can be argued that the subject of business dynamics is a technology unto itself. Certainly the subject can be contorted to fit the definition of technology presented in chapter 5, if psychology and sociology are used as the scientific underpinnings. However, for clarity, this discussion assumes that the business functions are not included in the definition of technology.

To accomplish its intended purpose effectively, the chapter is structured as follows: a partial model of a technology-oriented business enterprise is developed; this model integrates the technology functions discussed previously with some closely associated business functions. Those areas of business activity identified previously as unnecessary for the current presentation are not included in the model for the sake of clarity and brevity.

The model is used to provide a conceptual framework that is used to develop a number of concepts that are needed to place the technical discussions in context and to explain the approaches used. In previous chapters, many business-oriented inputs were used in defining technical activities, without the origin of these inputs being specified. Likewise, it was not previously possible to define the utilization of many outputs from technical functions, because their major purpose is business-related and not technically driven. This deficiency can now be corrected.

In addition to defining and describing this business model, three important observations will be discussed:

- A business requires many nontechnical activities to survive and thrive even in the most technology-dependent enterprise.
- The nontechnical and technical activities of an enterprise must be made symbiotic to assure a harmonious flow of information.
- All employees must understand the objectives and dynamics of an on-going business enterprise if they are to make the proper business decisions, whether or not their function is technology-based.

Unfortunately, technologists tend to ignore or misunderstand the business aspects of an enterprise, and business people tend to ignore or misunderstand the technology aspects. This has resulted in many inefficient and bankrupt businesses. This chapter is designed to address that problem at least partially.

You may need to read this chapter at least twice to understand the concepts presented. Because the model represents a closed cycle, it will take at least one trip around the concepts for all of the many interrelationships and interactions to manifest themselves. Many of the definitions and descriptions do not make sense on a stand-alone basis and require global knowledge of the complete process for correct interpretation.

BUSINESS DYNAMICS MODEL

Because business operation is a relatively convoluted and abstract concept, a model of it must meet a number of requirements:

- It must reflect business dynamics as well as static relationships.
- It must allow all necessary functions, interactions, and behaviors to be defined and examined without undue complexity.
- It must allow insight into the process as well as the derivation of specific results.
- It must be close enough to reality so that derived results can be utilized effectively.
- It must provide for a discussion of the overall business cycle as it applies to technology.

One such model is shown in figure 7.1. This model combines six functions, which are listed below in order of their approximate business/technology content ratio. Although not strictly a function *per se*, products and services are included in the model because they are the ultimate reason for the existence of the business.

• Business planning	Business-oriented
• Strategic planning	Business-oriented
• Marketing	Business-oriented
• Products & services	Result
• Technology management	Technology-oriented
• Development process	Technology-oriented

As would be expected, there are many interactions between the functional areas of the model. The major ones are marked on the figure with a letter indicator to facilitate fur-

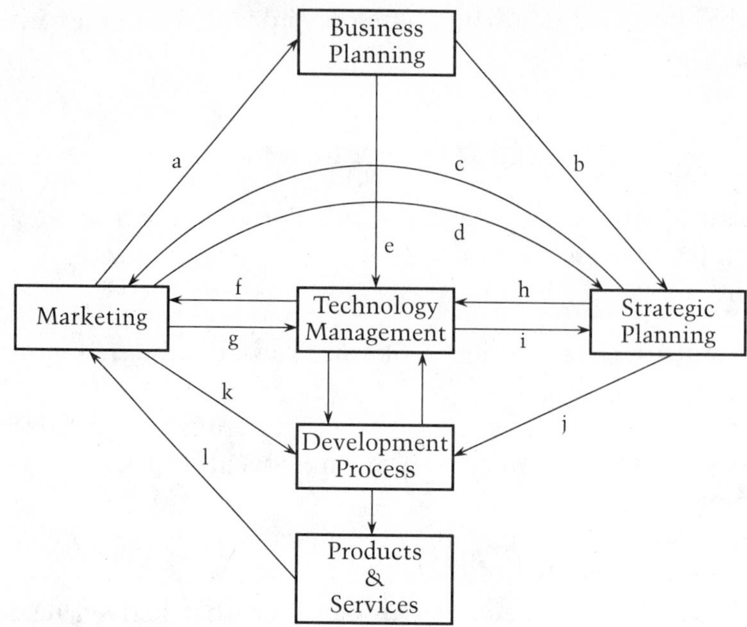

FIGURE 7.1 BUSINESS DYNAMICS MODEL

ther discussion. Those interfaces that have been discussed previously are shown but not identified specifically.

BUSINESS FUNCTION DEFINITIONS

The definitions of the business functions are presented in table 7.1 in outline form. These functions determine the overall directions of the business and define what capabilities (technical and others) are needed to enable the enterprise to reach its goals. Not only are these functions necessary in a viable business, the results of the processes must be disseminated throughout the organization so that all activities and decisions can be accomplished in a manner that will further the aims of the enterprise.

In order to accomplish this intrinsic utilization of business information in technical and nontechnical decision-making at all levels, the corporate culture must be such that this type

TABLE 7.1 BUSINESS FUNCTION DEFINITIONS

Function	*Purpose*
Business Planning	
Vision	Defines the organization dream
Mission	Defines the target business (as needed to reach the dream)
Strategies	Defines how the business will fulfill the mission
Operations model	Defines how the business will operate to accomplish the strategies
Strategic Planning	
Directions	Ways in which the strategies can be achieved
Goals	Quantified, measurable results (to enable the organization to follow the set directions)
Activities	Specific methods of achieving the goals
Marketing	
Research	Determine the characteristics of relevant markets, including needs, wants, size, and price elasticity
Product/service definition	Determine what products will meet the needs of the market
Customer relations	Service the continuing needs of current and prospective customers

of behavior is encouraged and rewarded. Although a discussion of corporate culture is beyond the scope of this book, it should be mentioned that without senior management attention to this aspect of corporate life, all of the policies, pronouncements, and meetings seeking to infuse the business goals into everyday business activities will have little or no effect.

To help present some of these rather abstract concepts and definitions, a specific example is used throughout the chapter. Where the characteristics of this example overlap with those of the example used in chapter 5, they will be made the same. Both examples assume a business that provides a wide range of network services to several clients. You are invited (and encouraged) to develop an example of your own choosing if it is more meaningful in your situation than the one outlined here.

Business Planning

The business planning function is a fundamental responsibility of senior management and is designed to establish the overall context under which the enterprise operates. The objective of this function is to determine at a high level what the business is, what it will become, and how best to accomplish the transition. Unless it is a monopoly or can exert monopoly powers — a rare condition — a business must operate in an environment over which it does not exert control. The planning process must be continuous to keep the enterprise adjusted to its environment and, in doing so, to achieve a form of harmony or at least coexistence. Details as to how to implement these high-level plans are left to the strategic planning process, which is discussed in the next section.

As an example of the business planning functions, assume an enterprise has just gone through the planning process and has a set of results from each of the steps that can then be used to guide the business. These results are presented in table 7.2. Notice that the outputs at this level are usually rather short. They need to contain only enough information to state the intent. Because no implementation detail is present, the wording can be brief. Another observation is that at this level any unnecessary restrictions should not be made. A dream is by nature large and all-encompassing. Enough restrictions occur naturally in the implementation process when reality must be considered.

Notice that even though this is a technology-based com-

TABLE 7.2 NETWORK SERVICES BUSINESS BUSINESS PLANNING RESULTS

Step	*Result*
Vision	Be the supplier of network systems and services that is the best known and most respected by the general public and industry.
Mission	Define, implement, and promote innovative network systems and services that provide an excellent benefit to the customer and a satisfactory profit to the company.
Operations model	The operations activities of the company will be governed by the chart in figure 7.2 (shown later in this chapter).
Strategies*	Market broad spectrum of system and service offerings
	Dominate market in selected areas
	Optimize internal productivity
	Be recognized as experts in network design
	Utilize state-of-the-art technology
	Provide single-stop service to customers

*The strategies shown here are the same as those presented in the discussion on technology management in chapter 5.

pany dealing in "high-tech" products, there is no mention of technology as a result of the business planning function, with only one relatively minor exception. This should not be surprising, because the technology is only an enabler. Customers want solutions. In general they do not care what means (read technology) are used to provide those solutions. This is true whether the technology pushes the business or the business pulls the technology.

Forming a vision and eventually defining activities that will implement that vision is similar to developing a system development methodology; each may be represented by a pyramid structure, as discussed in chapter 3.

The Vision The vision is stated informally, with no attempt to quantify words such as *best known, most respected,* and *network*. Is senior management really considering services for a water distribution network? Probably not, but again do not limit it at this time unless there is a good reason. Most people reading this vision probably would understand the writer's dream for the company — which is the only real objective of the statement.

Some organizations try to skip this part of the planning effort as "not practical" or unprofessional. Unfortunately, without the corporate vision as a guide, it is difficult to determine the proper direction to travel. This can lead to fragmentation of effort, and the usual result in any given activity is "too little, too late."

The Mission The vision or dream must now be interpreted and stated in terms that are meaningful and implementable by the enterprise. This is the function of the mission statement. The mission is not a restatement of the vision as such, although the mission and vision are sometimes incorrectly considered to be synonymous. A more accurate description of the relationship would be that the mission is a projection of the vision on the space of current and future business capabilities. As such, the addition of detail to the vision is a form of augmentation. Again, notice the lack of quantification in the mission statement for the example company. Even though some detail has been added, it still defines what is to be done — not the specifics of how to do it. This will not be addressed until later in the process.

The mission must be stated so that it is implementable. This means that it is in a form that can be used to verify the usability of the operations model and strategies in implementing the mission. If the mission is not stated in a way that can be implemented, it cannot be used in running the business and becomes meaningless words. Enough of such meaningless statements occur spontaneously in any business; more are certainly not needed.

The Operations Model The operations model, as it will be discussed in this section, is a "logical" model. It describes how the business needs to operate from an organizational point of view. The physical organization may or may not agree with this logical model. The only requirement is that the physical organization be able to act as if it were implementing the logical model. The concept of a "matrix organization" is an example of a logical organization that is product-based and a physical organization which is function-based. Without debating the advantages or disadvantages of such a structure, it should be noted that this type of logical/physical organization is used successfully in a number of enterprises.

The concept behind specifying separate logical and physical organizations is that logical organizations can be defined that are unambiguous, well behaved, and specifically suited to the needs of the organization without worrying about physical organizations, which are subject to corporate politics, individual quirks, less-than-perfect interpersonal relationships, and other messy realities of human behavior. By separating the two, the enterprise can define its operational needs clearly and yet allow for the vagaries of individual characteristics. It would be more effective and efficient if the logical and physical organizations were the same, but as a practical matter that may not be possible.

The operations model can be defined in a number of formats:

- Relationship chart
- Process flow chart
- Formal description

Whatever the format utilized, the purpose is to describe how the business will operate as an organization in order to accomplish the mission and support the strategies. For simplicity, it will be assumed that the example company uses the relationship chart format, as shown in figure 7.2. This chart is similar in format to a standard organization chart. However, its purpose is quite different. It defines the way the

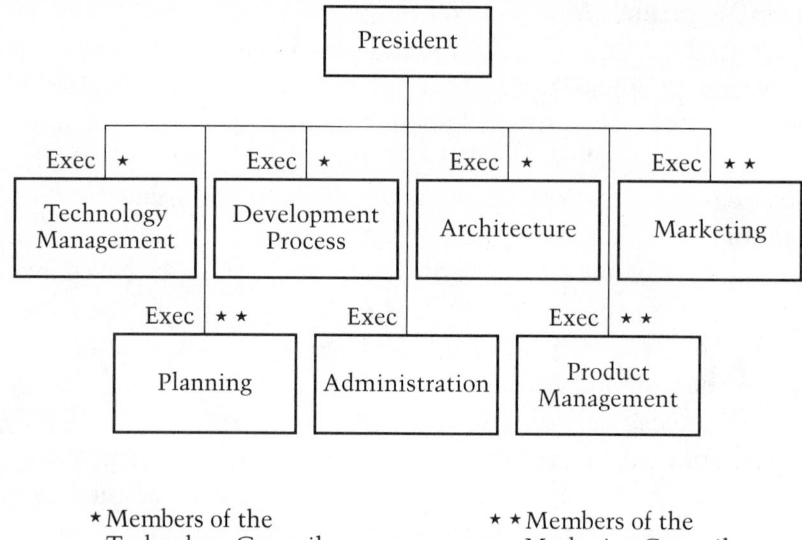

FIGURE 7.2 NETWORK SERVICES BUSINESS RELATIONSHIP CHART

business feels it has to operate and does not necessarily show the personnel reporting structure, although it may also do that if the logical and physical organizations are the same. If the two are different, a standard organization chart that shows the physical organization would be necessary.

Notice that the operations model for the example business gives technology management, development process, and architecture exposure at the highest levels. Furthermore, the responsible executives (no functional title is given or necessary for this definition) are all members of the technology council, in which fundamental decisions concerning technology in the enterprise are made. A similar structure governs the marketing responsibilities of the enterprise. General management executives are ex-officio members of both councils and act as the coordinators. This association will give general management personnel direct knowledge of these important aspects of business operation.

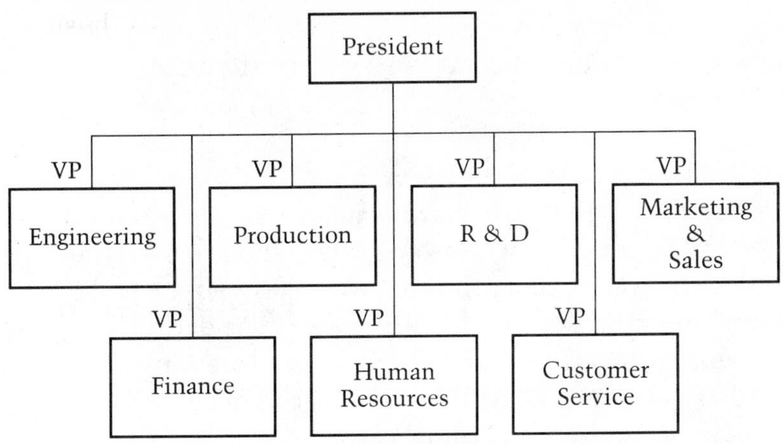

FIGURE 7.3 CLASSIC BUSINESS ORGANIZATION CHART

Because this chart is designed to show the importance given to different aspects of the business, it differs considerably from charts showing the classic physical organization of a technology-based company (see figure 7.3). This type of chart does not provide any indication as to how the business intends to operate or what the important business activities are. Many studies have shown that the real organization of an enterprise differs considerably from that published in the organization chart. The enterprise organization should not be allowed to fall into an arbitrary *de facto* logical structure. It must be defined and managed explicitly to insure that the enterprise is operating in the most efficient manner possible.

To fully define the operations model, additional levels of organization would have to be defined and added to the relationship chart. Definitions of each function and their major areas of interaction would also have to be provided. Space does not allow the inclusion of all of this detail, although as part of the marketing discussion later in the chapter, some additional definition of this function will be provided.

In general, the operations model is designed independently of the mission, although the basic characteristics of the enterprise are certainly considered. The relationship between the mission and the operations model thus becomes one of assignment.

The Strategies The strategies indicate how the business, operating through the operations model, is going to fulfill the mission. Because both the operations model and strategies are designed to support the mission, they must also be consistent and symbiotic with one another. The definition of the two must proceed in parallel and spring from an interactive specification process. An example of the necessary relationship between the operations model and strategies will be discussed in the definition of the marketing function for the example company later in the chapter.

The addition of detail to the mission statement is generally considered to be a decomposition process. Each statement in the mission is usually associated with multiple strategies designed to implement that statement. These implementing strategies do not overlap and are each designed to address a specific need of the mission statement. If multiple mission statements utilize the same strategy, it usually results from independently deriving the same strategy. Of course, a particular strategy needs to be stated only once.

Restrictions of a sort have been slowly entering the process even before the strategies are defined, because of the need for better definition at each level. However, the strategy definition is the first function in which restrictions become significant. Every enterprise has limited resources and cannot accomplish all of the activities that it sees as necessary to achieve its destiny. It must assign priorities and identify those areas which are perceived as having the highest payoff. Obtaining focus is the broad function of the strategies. In the case of the example organization, six areas are perceived as having the highest payoff. Others may also be important but they will have to wait for more resources or for the priorities to change.

This is an opportune time to observe that the strategies are one of the major inputs to the technology planning function that was discussed in chapter 5. For the sake of continuity, the strategies used for examples in that chapter and this are the same. The discussion in chapter 5 also showed that technology planning is a major input into the whole development process. As was inferred during that discussion but not demonstrated until now, all of the business and technical functions are highly interrelated. The many aspects of the enterprise must be developed together in order to avoid unnecessary incongruities during the conduct of the business.

Strategic Planning

Once the high-level business planning has been accomplished, the output from this process must be used to establish specific activities that can further the business vision and mission. This is a three-step process that is usually called the strategic planning function, because it consists of a decomposition of the business strategies. Strategic planning is usually a function of middle management in association with their staffs. Everyone in the corporation should have an opportunity to contribute to the planning process. Good ideas can come from any place. In addition, widespread involvement can help achieve the "buy-in" that is needed to make the process work.

Establishment of directions is the first step in the strategic planning process. Directions are used to determine the best way to proceed in accomplishing the strategies. Directions can be established through the use of formal "programs" that specify the way in which the strategy will be accomplished. The programs will contain goals and activities, which are defined as follows. *Goals* are milestones along the directions and are used not only to determine if the directions are being followed but also to indicate the progress that is being made. Because goals are milestones, it must be possible to measure

TABLE 7.3 NETWORK SERVICES BUSINESS STRATEGIC PLANNING DIRECTIONS

Strategy	Dominate market in selected areas
Directions	1. Define and develop a program to achieve market dominance in appropriate areas. 2. Define and develop a program to determine the financial justification for specific market dominance. 3. Define and develop a program that will measure the results of market dominance. 4. Define and develop a program to maintain market dominance when achieved.

when or how closely they have been achieved. This requires that the goals be stated in quantitative terms. Finally, activities are defined with the specific purpose of meeting the goals. Activities may be small or large, but their output is directly tied to one or more goals. Because activities are work projects, they must be assigned to one or more of the enterprise organizations for execution.

A number of new terms have been defined in the preceding discussion. To clarify their meaning and utility, additional details from the example company used throughout this chapter are presented here.

Partial data from each of the strategic planning steps for the example company is shown in tables 7.3 to 7.5. Full results are not presented, because the volume of information would be large if this process were performed in the detail necessary. A considerable amount of detail is required if the results are to be used to guide the company in the required directions. Notice that the goals are measurable and directly coupled to the defining strategy. The activities are also directly coupled to the goals and contain an overall implementation schedule. As mentioned previously, these results come from a classic decomposition process.

TABLE 7.4 NETWORK SERVICES BUSINESS STRATEGIC PLANNING GOALS

Strategy	Dominate market in selected areas
Direction	Define and develop a program to achieve market dominance in appropriate areas.
Goals	1. Identify candidate markets within six months.
	2. Select two target markets within eight months.
	3. Project activities to achieve market dominance available within two months after target markets are selected.
	4. Market dominance in target markets achieved one year after start of project.

As stated, activities are a form of internal project and must be managed with the same degree of attention and concern that a project for an external customer merits. For this reason, some organizations do not differentiate between internal and external projects. Others do because of the subtle differences in many of their characteristics. Either way is acceptable as long as the proper level of control is maintained.

Marketing

The marketing function can be defined and implemented in a wide variety of ways. The success of a particular organization depends on whether or not the necessary functions receive sufficient attention, either in marketing or elsewhere. As a basis for this discussion, the example company organization will be used. For this company, it will be assumed that marketing has three basic functions:

- Market research
- Product/service definition
- Customer relations

TABLE 7.5 NETWORK SERVICES BUSINESS STRATEGIC PLANNING ACTIVITIES

Strategy	Dominate market in selected areas
Direction	Define and develop a program to achieve market dominance in appropriate areas.
Goal	Identify candidate markets within six months.
Activities	1. Define market attributes relating to market share and dominance. (1/1/91 – 2/15/91)
	2. Identify an initial list of markets to be analyzed. (1/1/91 – 2/1/91)
	3. Identify market leaders and their apparent strategies for maintaining their position. (2/1/91 – 3/15/91)
	4. Develop characteristics for all markets on list, using defined attribute set. (3/15/91 – 4/10/91)
	5. Define a metric based on the market characteristics that will measure the desirability of achieving market dominance in that market on a relative scale. (2/15/91 – 3/25/91)
	6. Rank order markets in terms of desirability using previously defined metric and select the first ten as candidates. (4/15/91 – 5/15/91)
	7. Prepare a report for senior management that contains the results of the investigations and provides the requested set of recommendations. (5/15/91 – 6/20/91)

Those familiar with the definition of many marketing organizations will notice some amount of difference in the above assumptions from that of the classical marketing organization. The main difference is that product/service definitions (requirements definition) are made a part of the marketing function instead of the technically oriented system implementation function. Other differences will be discussed shortly. This type of specification is a continuation of the operations model definition that was initiated earlier in the chapter.

Market research has two basic functions — one is market-oriented and the other is product-oriented. The first function determines what markets would be suitable for the enterprise to compete in, the level of that competition, and the determination as to how well the process is proceeding. The other function determines what products/service classes would be suitable for those selected markets. This is a continuous process and, as discussed in chapter 5, the definition of these classes forms one of the primary inputs into the technology planning function.

The definition of the actual products and services developed by the company is also a part of marketing. A large part of this function is determining system requirements and obtaining the approval of the customers. This is one of the most important steps in the system development process. It is assigned to marketing to reinforce the concept that requirements determination is primarily a business function, not a technical function. The technical organizations certainly must be involved to estimate the amount of resources needed for the development, consult on any technical issues brought up by the requirements, and build a feasibility prototype as necessary. However, the final responsibility for the correctness of the requirements rests with marketing. Marketing must stay involved throughout the entire product development process, because the customer must be involved during each step of development. This involvement can be accomplished most effectively by continuing the same type of interaction as that utilized in the requirements definition phase.

Another difference in the example marketing operations model from that usually associated with technically based enterprises is that the sales function is made a part of the customer relations function. The customer relations function includes all contact with the customer, before, during, and after any product sales. Even the product/service requirements definition function utilizes the customer relations function as the direct customer interface. In fact, the following activities are also considered to be part of the customer relations function:

- Sales
- Training
- Customer service
- Consulting

This range of activities is designed to increase continuity and forestall any problems or product exceptions that may occur because of misunderstandings or other communication difficulties. The philosophy behind this particular operations model is that the customer relations function is responsible for any and all contact between the customer and the enterprise. The functions contained in the marketing organization must, of course, be tightly coupled in order to perform the required activities in an effective manner. Likewise, marketing must be tightly coupled to the other functions of the enterprise.

The definition of the marketing function is an excellent example of the way in which the model implements the portion of the mission which states ". . . promote innovative network services that provide an excellent benefit to the customer. . . ." It also supports the strategy, "Provide single-stop service to customers." The interrelationships between organizations and functions are again apparent.

INFORMATION FLOW

The definitions of each of the information paths shown in figure 7.1 are listed in table 7.6. The major information items have already been discussed in the previous sections, and it is not necessary to elaborate during the remainder of this

TABLE 7.6 INTERORGANIZATION INFORMATION TRANSFER

Path	*Contents*
a	Market characteristics Potential opportunities Problem areas
b	Vision Mission statement Operations model Strategy definitions
c	Market characteristics Potential opportunities Customer requirements Competition activities
d	Direction statements Goal definitions Activity plans
e	Business operations model
f	Technical assessments Education and training programs Project estimation analysis
g	Product/service class definitions Competition activities
h	Direction statements Goal definitions Activity plans
i	Technical assessments Education and training programs
j	Development model and process Characterization
k	Product/service requirements
l	Deployment results Operational results Needed changes

discussion. The main thrust of this section is the considerable amount of nontechnical information that is being transferred between organizations and the high degree of interaction that is necessary for the business to function.

The flow of information does not happen automatically; it must be planned for and made an integral part of the organizational definition. Although most of this data does not constitute even a partial technology transfer as defined in chapter 6, many of the same characteristics are required. There must be a willingness on the part of the receiving organization to accept and utilize the information presented, and there must be experienced personnel in both the receiving and transferring organizations.

Although the information flow is shown diagrammatically to be in one direction, because it is meant to indicate the final disposition of the flow, the actual transfer is an iterative process, and a great deal of interaction is necessary for a successful conclusion. Ensuring that the information flow takes place in an efficient and effective manner and that all involved have a common understanding of the information is the responsibility of all management personnel but must be made the specific direct responsibility of senior management.

BUSINESS CYCLE

Now that all of the functions, interfaces, and interactions of the model have been defined and discussed, it is possible to step through a complete cycle of the process. At a high level, this will provide a feeling for the overall dynamics of the organization. Because the process is continuous, any function can be used as a starting point. For convenience, the discussion will start with the business planning function. The time to complete one cycle of the model for most businesses is one year, and this period is generally called the *planning period* or *cycle.* However, individual functions may be performed many times within this period depending on the use-

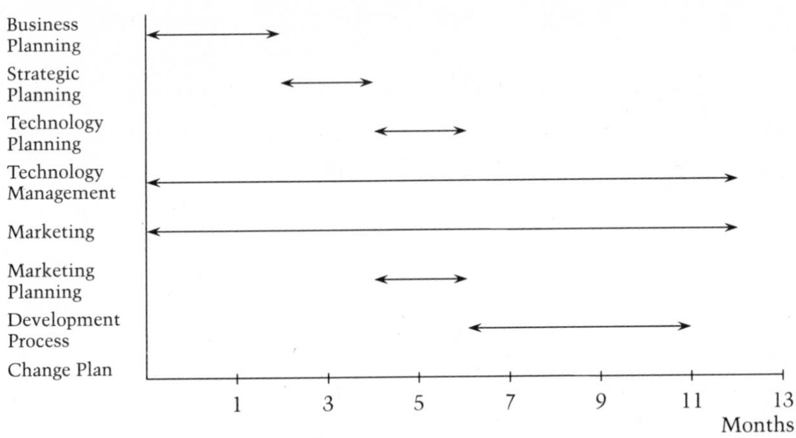

FIGURE 7.4 BUSINESS FUNCTION TIMING EXAMPLE

ful life of the information obtained. Because the following discussion cannot adequately present the complex timing relationships inherent in the planning cycle, figure 7.4 is provided as an aid in determining the relative schedule of each activity. This data is meant to be utilized as an example only. Individual enterprises will define processes that are tuned to their own needs and organizations. It is necessary only that all of the functions be performed; the exact sequences are somewhat arbitrary.

Business planning produces the vision, mission statement, operations model, and strategies. The first three change slowly, and the objective of the periodic review is to "fine-tune" these items. Only rarely do wide-scale changes need to be made. The strategies, however, are subject to considerable change depending on the needs of the enterprise during the coming planning period. Usually, strategies are defined with one-, two-, or three-year lifetimes so that there is some amount of continuity in this process. After approval, the strategies for the coming period are then sent to the strategic planning function for further decomposition. In addition, as discussed earlier, they are disseminated throughout the enterprise.

As part of the initial strategic planning function, the direction statements from the previous year are updated to reflect the new set of strategies. Changes in direction are always painful, and care should be taken to make the minimum changes necessary while still supporting the strategies. This is especially necessary for the direction that determines the structure and content of the development process. Usually, only minor changes are required in this area, because the development process tends to remain relatively stable. If this were not the case, the instability of the development process would adversely affect the economic and technical viability of the systems produced.

Once the directions have been defined and set forth in appropriate detail, the goals and activities that implement them are defined. These are then sent to the appropriate functional areas for assignment, addition of detail if required, and, finally, implementation.

During the previous planning period, technology management has been conducting assessments and tracking a number of current and emerging technologies. This information is made available to strategic planning, marketing, and development for use when required in their respective planning functions. Strategic planning, for example, will make extensive use of the current technological environment in determining the directions, goals, and activities. In turn, technology management takes the outputs of strategic planning and marketing in order to develop the technology plan. This plan is usually formulated after the strategic planning process so that any technology support can be defined and started. Because of the long lead time in many of the technology management activities, there may be considerable time between the start of an activity and the availability of results.

The development process examines the relevant requirements of strategic planning, as well as the available technology environment from technology management, and updates its procedures as necessary. Because of the difficulty in changing the development process, the actual updating is usually performed only once a year. Multiple-year phase-in plans are not uncommon for significant alterations. Planning for any change usually takes considerable resources and time, and for this reason, some type of change planning may be in progress throughout the plan year.

System requirements information may be sent from marketing to the development process whenever necessary during the development of new systems. This type of information is not related to the planning cycle and may occur at any time during the year depending on sales and customer needs. It must, however, be considered as an integral part of the business dynamics.

Marketing continuously performs its function as the interface to the customer. Although most of the information obtained from this interaction is used only periodically (except for the development process, as explained above), it nevertheless is vital in keeping the business current and responsive to changes in its customer environment. Marketing-developed competitive data and product/service class information is used by technology management in developing the technology plan. Strategies must be defined to follow the market and customer base. Business planning needs to know if fundamental shifts are taking place or when lucrative new opportunities occur. Ad hoc queries are made to marketing continuously during the planning year by senior and middle management seeking various types of information necessary to perform their jobs on a day-to-day basis.

In the face of significant unforeseen occurrences, the timing of one or more of these functions may have to change. Although there is usually great reluctance to make such changes, because they cause considerable disruption in the usual orderly flow of corporate events, it is desirable to have the flexibility to allow this alteration. One of the great criticisms of any business (especially large business) is that its policies and procedures become cast in concrete, and it cannot take advantage of significant opportunities because of the inability to dynamically change its planning functions or program activities as necessary.

EXPANSIONS ON THE THEME

You should now have a good grasp of the major functions and activities of both the business and technical areas of "high-tech" enterprises, in addition to an appreciation of the close interaction of these areas and the need to coordinate fully between them. Unfortunately, it was possible to provide only an overview of most of the concepts presented in this book. Effective utilization in most cases requires that more details be added and additional study be undertaken. In some cases, this further definition may be obtained from the open literature, especially in those areas which are concerned with well-known concepts (for example, individual technology characteristics). Other concepts are new to this book, and further research and development must be performed to harden them into commercially viable solutions (for example, the development process model).

Two of the most important concepts covered, the systems architecture and the implementation methodology, are treated in greater detail in two companion books: *Network System Architecture* and *Information Networks: A Design and Implementation Methodology.* The treatment in these books is highly recommended for anyone needing a more comprehensive treatment of these subjects.

EIGHT

EPILOGUE

LOOKING BACK

At the end of any project, successful or unsuccessful, it is always wise to examine the significant events encountered in the context of the entire effort. Typically, this examination is called a *postmortem*. I object to this term because this so-called examination of the dead may be done on a very live patient. A better word is *retrospective,* which implies a considered, thoughtful analysis of the project. This chapter is such a retrospective, albeit brief, of the project that created the book, the result it produced, and my perception of the use to which it will be put.

FAILINGS AND FUTURES

The complex process of explaining the premise of the book — that modern network systems and associated services require the integration of a large number of technologies and business considerations in order to be successful — almost certainly resulted in many loose ends and unanswered questions. This problem is a direct result of the necessity to limit the scope of the discussion in order to keep the book to a reasonable size. Any modern book on the design of complex systems shares this problem. In this respect, the book is not able to deliver everything readers might desire. However, it does provide the opportunity for other publications to enlarge on selected areas. The two current companion volumes, *Network System Architecture* and *Information Networks: A Design and Implementation Methodology*, are a step in this direction. It is my intention to provide other expanded discussions as necessity and circumstances permit. The information in this book will give you sufficient information and background to enable you to read and understand the relevant literature as it is published.

INFORMATION BOOKS VERSUS COOKBOOKS

There are few hard and fast answers in the area of network system design that can be looked up in a reference manual or derived through a formula. The success or failure of any product or service has always rested on the business considerations and the vagaries of the marketplace, as well as the technical factors inherent in its design. This is even more true today in an era of increased competition and technological change. The material in the book has attempted to point out the synergy and interaction between business and technology that are required in the current and future network environment in which enterprises must operate and make available products and services.

This book is obviously an information book. It is intended to provide a level of understanding and knowledge sufficient to begin the network and network product and service design process. The missing ingredient is, of course, actual experience. This can be obtained only by participating in the design process. Otherwise, the information presented in this and other publications cannot be put in its proper context. This will be illustrated through a short scenario — a story that has been told many times but that is appropriate here to close out the issues and discussions presented in the book.

A SHORT, SAD STORY

Engineer Jones, working in the research and development department of a small company, invented an amazing new product called the Percom, which was going to revolutionize the communications industry. The product was technically elegant and met a perceived need in the market. At the heart of the Percom design was a hole required to be located to a precision of .00001 inch both to its location and its size. The hole was not quite a circle and had to be machined according to a complex calculation. The cost of machining this hole accounted for approximately two-thirds of the entire cost of the product.

Initial market trials went well, and the unit was placed into production and quickly became the main product for the company. The president of the company was an engineering graduate from a large prestigious engineering school. He delighted in telling all who would listen of the great technical breakthrough that had been achieved by the product and the importance of the machining of the hole that gave it its necessary characteristics.

In performing further R&D work on Percom, it was discovered that in conjunction with other changes, a round hole machined to within one-tenth of an inch as to its center and radius would also work, but would reduce the effectiveness of the product by approximately 40 percent. Because of the increased simplicity of manufacturing, the cost of the product was also reduced by a factor of two-thirds. However, enamored by the technological elegance of the initial product, the president and engineering staff overruled the marketing department when it sought to market the degraded but much cheaper product.

Further R&D work revealed that with additional changes two holes could be utilized instead of one. This would reduce the cost by one-third instead of the two-thirds that could have been achieved with the single round hole. Further, the change would decrease the effectiveness by only 15 percent. After many discussions between engineering and marketing, a product based on this new discovery was also overruled by the president for the same reasons as were used to overrule the product with a single round hole.

Because of the high cost of the Percom product, the potential market was saturated in approximately six months after its introduction, and gross sales of the small company began to decline rapidly. At this point, the president was replaced by the vice president of marketing through the action of the investors. The new president, reacting to the high cost of the present product, immediately decreed that a new version of Percom would be based on the initial discovery that a single round hole would work even though it would degrade the usefulness of the product by 40 percent.

The new product was brought out quickly and hit the marketplace. In spite of the greatly reduced cost, however, sales were few. This occurred because the efficiency of the product did not meet the needs of most of the potential users. When asked to bring out an additional product based on the second discovery of the two round holes, the president declined, citing cost containment as the principal reason. Within six months the company was bankrupt.

Of course, the story is constructed to make it obvious what would happen to the Percom Company. The engineering people wanted a product with technical elegance and were unwilling to compromise. The marketing people did not care about the engineering but only wanted the cheapest product possible to go into the marketplace. In the end, neither of these strategies worked. The product that would have assured the success of the company was the one using the two-hole design, which unfortunately met the requirements of neither group.

That is the lesson to be learned from the information presented in this book. Any new product, especially those associated with networks, must be designed and deployed using a combination of factors. If any of these are left out, a high potential exists for disaster.

A FOND HOPE

I look forward to the many innovative systems and services, utilizing the coming intelligent network environment and based on sound technical and business considerations, that will enhance and enrich the lives of us all.

BIBLIOGRAPHY

The references selected for inclusion in this section serve one of three purposes: they relate directly to specific material discussed in the book, they provide background information or additional detail for those areas, or they cover subjects that are mentioned but not presented in detail. The references have been selected to favor the most recently published information that will adequately cover the subject. When there has been no suitable replacement, the original or classic publication in a subject area has also been included. Because a great deal of material in the book is new, no previous publications are directly applicable. In this instance, references have been selected that provide a suitable background in the general subject area.

Because of the breadth of the material covered in the book, the references have been arranged by chapter to facilitate their use. When a given reference could be placed in more than one chapter, it has been assigned to the chapter that seems most appropriate. This process seems preferable to duplicating references. Because of the number, a comprehensive bibliography in all the subject areas is not feasible. However, it is anticipated that the references provided will give you a good start in finding additional information about the subject of interest.

CHAPTER ONE

Allen, Robert E. "The Effects of Regulatory Policy on the International Telecommunications Market." *IEEE Communications Magazine.* Vol. 27, no. 1 (Jan. 1989): 26–28.

American National Standards Institute (ANSI) Standards. American National Standards Institute, Inc., 1430 Broadway, New York, NY 10018.

Comité Consultatif International Telephonique et Telegraphique (CCITT) Recommendations. United States Department of Commerce, National Technical Information Service, 5285 Port Royal Road, Springfield, VA 22161.

Electronic Industries Association (EIA) Recommendations. EIA Engineering Department, Standards Sales, 2001 Eye Street NW, Washington, DC 20006.

European Computer Manufacturers Association (ECMA) Standards. European Computer Manufacturers Association, 114 Rue du Rhone, 1204 Geneva, Switzerland.

Federal Standards. General Services Administration, Specification Distribution Branch, Building 197, Washington Navy Yard, Washington, DC 20407.

Foits, Harold C., editor. *Data Communications Standards.* New York: McGraw-Hill, 1986.

Hollander, Adrian W., "Translating Computerese." *Illinois CPA Society News Journal.* (July 1989): 25.

International Standards Organization (ISO) Standards. Available from the American National Standards Institute (see above).

Klasson, Kerstin. *Developments in the Terminology of Physics and Technology.* Stockholm: Almqvist & Wiksell International, 1977.

McDonald, John C.. "The Regulatory Challenge of Broadband Technologies." *IEEE Communications Magazine.* Vol. 27, no. 1 (Jan. 1989): 71–74.

Omnicon Index of Standards. New York: McGraw Hill, 1989.

Prigge, R. D., M. F. Hill, and J. L. Walkowicz. *The World of EDP Standards.* Blue Bell, PA: Sperry Univac, 1978.

Reingold, Howard and Howard Levine. *Talking Tech: A Conversational Guide to Science and Technology.* 1st ed. New York: Morrow, 1982.

Weidenbaum, Murray L. *The Future of Business Regulation.* New York: AMACOM, 1979.

CHAPTER TWO

Appleton, Daniel S. *Business Rules: The Missing Link.* Datamation, October 15, 1984.

Barton, Michael H., Erik L. Dagless, and Gerard L. Reijns. *Proceedings of the IFIP WG 10.3 Working Conference on Distributed Processing.* Amsterdam, The Netherlands, October 5–7, 1987. New York: North-Holland, 1988.

Bolc, Leonard (ed.). *Computational Models of Learning*. Berlin and New York: Springer-Verlag, 1987.

Chorafas, Dimitris N. *Data Communications for Distributed Information Systems*. New York: Petrocelli Books, 1980.

Chorafas, Dimitris N. *Fourth and Fifth Generation Programming Languages*. New York: McGraw-Hill, 1986.

Cieslak, Randy, Ayman Fawaz, Sonia Sachs, Pravin Varaiya, Jean Walrand, and Albert Li. "The Programmable Network Prototyping System." *Computer*. Vol. 22, no. 5 (May 1989): 67–76.

Federal Software Management Support Center, *Fourth Generation Languages: Issues and Impacts*. Falls Church, VA: Office of Software Development and Information Technology, 1986.

Figenbaum, Edward A. and Pamela McCorduck. *The Fifth Generation: Artificial Intelligence and Japan's Computer Challenge to the World*. Reading, MA: Addison-Wesley, 1983.

Fisher, Gary E. *A Functional Model for Fourth Generation Languages*. National Bureau of Standards, 1986.

Head, Charles S. "Intelligent Network, A Distributed System." *IEEE Communications Magazine*. Vol. 26, no. 12 (Dec. 1988): 16–20, 63.

Jordan, Pamela W., Karl S. Keller, Richard W. Tucker, and David Vogel. "Software Storming: Combining Rapid Prototyping and Knowledge Engineering." *Computer*. Vol. 22, no. 5 (May 1989): 39–48.

Laird, Philip D. *Learning from Good and Bad Data*. Boston: Kluwer Academic Publishers, 1988.

Martin, James. *Computer Networks and Distributed Processing: Software, Techniques, and Architecture*. Englewood Cliffs, NJ: Prentice-Hall, 1981.

Meltzer, Morton F. *Information: The Ultimate Management Resource*. New York: AMACOM, 1981.

Mueller, Robert Kirk. *Corporate Networking: Building Channels for Information and Influence*. New York: Free Press, 1986.

Samuelson, Kjell, H. Borko, and G. X. Amey. *Information Systems and Networks: Design and Planning Guideline for Managers, Decision Makers, and System Analysts*. New York: North-Holland, 1977.

Schultz, George P. *The Shape, Scope, and Consequences of the Age of Information*, U.S. Department of State, Bureau of Public Affairs, 1986.

CHAPTER THREE

Abbott, Russell. *An Integrated Approach to Software Development.* New York: Wiley, 1986.

Appleton, D. S. "Information Asset Management." *DATAMATION* (February 1986): 71–76.

Awani, Alfred O. *Data Processing Project Management.* Princeton, NJ: Petrocelli Books, 1986.

Cohen, B., W. T. Harwood, and M. I. Jackson. *The Specification of Complex Systems.* Reading, MA: Addison-Wesley, 1986.

DeMarco, T. *Structured Analysis and Systems Specification.* Englewood Cliffs, NJ: Prentice-Hall, 1979.

Gilb, Thomas and Susannah Finzi. *Principles of Software Engineering Management.* Reading, MA: Addison-Wesley, 1988.

Hale, Bob. *Abstract Objects.* New York: B. Blackwell, 1987.

Jackson, M. A. *System Development.* Englewood Cliffs, NJ: Prentice-Hall, 1983.

Jones, T. C. "Reusability in Programming: A Survey of the State of the Art." *IEEE Transactions on Software Engineering.* (September 1984): 488–94.

King, David. *Current Practices in Software Development: A Guide to Successful Systems.* New York: Yourdon Press, 1984.

Orr, K. T. *Structured Systems Development.* New York: Yourdon Press, 1977.

Swanson, M. E. and S. K. Curry. "Results of an Asset Engineering Program." *Information & Management.* Vol. 16 (1989): 207–16.

Weinberg, Julius Rudolph. *Abstraction, Relation, and Induction.* Madison, WI: University of Wisconsin Press, 1965.

Yourdon, Edward. *Managing the Structured Techniques: Strategies for Software Development in the 1990s.* 3rd edition. New York: Yourdon Press, 1986.

Yourdon, E. and L. L. Constantine. *Structured Design: Fundamentals of a Discipline of Computer Program and Systems Design.* New York: Yourdon Press, 1979.

Zimmer, J. A. *Abstraction for Programmers.* New York: McGraw-Hill, 1985.

CHAPTER FOUR

Anderson, David. *AI and Intelligent Systems: The Implications.* New York: Halsted Press, 1988.

Beck, L. L. and T. E. Perkins. "A Survey of Software Engineering

Practice: Tools, Methods and Results. *IEEE Transactions on Software Engineering*. Vol. 9, no. 5 (1983): 541–61.

Bolc, Leonard (ed.). *Natural Language Parsing Systems*. Berlin and New York: Springer-Verlag, 1987.

Doebelin, Ernest O. *System Modeling and Response: Theoretical and Experimental Approaches*. New York: Wiley, 1980.

Douglas, J. H. "New Computer Architectures Tackle Bottleneck." *High Technology* (June 1983): 71.

Eaton, John, Jeremy Smithers, and Susan Curran. *This Is It: A Manager's Guide to Information Technology*. 2nd edition. Highlands, NJ: Philip Allan, 1988.

Fairley, Richard E. *Software Engineering Concepts*. New York: McGraw Hill, 1985.

Foley, James, Won Chul Kim, Srojan Kovacevic, and Kevin Murray. "Defining Interfaces at a High Level of Abstraction." *IEEE Software.*" (January 1989): 25–32.

Gladney, H. M. "Data Replicas in Distributed Information Services." *ACM Transactions on Database Systems*. Vol. 14, no. 1 (March 1989): 75–97.

Goshawke, Walter, Ian D. K. Kelly, and J. David Wigg. *Computer Translation of Natural Language*. New York: Halsted Press, 1987.

Graubard, Steven R. (ed.). *The AI Debate, False Starts, Real Foundations*. Cambridge, MA: MIT Press, 1988.

Halsall, Fred. *Data Communications, Computer Networks, and OSI*. Reading, MA: Addison-Wesley, 1988.

Hartson, Rex. "User-Interface Management Control and Communication." *IEEE Software* (January 1989): 62–70.

Houy, Edward H. *Generating Natural Language under Pragmatic Constraints*. Hillsdale, NY: L. Earlbaum Associates, 1988.

Hu, S. David. *Expert Systems for Software Engineers and Managers*. New York: Chapman & Hall, 1987.

Pressman, Roger S. *Software Engineering: A Practitioner's Approach*. New York: McGraw-Hill, 1983.

Ray, Asok, Seung Ho Hong, Suk Lee, and Pius J. Egbelu. "Discrete-Event/Continuous Time Simulation of Distributed Data Communications and Control Systems." *Computer Simulation*. Vol. 5, no. 1 (January 1988): 71–85.

Rouse, William B. *Systems Engineering Models of Human-Machine Interaction*. New York: North Holland, 1980.

Taylor, William A. *What Every Engineer Should Know about AI*. Cambridge, MA: MIT Press, 1988.

Tugal, Dogan A. and Osman Tugal. *Data Transmission*. 2nd edition. New York: McGraw-Hill, 1989.

Weisser, Frank J. and Randall L. Corn. "The Intelligent Network and Forward-Looking Technology." *IEEE Communications Magazine*. Vol. 26, no. 12 (December 1988): 64–69.

Williams, Fredrick and Herbert S. Dordick. *The Executive's Guide to Information Technology: How to Increase Your Competitive Edge*. New York: Wiley, 1983.

CHAPTER FIVE

Monger, Rod F. *Mastering Technology: A Management Framework for Getting Results*. New York: Free Press, 1988.

Morone, Joseph G. and Edward J. Woodhouse. *Averting Catastrophe: Strategies for Regulating Risky Technologies*. Berkeley, CA: University of California Press, 1986.

Porter, Alan L. *A Guidebook for Technology Assessment and Impact Analysis*. New York: North Holland, 1980.

White, Blake L. *The Technology Assessment Process: A Strategic Framework for Managing Technical Innovation*. New York: Quorum Books, 1988.

CHAPTER SIX

Ackerman, A. Frank, Lynne S. Buchwald, and Frank H. Lewski. "Software Inspections: An Effective Verification Process." *IEEE Software*. (May 1989): 31–36.

Boyer, R. S. and J. S. Moore, (eds.). *The Correctness Problem in Computer Science*. New York: Academic Press, 1981.

Conte, S. P., H. E. Dunsmore, and V. Y. Shen. *Software Engineering Metrics and Models*. Menlo Park, CA: Benjamin/Cummings Publishing Co., 1986.

Crosby, Philip B. *Quality Is Free: The Art of Making Quality Certain*. New York: McGraw-Hill, 1979.

Deutsch, Michael S. and Ronald R. Willis. *Software Quality Engineering: A Total Technical and Management Approach*. Englewood Cliffs, NJ: Prentice-Hall, 1988.

Fagan, M. E. "Design and Code Inspections to Reduce Errors in Program Development." *IBM Systems Journal*. Vol. 15, no. 3 (1976): 182–211.

Garvin, David A. *Managing Quality: The Strategic and Competitive Edge*. London: Collier Macmillan, 1988.

Londeix, Bernard. *Cost Estimation for Software Development*. Reading, MA: Addison-Wesley, 1987.

Musa, John D. and Frank A. Ackerman. "Quantifying Software

Validation: When to Stop Testing." *IEEE Software* (May 1989): 19–30.

Proceedings/Sixth Symposium on Reliability in Distributed Systems, 17–19 March, 1987. Washington, DC: IEEE Computer Society Press, 1987.

Rogers, E. M. *Diffusion of Innovation*. 3rd edition. New York: The Free Press, 1983.

Smith, David John. *Engineering Quality Software: A Review of Current Practices, Standards, and Guidelines, Including New Methods and Development Tools*. New York: E. L. Sevier Applied Science, 1987.

Wallace, Dolores R. and Roger U. Fujii. "Software Verification and Validation: An Overview." *IEEE Software* (May 1989): 10–18.

CHAPTER SEVEN

Bjorn-Anderson, Niels, Ken Eason, and Daniel Robey. *Managing Computer Impact: An International Study of Management and Organizations*. Norwood, NJ: Ablex, 1986.

Blau, Peter M. *On the Nature of Organizations*. New York: Wiley, 1974.

Block, Robert. *The Politics of Projects*. New York: Yourdon Press, 1983.

Brooks, F. *The Mythical Man-Month*. Reading, MA: Addison-Wesley, 1975.

Drucker, Peter F. "The Coming of the New Organization." *Harvard Business Review*. Vol. 66, no. 1 (January-February 1988): 45–53.

Goldhaber, Gerald M. *Organizational Communication*. 2nd edition. Dubuque, IA: W. C. Brown, 1979.

Hage, Jerald (ed.). *Futures of Organizations: Innovating to Adapt Strategy and Human Resources to Rapid Technological Change*. Lexington, MA: Lexington Books, 1988.

Jackson, Barbara B. *Computer Models in Management*. Homewood, IL: R. D. Irwin, 1979.

Kantrow, Alan M. *The Constraints of Corporate Tradition: Doing the Correct Thing, Not Just What the Past Dictates*. New York: Harper & Row, 1987.

Lorange, Peter (ed.). *Implementation of Strategic Planning*. Englewood Cliffs, NJ: Prentice-Hall, 1982.

Lu, Ming-te and Crumpton Farrell. "Software Development: An International Perspective." *The Journal of Systems and Software*. Vol. 9 (1989): 305–309.

Naylor, Thomas H. *Corporate Planning Models*. Reading, MA: Addison-Wesley, 1979.

Naylor, Thomas H. (ed.). *Simulation Models in Corporate Planning*. New York: Praeger, 1979.

Perkins, Dennis N. T., Veronica Nieva, and Edward E. Lawler III. *Managing Creation: The Challenge of Building a New Organization*. New York: Wiley, 1983.

Robbins, Stephen P. *Organization Theory: Structure, Design, and Applications*. Englewood Cliffs, NJ: Prentice-Hall, 1987.

Roberts, Karlene H., Charles L. Hulin, and Denise M. Rousseau. *Developing an Interdisciplinary Science of Organizations*. San Francisco, CA: Jossey-Bass, 1978.

Toffler, Alvin. *The Adaptive Corporation*. New York: McGraw-Hill, 1985.

Torbert, William R. *Managing the Corporate Dream: Restructuring for Long Term Success*. Homewood, IL: Dow Jones-Irwin, 1987.

INDEX